Pursuing Whitey Bulger,

the Murderous Mob Chief the FBI Secretly Protected

MOST WANTED

THOMAS J. FOLEY
and John Sedgwick

A TOUCHSTONE BOOK
Published by Simon & Schuster
New York   London   Toronto   Sydney   New Delhi

Touchstone
A Division of Simon & Schuster, Inc.
1230 Avenue of the Americas
New York, NY 10020

Copyright © 2012 by Thomas J. Foley and John Sedgwick

First Touchstone hardcover edition May 2012

TOUCHSTONE and colophone are registered trademarks of Simon & Schuster, Inc.

For information about special discounts for bulk purchases, please contact Simon & Schuster Special Sales at 1-866-506-1949 or business@simonandschuster.com.

The Simon & Schuster Speakers Bureau can bring authors to your live event. For more information or to book an event contact the Simon & Schuster Speakers Bureau at 866-248-3049 or visit our website at www.simonspeakers.com.

Designed by Joy O'Meara

Manufactured in the United States of America

10 9 8 7 6 5 4 3 2 1

Library of Congress Cataloging-in-Publication Data
Foley, Thomas J.
  Most wanted : pursuing Whitey Bulger, the murderous mob chief the FBI secretly protected / Thomas J. Foley and John Sedgwick.
      p.   cm.
  Includes index.
  1. Bulger, Whitey, 1929–   2. Gangsters—Massachusetts—Boston—Biography.
  3. Murderers—Massachusetts—Boston—Biography.   4. Organized crime—
  Massachusetts—Boston—Biography.   I. Sedgwick, John, 1954–   II. Title.
    HV6452.M4F65   2012
    364.1092—dc23   2012005940

ISBN 978-1-4516-6391-4
ISBN 978-1-4516-6394-5 (ebook)

I want to dedicate this book to my wife, Marguerite.
She has been my wife and best friend for thirty-five years.
Without her love, support, and understanding during a very
demanding career, I would not have been successful.—TF

For my moll, R.—JS

— CONTENTS —

PART ONE
Where I'm Coming From

— CHAPTER 1 —

I was dead asleep when the call came in that June night in 2011, and I had to grope for the phone by the bed. It was Colonel Marian McGovern, the superintendent of the Massachusetts State Police, my old job. She was telling me something about Whitey Bulger, but I couldn't quite follow it.

"Sorry. Can you say that again?" I asked. "What was that?" I was sure I was dreaming.

"Whitey Bulger, Tommy," she repeated. "He was captured in California."

"Wait. What?" I was fully awake now. My wife pulled herself up in bed beside me.

The colonel still had to say it all one more time before it could sink in. "When did this happen?"

"About an hour ago. The FBI captured him in Santa Monica. I got a call from Special Agent DesLauriers." He was in charge of the FBI's Boston office. "I thought you'd want a heads-up."

"Santa Monica," I repeated. "Jesus."

"A few blocks from the beach. He'd been renting an apartment there with his girlfriend." Catherine Greig, the woman he'd fled Boston with, back in 1995. I remembered her well. A real ballbuster, over twenty years younger than Whitey. We'd wanted to search her town house for Whitey the night he fled, but we'd been running all over the place trying to find him. When we showed up at her door, she refused to let us in. "No warrant?" she sneered. "Then go fuck yourselves." Then she slammed the door in our faces.

That was our last chance of catching Whitey that night. Or for the next sixteen years. Over time, he got up to second—just behind Osama Bin Laden—on the FBI's most wanted fugitive list, with a $2 million reward on his head. And then he was number one.

"Where's Whitey?"—that game was always fun to play. I had him in Cuba. I figured his money would hold up, it had great beaches, and there was no extradition treaty with the United States.

I had the beach part right, but I certainly didn't pick him for Santa Monica. And not in the same third-floor apartment, steps from the piers, for the last fourteen years. Nobody guessed that.

When I finished the call, I filled in my wife, Marguerite, who'd suffered through the Whitey investigation even more than I did. "They got him," I told her. "In Santa Monica." I didn't have to say who.

You might think I'd feel frustrated not to have bagged the guy myself, but I was just glad that somebody got him. It didn't matter to me who it was, and it still doesn't. Just so long as Whitey rots in prison now.

I called up Danny Doherty and Stevie Johnson, two members of the Whitey team I put together, and told them the news. They wouldn't mind being woken up for this.

"Well, it's about time," Stevie said.

All three of us—Danny, Stevie, and me—had been afraid we'd never get him. Either he'd slip away forever, or he'd turn up dead. He'd just stay out there somehow, permanently out of reach.

"They better hang on to him," Danny said. "That's all I can say."

———

It wasn't for another day or so that we got pictures. Bulger bald, with a monk-ish white beard and a loopy grin on his face, Greig looking gray and defeated. Both of them stooped with age. Some people thought Whitey might be seriously ill. I don't know about that, but he did look weak. He'd always been about power—having it, projecting it. He was not a big man, but his arms and shoulders had always been heavily muscled. Now that strength was all gone, and he looked like just another tired old man, maybe a few years away from using a cane or a walker.

For a guy who was one of the most sought-after fugitives in the entire world, he'd proved surprisingly easy to apprehend. The FBI had been tipped off about his name and address, lured him into the garage, clapped the handcuffs on him, and that was it. You had to wonder how hard the FBI had been trying for the past sixteen years. That whole time, Whitey had been hiding in plain sight, lying out on the beach, maybe a little quiet with the neighbors, his bedroom window blacked out. It took sixteen years for someone at the Bureau to figure out—how about we try looking for her? She's probably not as careful as a mobster about hiding her tracks. It seemed pretty basic to me, but apparently not to the FBI.

————

When Whitey was captured and flown back to Boston, he was the talk of the city, and much of the country, too. I knew him as a fiendish killer, but to lots of people in Boston he was just a character. That's how he was seen in the tony parts of town like Cambridge, the Back Bay, and Beacon Hill. In tougher neighborhoods like Charlestown, the North End, and Southie, Whitey was almost the unofficial mayor, as plenty of people there thought of him as a Robin Hood who always had a few bucks for some turkeys to give to the poor at Thanksgiving. That drove me nuts. Whitey Bulger sure as hell didn't give anything away. He was a murderer, a drug dealer, an extortionist, a thug. He was like the Boston Strangler or Joe "The Animal" Barboza or Johnny Martorano, only worse because he did more damage over a much longer time. These were not gentle guys, and Whitey wasn't gentle either.

Lots of people lined the streets to watch Whitey be taken by police SUV and, escorted by state troopers, from Logan Airport to the new Joseph A. Moakley federal courthouse on the South Boston waterfront. On TV, I watched Whitey emerge from the SUV, and he walked, in handcuffs and leg irons, to the courthouse, a federal Marshal on each arm. I saw the halting gait, the hunched shoulders. Waiting for him inside was his brother, the former state senate president, Billy Bulger, who'd lost his job as president of the University of Massachusetts for refusing to tell a congressional committee what he knew about his brother's whereabouts during Whitey's flight. This first court appearance of Whitey's was brief, since it was to see if he qualified for bail. Since he had been the most wanted fugitive in America, the answer would be no.

It wasn't for another month that I laid eyes on him myself. I'd been waiting for that moment ever since we first started up the investigative unit to get him in 1990. That was over two decades, a good chunk of my life spent on Whitey Bulger, but I'd never once seen him, at least not definitively. In late July after his capture, though, he was to be formally arraigned, and I drove in from my home in Worcester to see him in the federal courthouse. I sat with the victims' families in the small spectators' gallery. I'd done what I could to find out what had happened to their loved ones; before our investigation, many of them had never known for sure. The news wasn't happy. In every case, a member of their family had been murdered by Whitey, often in a hideous fashion. But, painful as that was, they were grateful to know. Now they came up to shake my hand, with some warm words. Some of them were tearful. I sat next to Steve Davis, the burly brother of Debbie Davis. Starting in her late teens, she'd been the girlfriend of Stevie Flemmi, Whitey's close associate. When Flemmi tired of her, Whitey strangled her for him. We'd found the corpse, buried on a beach not far from where Whitey lived with Catherine Greig. Now Steve Davis greeted me with a clap on the back like a family member.

Finally, a door opened, and there was Whitey. Clad in an orange prison jumpsuit, his legs clapped in irons, he shuffled into the court, a U.S. Marshal holding tight to each arm. His brothers Jack and Billy Bulger were there in front-row seats, and he shot them a look of hello, with a little wave. The brothers nodded back with half smiles. Beside me, I could tell Steve Davis was tensing up, his breath coming heavy, obviously infuriated to see his sister's killer a few feet from him. I was afraid he might leap from his seat and charge at Bulger. Instead, he blew out several long breaths and dried his hands on his pants. Whitey took a seat in a chair at the defendant's table, facing the judge, his back to us. All around me, the victims' families stared hard at Whitey's back, their gaze like bullets.

Whitey was detestable, yes. But mostly what he seemed to me right then was small. And old. Beaten looking. All the life had drained out of him. He was just a wisp of a guy shuffling around, his rough voice all that was left of the vitality that had once terrified an entire city.

But that thought didn't bring me peace. I was pleased to see him captured, no question. But what kept coming back as I looked at this old man was the cold fury that had so often surged through me on this case. I'm not the type to yell and scream. People say I show my anger in my eyes. Just seeing how old Whitey was as he sat, his shoulders curved, on that chair—it reminded me of how long he'd been gone, and that made me think of *why* he'd been gone so long. And why he hadn't been rotting in prison as he deserved. And that went back to why we hadn't been able to arrest him that day that Catherine Greig tossed us off her front steps, or any day since. And that only raised other questions, the same old questions, as to why someone like Whitey Bulger had been able to stay in business for so long, killing, extorting, dealing drugs, terrorizing. And, finally, why had this outrage *still* not been addressed? How could it *still* fester, wrecking more lives, like those of the families of the victims sitting around me?

— CHAPTER 2 —

At Christmas in 1991, we were about a year into the Bulger investigation. I was with a few guys from my team at Joe Tecce's, the big, splashy restaurant in the North End. Big John Tutungian, Sly Scanlan, our hookup guy Chuck Hanko, and a few others. It was the annual Christmas party of the Boston office of the FBI for a lot of law enforcement people around New England.

FBI special agent John Connolly, one of the bigger showboats, always played the host. Remember, this was when the local FBI and the State Police were supposedly working night and day to get Whitey Bulger arrested and sent away. Guess where the booze came from. A liquor store called the Rotary Variety in South Boston that was owned by Whitey Bulger himself. That was the rumor back then, that Connolly picked it up there himself, and it turned out to be the truth: we were drinking Whitey's booze.

My guys were bothered by the idea, needless to say. We drank, sure, but the beer did not go down easy. But, starting with Connolly, a lot of FBI agents seemed to think it was a matter for a few jokes, some hearty claps on the back, and maybe another round on Whitey.

The U.S. Attorney's Office in Boston also had some law enforcement people in from around New England for a little get-together from time to time. A bunch of FBI agents swung by for one of them that year, 1991, and some "Staties," including me. By then, we'd started to make some serious progress on the Bulger investigation, and I was feeling good about how things were coming along. A couple of agents clanged beer bottles together and yelled for quiet and then they announced they wanted to make a presentation. They did it up big, asked all of us to crowd around, and got all solemn. When everyone was quiet, one of the FBI agents called out: "Everyone, this is a very special occasion for all of us here, and we'd like to present an award to a distinguished trooper from the State Police. Would Corporal Tom Foley please step forward?"

There was a little too much tittering in the crowd. My friend Fred Wyshak, the assistant U.S. attorney, had been given an "award" from the feds just the year before, and he didn't appreciate his very much. So I stayed right where I was.

"Tom Foley, please?" one of them repeated.

By now, the room was dead silent. I still didn't move, so the feds came toward me, and drew many of the attendees, many of them my superiors in the State Police, in a ring around us. One of the agents made a little unfunny speech about my investigative zeal in the Bulger case. That got some laughs, but not many.

Then the two agents handed me my award, which was wrapped up in tissue paper. "Go ahead, Tom, open it up," one of them told me.

I pulled the tissue paper away, and scanned the plaque. It read: "The Most Hated Man in Law Enforcement." It had a picture of me with my name underneath.

They wanted me to read it out to the crowd, but no way. So one of them did the honors, while I just glared at him.

The FBI agents in the crowd got a chuckle out of it, but not too many other people did, and I certainly didn't. Still, the agents shook my hand, looked me dead in the eye, and said, "Congratulations, Trooper, you've earned it."

I still have that trophy someplace, and whenever I want to remember what it was really like to work on that case, I take it down and look at it. Then everything comes rushing back.

———

The most hated man in law enforcement. I'm proud of that, prouder of that than I have been of any other award I have ever received. This book is about how I earned that honor. It's the story of my twenty-year quest to bring Whitey Bulger to justice when hardly anyone outside my little band of overworked State Police investigators—like Tutungian, Scanlan, and Hanko; and a dogged agent from the DEA named Dan Doherty; and a few others who came later—gave a shit, quite frankly, and the FBI did about everything in its power to stop us.

In 1990, when our investigation kicked in, Whitey Bulger was by far the most dominant figure in the Irish mob. The Mafia had started to flame out, leaving the Irish mob about the only mob with any impact in Boston. Steve Flemmi, or Steve "The Rifleman" Flemmi, as the newspapers always put it (so named for his lethal shooting skills as a paratrooper during the Korean War), came in second to Whitey. Flemmi was up there largely because he was tight with Bulger; Whitey would have ranked regardless. Still, Flemmi was the only mobster Whitey trusted, had ever trusted, or even spoke to on any kind of regular basis. Third was probably "Cadillac Frank" Salemme, so named for his favorite car, who had recently emerged from prison to claim control of what was left of the New England Mafia. He'd relied on Flemmi for help in getting established, which meant that he was drawing on Whitey's reputation, too. In the Boston mob scene, Whitey had all the power—others simply borrowed it. But all three of these men were woven in tightly to our case.

By 1990, Bulger was sitting on a criminal empire the newspapers pegged at $50 million. It came from his marijuana smuggling, cocaine dealing, extortion, illegal liquor distribution, pilferage, racketeering, gaming, and loan-sharking, but he'd do about anything if enough money was on the table. Although he was rarely seen around town, even in South Boston, his presence was everywhere. If there was a crime anywhere in the city that involved scaring the crap out of someone, it was probably Whitey's doing. If there was a legitimate business to be muscled in on, Whitey again. If someone needed to be made an example of, Whitey.

Whitey was just plain smarter than the other mobsters, better connected, with keener instincts. But most important of all, he was utterly ruthless. More than most gangsters, Whitey could always think several steps ahead, sure. But it was his ability to scare the shit out of people that made the difference. Terror was his business. It wasn't just killing people. All mobsters killed people. By now, Whitey's official tally is up to nineteen, but the real count is probably twice that, if you add up all the virtual unknowns from the gangland wars earlier on when he was making a name for himself as a killer. Those victims weren't widely missed after their bodies were dropped into the trunk of a car, or dumped in some alley. But more than the numbers, it was the way he killed, at extremely close range, the tip of the gun right up in the victims' faces, so that last thing they saw on this earth was Whitey Bulger hovering over them, relishing it, before he blew them away, the blood splattering on him, like that brought him the greatest satisfaction there was. People who were there told us that Whitey liked to lie down afterward, and a weird calm would descend over him. "Like he'd taken a Valium," one of them said. And the whole scene was so grotesque, so horrible, he knew that word would get out about what he'd done, and that this would be good for him, too. Do that enough, and you have to do it less. Whitey Bulger has to be the most cold-blooded killer in Boston's history. If he isn't, I wouldn't want to know the guy who is.

None of this was a big secret in Boston. Most people knew the basics of what Whitey was about. But until we came along, no one in law enforcement had been able to do what law enforcement is supposed to do— get a bastard like that off the street before he kills somebody else. Whitey had been at large since 1965, when he emerged from his only prison stint, served mostly in Leavenworth and Alcatraz for a string of bank robberies, the last one in the Midwest. Since then, he hadn't been touched by law enforcement. Never questioned, never indicted, never arrested. Not once. It was as if Whitey Bulger was a model citizen.

To the FBI, it was like Bulger didn't matter. Despite his fearsome reputation, he had nothing to do with anything. Well, we thought differently. There are plenty of things to say about the FBI, but I'll save most of them for later. For now, I'll just say that I have never known any other organizations, or any individuals, where what they said and what they did had so little to do with each other. But the funny part is that the FBI thinks this is fine, even now. Since I got that Most Hated award, federal judges, congressional committees, and countless newspaper accounts have all agreed that the FBI's problems go very deep. They did here. The feds stymied our investigation of Whitey, got *us* investigated on bogus claims, tried to push me off the case, got me banished to a distant barracks, phonied up charges against other members of the State Police, lied to reporters, misled Congress, drew in the president of the United States to save themselves, nearly got me and my investigators killed, and—well, I'll tell you *and*.

The Most Hated Man in Law Enforcement, indeed.

— CHAPTER 3 —

Whitey Bulger was born in the Depression year 1929 and grew up in the Old Harbor, one of the first public housing developments in the country. It was a dreary collection of spare brick buildings not too far from the water. Like South Boston itself, the project was a tough place to live, and, like the neighborhood, it has spawned a disproportionate number of gangsters and thugs.

Whitey was the first of seven children. Billy was the next oldest son. When they were growing up, Billy was everything that Whitey was not. Obedient, studious, Billy was nicknamed Beam for the desk light that was always on. Whitey—actually James Bulger Jr.—got his nickname for the lightness of his hair, but anyone close to him knew not to use it to his face. In person, he was always to be called Jim.

The family qualified for public housing because Whitey's father, James Bulger Sr., had been unable to work at his job in the railroad yards after his left arm was crushed when two boxcars slammed together. For whatever reason, Whitey was a hellion from the beginning. In his early teens, he ran off to join the circus, literally—Barnum & Bailey's, as a roustabout. He returned all mouthy, ready to take anyone on for any reason, and would beat kids up for fun. He soon fell in with a gang of young Southie toughs who called themselves the Shamrocks, and made easy money hijacking goods off the back of trucks. Whitey started in on a rap sheet at thirteen when he was arrested for larceny. Before long, he went on to grand larceny and other crimes, and finally rape. There are some claims that Whitey pimped himself out as a gay hooker when he was a teenager, but I don't buy it. He's into power and control, and that's always been pretty much it.

———

I was born a quarter century later, in 1954, and raised in a triple-decker in Worcester. Growing up, I was an altar boy, but don't make too much of that. I went to Catholic school, and there were plenty of altar boys. Often forgotten, Worcester is probably best known for the huge cold storage warehouse fire in 1999 that cost the lives of six firefighters. My father, John J. Foley Sr., was a firefighter, but he'd retired by then. When he was working, he chased fires during the day, then lugged beef at a meatpacking plant after hours for extra money. He'd sometimes come home with angry burns, or maybe not come home at all because he'd been hospitalized for smoke inhalation. Once, he fell through three floors of a burning house. He was all banged up, but he went to work the next day.

Public service is important in our family, and it's a big reason why I went into law enforcement. Maybe it's old-fashioned, but it's all about trying to help people out.

After twelve years of parochial school, I picked up a criminology degree at Westfield State, hoping for a chance to join the State Police, which had been my dream for a while. There were no openings that year, so I applied to the Massachusetts Department of Corrections, and got assigned to MCI Walpole, the biggest and most dangerous penitentiary in the state. It's one huge, echoing warehouse for convicts—a horrible place to be a guard, let alone a prisoner. And it was even worse to be a rookie guard, since the convicts figured they could take advantage of you, and the veteran guards hated you because they assumed that, as a college grad, you'd be their boss one day.

But the guards needed one another, because at Walpole we were locked inside a big cage with the prisoners. It was like we were doing time, too. In my section, I was in with forty-five convicts, with three levels of private cells going up one wall.

We had nothing to protect ourselves either. No gun, no knife, nothing. Any weapon we had the prisoners might grab and use on us. All we had was the key to our cell block. If we saw trouble coming, we were supposed to sprint to the door, shove the key into the lock, get out as quickly as possible, and slam the door as hard as we could. The sound would bring guards running. If I couldn't make it, I was supposed to throw the key through the bars and up high enough in the air that when it landed it clanged on the concrete floor, and other guards would hear it and come running.

We never strayed very far from that door. But even so, we weren't exactly safe. At any moment, an inmate could jump up and grab my key, or sneak up behind me and bury a shiv—a homemade blade of some sort—in my back. Everybody had scares. One time, an inmate came up to shoot the breeze at my desk while one of his pals way up on the third tier of cells, maybe forty feet up, positioned himself over me, lining up a big can of soup directly over my head. Then he let go. It was like a bomb coming down. By luck, I just happened to lean forward onto my desk right then, and the can slammed into the back of my chair with this terrible *crack*. The prisoner who'd been talking to me just walked away whistling.

It gets to you, that sort of thing. I was taking courses in a college graduate program by then, and sitting there in the classroom, I couldn't get comfortable unless I sat with my back against the wall so I could see everything in front of me. Even so, if there was a sudden slamming of the door, I'd want to jump out of my chair.

At Walpole, you had to be alert. And that was great training for the State Police. I learned to focus, to see everything like my life depended on it. At Walpole, I was up against some of the most devious minds anywhere, many of them bent on finding ways to kill me. I learned what to watch for—the little tics, the things out of place—and I learned to depend on others. I'd watch their backs; they'd watch mine.

———

I didn't get caught up in figuring out which inmate was in for what. But I knew there were a few mobsters in there. Most of them were just quietly doing their time. That's old-school Mafia. But one of them was a scrappy kid named Ricky Costa. I didn't know he was in the mob until he came back from the prison visiting room, and I was patting him down. The visit mustn't have gone too well, because Ricky was in a shitty mood. A lot of prisoners wear shoes with hollowed-out heels so they can sneak in drugs. When I asked Ricky to take his shoes off so I could check them out, he screamed, "Fuck you," and started grappling with me. Some other guards rushed over, and we hustled him off to solitary to chill out for a couple of days.

Afterward, a few of the guards came up to me and asked me if I had a death wish.

I didn't know what they were talking about.

"Don't you know who that is?" one of them asked.

"Yeah," I said. "It's Ricky Costa."

"But, Foley, jeez—what are you, stupid? He's in the mob! He's Angiulo's godson."

Jerry Angiulo ran the Mafia in Boston. I went silent, trying to think that one through.

They started laughing. "You're really fucked now. Somebody's going to come after you."

I had nothing to say to that. If somebody was, he was. I wasn't going to worry about it. Maybe that's fatalistic, but to me it was just being practical. If there's nothing to do about something, I just let it go.

————

Whitey got into the air force somehow, based in Montana. He was up on rape charges there when he was honorably discharged. Back home, he returned to his old ways, "tailgating," as these truck heists were called. In one case, he attempted to steal an entire beer truck. It was a good line, since most of the thefts were inside jobs—the driver was in on the deal. At first, there was a fair amount of competition, but a lot of it faded as one thief or another was picked off by the cops, the victim of a stool pigeon no one could locate.

Whitey teamed up with a burglar from Cambridge to put together a gang of bank robbers, who knocked over a bank in Providence, then another in Boston, before hitting the road, first to Florida and then to Indiana, where they cased one bank in Hammond and hit another. Whitey was carrying two handguns when he burst in with his pals, and immediately leaped up onto the counter and screamed at everyone to get down and shut the fuck up while a confederate scooped up the money from the tellers' cages. The haul was over $12,000. The gang split it up and then dispersed. Whitey had a girlfriend then, and they drove to back to Florida and then to Boston, and then hopped about the country. To disguise himself, Whitey dyed his hair black, wore horn-rim glasses, and chomped on an unlit cigar.

By then, the FBI had already been keeping an eye on him for some time. An agent in Boston named H. Paul Rico knew all about Whitey. An "extremely dangerous character," Rico called him, with "remarkable agility" and "reckless daring in driving vehicles." Most noteworthy, though, were his "unstable, vicious characteristics."

When Whitey returned to Boston in March 1956, Rico picked up a tip that he could be found in a nightclub in Revere. Some FBI agents grabbed him one night as he stepped out of the club to get his car. Whitey received a twenty-year sentence but served only nine, most of them in Leavenworth, a real hellhole back then. He was just twenty-seven when he was sentenced. In some ways he was lucky. Back in Boston, a gang war was raging between two Irish gangs, the McLaughlins and the McLeans, that could easily have been the end of him.

Still, in prison, confinement gnawed at him, and that only made the hard time harder. He spent months in solitary for fighting and mouthing off. When he was caught plotting his escape, Whitey was sent to Alcatraz, out on its solitary rock in San Francisco Bay, a prison from which no one ever gets out before it's time. To shave a few months off his sentence, he agreed to take part in some CIA experiments with LSD. The program was called MK-ULTRA and was a test of mind-altering drugs that the agency thought might yield a truth serum. In some notes of his that were found later, Whitey complained that these drugs gave him nightmares and insomnia for years afterward. Murder, by contrast, never troubled his sleep.

The rest of the time he spent reading just about everything in the prison library. He pored over the major battles of World War II, scrutinizing them both from the viewpoint of the Allied general and from that of the Nazi commander. He was fascinated by the moves, countermoves and counter-counter moves—by the way everything could be anticipated if you thought about it hard enough. It was his graduate school, and it made him a far more disciplined criminal, teaching him that everything he did had consequences, and those consequences had consequences, too.

Even though he was a hardened ex-con when he was finally released in 1965, he came back home to live in the Old Harbor with his mother, a widow now. He took a job as a janitor at the Suffolk County Courthouse that his brother Billy had arranged. He stuck it out for a few years, and then returned to his old life, quickly creating a reputation for himself as the most frightening SOB in Boston. This time he'd be professional about it—strike with a vengeance, but be smart. Maximum impact, minimum exposure.

And he wasn't going to waste his ammo on targets he could not take. So now, instead of giving the cops lip, he'd be respectful, suggesting they were all in the same business together, cops and criminals both, and trying to make nice. But when he struck, he struck hard. When you give somebody a beating, he once counseled a younger gangster, "don't just knock him out. Bite his fucking ear off, bite his face off, lift his arms up and break his fucking ribs, break his ankles, hit all his spots, his nonlethal spots." Do everything but kill him, in other words. That way, the guy remembers it, and so does everyone else.

———

After I'd been a screw for a while, I took another shot at the State Police exam in 1979. They only had space for a couple hundred students at the academy, but twenty thousand guys applied. Fortunately I did well enough on the test to land one of the spots. I was thrilled to get a shot at the State Police, which had been an ambition of mine since my teens. And I didn't mind at all the thought of getting out of Walpole either.

The State Police Academy was no picnic. The training went on practically around the clock with course work, physical training, practice on the firing range, and a lot more, since police work involves a bit of everything. Believe me, when I was done at the end of the day, I was dead. But I loved it. I loved the structure, the discipline, the clarity. Every minute I was there would make me a better cop, and nothing could feel better to me than that.

When I graduated, I got stationed out near Northampton. Lots of farms and small towns along the Connecticut River, just east of the Berkshires. It's a pretty part of the world, with some famous colleges like Amherst and Smith. I was married by then, to Marguerite Cawley, who I met in college. Her father had been a firefighter like my dad.

When you're just starting out, you pair off with a veteran trooper and ride with him for a few months so he can show you the ropes. Every cop has a thing about his cruiser. It's private, like his office, or maybe even his bedroom. When you're there as a rookie cop, and you climb in, you see a lot of what is going on. You see the paperwork he's going to need for arrests and citations, the stack of case files he's working on, maybe even his mail. In the back, there's probably a rifle on the gun rack over the seat. In the trunk, there's firefighting equipment, a medical emergency kit, road markers. It is a tight fit.

Riding with a veteran, I learned things I didn't get in the academy, key things for working the road—how to approach a stopped car, what to check for in the vehicle, bureaucratic procedures, legal stuff, what to worry about, what not to worry about.

After a few months of this, I had my own cruiser. It was a Chevy Impala, loaded up with the police package, with maybe 100,000 miles on it. It rode a little rough, but it said Massachusetts State Police in bold white letters against pale blue, and it was all mine. It was a great moment when I slid behind the wheel of that car that first time.

At first, the work was mostly patrolling the north-south highways in the western part of the state. Drivers coming up from New York and bound for a getaway in Vermont would come screaming through there at eighty or ninety miles an hour. Late one night, I was out on Route 84, when a car with New York plates came flying up from Connecticut, doing ninety, easy.

I pulled out, got the siren and the blue lights going, and tore after it. It was just that car and me for maybe five miles, but I finally got it to pull over. A Saab, dark blue. There were four guys in it, two and two, and all eyes were on me when I came to the window with my flashlight to ask for license and registration. They kept their eyes on me, but I could see they were shifting stuff around in their seats in an odd way, as if to hide something. I grabbed licenses from all of them and returned to the cruiser to call in the license numbers to the dispatcher. This was years before cruisers had laptops. After a few minutes, word came back. None of their IDs checked out.

I looked back at the car. Shit. Four of them, one of me. Now what?

I decided to play it cool, strolled back to the car, and asked them if they'd mind if I took a look in the trunk.

"No problem, officer," the driver told me.

He came around and popped the trunk with his key. There was a big heap of laundry, and I went through it all. Shirts, pants, shoes, everything. I'd been trained to be thorough, and as I peered inside one loafer with my flashlight, I noticed a number written there under the tongue. W134506. It was a Walpole ID. As I knew well, every inmate has one, and it goes on everything he owns. I jotted it down, closed the trunk, and told the four guys to hold tight a few more minutes. I'd be right back. I returned to my cruiser, called in to the barracks, and asked the staff to call the number in to the office at Walpole. They called me back right away, It belonged to a man I'll call Marcus Dupree. There was a federal indictment out on him for drug trafficking and intent to murder.

Normally, I'd call for backup, but I was going to make only one arrest, since I had no evidence on the others. I returned to the car and asked Marcus to step out for a moment. He was in the front passenger seat, and he acted sullen as he climbed out. As soon as Dupree shut the door behind him, I had him up against the side of the car, his hands behind his back, and cuffed. Once I had backup, we pulled the rest out of the car. We found some pills and a few bags of dope in the car. Small stuff compared with what I did later, but big to me then.

I made a lot of arrests like Dupree. But I spent plenty of time off the highway and in the towns, too, handling housebreaks, domestic cases, street crime. Small cases, you might say, but no case is ever small to the victim.

Occasionally you'd be involved in a high-profile case. One of them involved the murder of a state trooper. Horrible. I'd been working a drug case in Southbridge, a little town south of Worcester. I was in the dealer's apartment, ripping the place apart looking for his stash, when there was a frantic call over my radio: "Trooper down! Trooper down!" That's always a bad moment for a cop. This time it was George Hanna, one of the veterans on the force, a real good guy. He'd taken my patrol in Auburn near Worcester while we hit the Southbridge house.

We jumped into our cruisers and raced over to where George had been hit, but he'd been rushed to the hospital, and soon died there. Apparently, he'd spotted three guys getting set to knock over a liquor store on Route 20, one of the big streets through town. When he confronted them, one of them opened fire. George went down with a ton of bullets in him. He didn't have a chance.

After the medics got George onto a gurney to take him to the ambulance, a bystander picked a wallet up off the ground and handed it to a State Police sergeant, Tom White, who'd been securing the crime scene. Figuring it was George's, White put it aside. When he opened it up later, he found that it had no identification, only a few dollars, and a lot of papers in Spanish. It obviously wasn't George's. I had a Spanish-speaking kid with me to break in as a new trooper, and he translated the contents for us. One of the pieces was a ticket stub for a softball raffle at a bar in Worcester. Just the stub, but we figured the rest of the ticket would be back at the bar, and it would have the name. So another trooper and I rode over to the bar, and we explained the situation to the owner. He found the original book of tickets and matched the stub to a man named Emelio Otero, and it gave Otero's address. Early the next morning, two troopers found Otero driving with two other passengers. I was part of the backup team, and we found a small bag on the floor by the front seat. Inside was George's gun.

———

All crime is cruel, and some is savage. Regardless of its severity, I never got over how it affected the victims. That was why we did our job. And I quickly learned that most criminals aren't geniuses. Crime is difficult—committing it, concealing it. A lot of criminals just don't have the right mentality, and they mess up in the most obvious ways. Most of them do crime because they can't do anything else, and they're impulsive besides. They do the crime, but they don't think much about what's going to happen *after* they do the crime. They think they can just walk away and that's it.

For example, two inmates busted out of the Concord jail and started sticking guns in the faces of convenience store clerks and swiping all the money from the till. A State Police detective called to tell me that he and his partner had the robbers holed up in an apartment in Fitchburg. They were set to burst in and grab them, but they needed someone in a State Police uniform to go first, so the robbers would know they were dealing with the cops. Could I help them out?

It can be scary to rip through a door not knowing what's on the other side. But it's a job; we're trained for it. When doctors open you up for heart surgery, they don't get the jumps. I'd have a shotgun—and surprise—on my side. Of course, they might, too.

"Sure," I said. "No problem."

I get pumped for something like that, all the same. The two detectives ripped open the door with a sledgehammer while I stood off to one side with my shotgun. As soon as the door was down, I charged inside. It's all about speed, to get them before they can get you, but also to get them before they can dump the drugs down the toilet. The lead guy had been watching TV with his girlfriend. He sprang off the couch and dug under his pant leg for his knife, but he was too late. I had the tip of my shotgun up hard under his chin.

"Drop the knife," I told him. "Do it!" It wouldn't do him much good anyway. No point bringing a knife to a gunfight, right?

"Now put your hands up, or I'll blow your head off."

Staring down at the barrel of my gun, he didn't have much choice, and his hands went up toward the ceiling.

Meanwhile, the detectives chased my guy's partner up the stairs and I could hear them scrambling down the hall, the detectives' shoes sounding heavy through the ceiling. Then silence, and then the detectives shouting, "Get the fuck out of there!"

The partner had tried to hide under a pile of dirty laundry.

That's when it clicked in about the guy at the other end of my shotgun. Geroux! Fat, pimply guy—had to be one of the dumbest criminals ever. He simply could not stay out of prison. This was my third run-in with him, and the other two had gone just as badly for him.

Last time, I'd been in a Worcester toy store buying a Christmas present for my nephew when I noticed a guy wandering around the place like he was casing it. Next thing I knew, three guys came bursting in wearing Halloween masks. One of them had a shotgun, and he went right for the cash register. The other came around to me and demanded my wallet. I was afraid I'd left my badge in it. Now I was afraid that if the guy saw it, he'd freak out and shoot me. So I dropped the wallet onto the floor and kicked it down the aisle, hoping it would slide under one of the cases. No such luck.

The guy bent down, picked it up, and flipped it open. Then he looked at me.

No badge, thank God.

He failed to make me, but when he looked at me straight on, I made him. Because I had known him before that. From Walpole, where he'd been doing a three-year hitch for larceny. Fat, pimply Geroux. One more time.

There, in the toy store, he slid the cash out of my wallet—all I had was fifteen bucks—and shoved it into the front pocket of his jeans, and then he flipped my wallet back onto the floor. Then the robbers all scrammed. The cops caught him that night, of course. There were plenty of eyewitnesses, and it wasn't hard to get a name. Geroux.

I testified against him. Back he went to Walpole.

Now, at the apartment in Fitchburg, I was staring at the very same Geroux, who had nearly killed me, and I pressed the tip of the shotgun against his neck a little tighter.

"Geroux, right?"

He seemed startled.

"Don't you remember me?"

He looked blank.

"I remember you." I didn't say how, and he didn't ask.

The two detectives handled the other guy, while I took Geroux to the Fitchburg PD in the back of my cruiser. I watched him in the rearview. He said nothing, just looked dead ahead, with about as unhappy a face as you'll ever see.

"Aren't you curious?"

"Curious what?"

"How I know you."

"Fuck no."

I told him anyway. First Walpole. Then that toy store.

"Shit," he said.

Geroux. Some guys, they start to go off at the wrong angle, and then they just keep going.

––––––––

By the time Whitey got out in 1965, Boston was in the midst of another of the great gang wars that surged over the city every decade or two, dropping carnage in back alleys and abandoned cars. He'd missed the McLaughlins and McLeans, but this was another pair of rival Irish gangs called the Mullens and the Killeens, and they went at it like the Hatfields and the McCoys with machine guns. The battle had begun when a Mullen and a Killeen had gotten into a scrap at a Killeen bar in Southie called the Transit, and the Killeen ended up biting off the nose of the Mullen. The Mullens charged into the Transit to seek retribution. The Killeens expressed outrage at the disrespect, and all around the city, bodies got bullets in them.

By then, Bulger had thrown in with Donald Killeen, the South Boston bookie who served as the Killeen chieftain. Bulger was his bodyguard, watching Killeen's back. In a flash of power, Whitey blasted Mullen's ally Buddy Roache, brother of the future Boston police commissioner, not killing him, but paralyzing him for life, and, for good measure, he knocked off Donald McGonagle, although that one may have been in error, since McGonagle hadn't taken sides in the conflict. The Mullens took revenge by popping a Killeen loyalist named O'Sullivan. And on it went. Move and countermove. Whitey was not touched.

Things were not going well for the Killeens, and Whitey blamed Donald, who may have seemed a little soft to run a war like that, and he'd left his organization overextended. And the Mullen group of Paul McGonagle and Patrick Nee kept squeezing and squeezing. To Whitey, the choice was to protect Donald Killeen or protect himself. That one was easy.

He threw Donald Killeen over, and, caught between the Italian mob he detested for its pomp and extravagance and the vengeful Mullens who wanted to kill him, he took the third course: he joined up with the oversized Howie Winter, who ran the Irish mob operation out of a garage on Somerville's Winter Hill. Winter was friendly with the Mullens, but not to the point of joining their war with the Killeens. And they were friendly enough with him that they didn't kill him.

Safely in the Winter Hill camp, Whitey knew better than to wait for Donald Killeen to send out someone to slaughter him. He struck first. Donald was attending his son's fourth birthday party at his house in Southie when he received a phone call that sent him out to his car. A man with a machine gun was watching from a nearby stand of trees. When Killeen closed his car door, the man charged toward him, his machine gun leveled. Frantic, Killeen groped for the pistol under his seat, but too late. The gunman rammed the machine gun through the window and into his face and let loose fifteen bullets that nearly ripped Donald Killeen's head off. No one doubts that it was Bulger.

Having made his statement, Whitey was the one to end the violence a few weeks later. He was waiting in his car with three other men when Donald's youngest brother, Kenneth, came jogging by. It was Kenneth who'd bitten the nose off the Mullen at the Transit months back, starting the war. Now he'd be the one to end it.

Bulger rolled down the window. "Hey, Kenny!" he shouted. Kenneth turned and saw Whitey's face looming up, and a gun leveled at him at eye height.

"It's over," Whitey snarled. "You're out of business. No other warnings."

And that was it. The Killeens just . . . stopped. To fend off further attacks from Whitey, the cowed Killeens offered him control of the gang. With that opening, Whitey persuaded Winter to move into the vacuum with him, and the two rounded up some other Winter Hill heavyweights and went at the Mullens harder than the Killeens ever had. Whitey took out six of them in a single two-day spree, and he'd slaughtered a full dozen by 1975. When Whitey was done, the gang landscape had changed. Now there was Jerry Angiulo's Mafia operation based in the North End, and Howie Winter's Winter Hill gang in Somerville, and that was pretty much it. Except that inside Winter Hill, people were starting to listen to Whitey, not Howie. He'd branched out to take personal control of all the rackets in South Boston, and he was making inroads among the bookies in the North End, too. There was nothing that Winter could say about it, even though it was cutting into Winter's revenue so bad that, at one point in the 1970s, he had to go to Angiulo for a loan. Then, scrambling to pay the interest, he started rigging horse races, which was not his game. It cost him. Acting on a tip, the feds arrested him for race-fixing in 1979. He was sent to prison with most of the Somerville crew, except for Whitey Bulger and Steve Flemmi. They were Winter Hill now. But everyone knew which of the two called the shots.

— CHAPTER 4 —

I was a trooper for four years altogether, and the work went well. I was a producer, so I was in on a lot of police action, arrests especially, which get you noticed.

After a while you develop a reputation, good or bad, and opportunities come with it. I was approached several times about joining the district attorney's drug unit, but it would take something more for me to move to a different assignment. I liked the job I had.

That year, 1984, Colonel Canty asked Dave Mattioli, a sharp, young lieutenant in the State Police, to start up an Intelligence Unit to focus on organized crime. Mattioli was a real up-and-comer, smart and well liked, and when the colonel gave him that assignment, it meant the top brass was going to get behind it. The State Police already had an OC unit called Special Services commanded by Lieutenant Charlie Henderson, but it concentrated more on gaming than on more serious mob crimes. Mattioli's unit would strike at the OC hierarchy, working with the FBI to do it. In fact, the unit was the FBI's idea.

Dave told me all about it one night. I was out on patrol, and he got me by radio and asked me to meet him at a Friendly's in Worcester. We were in a booth there when he laid it all out.

"So, would you be interested in joining it?" he asked me.

"Absolutely," I told him. It was no decision at all. Working with Mattioli *and* with the FBI on serious stuff like the mob? Count me in.

Organized crime had always been a federal topic. The FBI had started hitting mobsters with its Top Hoodlum Program of 1953, and it had made a famous score in 1957, when it rounded up a slew of baffled mafiosi at what was supposed to be their top-secret gathering in Bingham-ton, New York. But the Bureau had been more preoccupied with headline targets like bank robbers and Communists, and it never went all that hard against syndicates, as they were known, until Hoover decided to make the syndicates a top priority during the Kennedy administration. One of the first mobsters he went after was Raymond Patriarca Sr., in Providence. Crawling with mobsters in those days, Providence was the Mafia head-quarters for all of New England.

Still, the FBI didn't have much luck against the mob until 1970, when Congress passed an antiracketeering act, RICO, that made it illegal to be in a mob at all. Since RICO is federal, only the feds can act on it, so they'd been doing the bulk of the OC work. But recently, some state police had started to move in on the OC action, seeing how much the mob was eat-ing away at their cities.

Plus, the Intelligence Unit was designed to work closely with the FBI, following up on leads that the feds had been developing. They'd just had those indictments that hit hard at the leadership of the Italian mob, start-ing with Jerry Angiulo, and going pretty deep, after they bugged the mob's headquarters on Prince Street in the North End.

A nervy FBI agent, Ed Quinn, arrested Angiulo at a North End restau-rant. It was one of those moments the FBI loves to publicize, and it sure impressed me when I heard about it. After Quinn cuffed him, Angiulo was so sure the charges would never stick that he told the waiter at the restaurant to leave his pork chops on the table. He'd be back before they got cold. They must be icy now. At the time, I had to hand it to Quinn. That was a hell of an operation, and it is hard to tell the story without a chuckle.

In those days, I had nothing but admiration for J. Edgar Hoover and his G-men. I viewed them all as solid professionals—highly qualified and well trained and all the rest of it. They were the elite of our profession. And that wasn't just a line. I really believed it. And if I had any doubt, all those skills were on full display in the Angiulo investigation. It was no easy thing to penetrate a secretive and deadly organization like La Cosa

Nostra—the LCN—but the feds did, and they got a raft of indictments out of it. The whole idea was really exciting. I couldn't wait.

————————

The FBI offices were up in the McCormack Building at that time, across the plaza from City Hall. From up there you can see up the Charles, and out to Boston Harbor. By contrast, Mattioli's group would be working out of offices in suburban Framingham in a low-rise that looked out onto a parking lot. Jim Ring ran the FBI's organized crime unit of the Boston office, the one we'd be allied with. The Boston office was a bigger deal than you'd think. It didn't just run Boston, but all of New England. Hundreds of agents took their orders from the Boston office; many of them worked there in the McCormack Building, and the others spread out to branch offices throughout the six states.

Strangely enough, everybody seemed to have worked in Worcester. Not just Mattioli and Henderson, but Ring, too. He'd worked out of the FBI branch office there. I didn't know him, but he knew Mattioli and Henderson. It seemed to me that this would help everybody get along, but it didn't. For one thing, Henderson didn't get along with Ring, and I soon realized that few people did.

It wasn't until I spent some time with Ring myself that I got it. He smoked a pipe—a rarity in any office and unheard-of in law enforcement—and he liked to sit back in his chair, puffing out a cloud of pipe smoke, occasionally sending a little of it your way, as he went on and on about something that, often, didn't have much to do with anything.

Ring chose Nick Gianturco to be his case agent, the one in charge of any investigation we did from the FBI side. I'd do that on the State Police side. So Nick and I were set up to work together, and to show how the Staties and the feds can get along. And we did that. We actually were friends, up to a point anyway. Nick talked with his hands and was full of laughter. A fun guy. Everybody liked him, and I did, too. And we opened up to each other a fair amount.

Still, it didn't take long for me to figure out that, as much fun as he was, Nick set firm limits on any friendship. It would never go beyond his loyalty to the FBI even if the FBI was wrong. So I knew where I stood with Nick. His friendship was conditional.

When I got into organized crime investigations, it took me a while to see the big picture. Usually with homicides, when you have a dead body at your feet, the explanation is right there—somebody got mad, or greedy, and the gun came out. But with a mob hit, the explanation always lies somewhere else, often far away. It takes a while to figure out.

Also, one mob is not like another one. The Italian mob is night and day different from the Irish mob. The Mafia is like a little army, with military ranks like all that capo and consiglieri stuff they take very seriously. The Irish mob is more like a gang, one that doesn't have much order beyond the fact that the toughest bastard in the group usually runs it.

When you look at it like that, it's pretty clear, but it gets blurry at the borders, when you see Italians bringing the Irish in on something, and the Irish doing a favor for the Italians back, and both groups working together if the money is right. And there are times when someone from one mob gets wasted by someone from the other. That can be shrugged off or lead to total war, and it's anyone's guess which.

I wasn't the only one having trouble figuring it out. In April 1986, a couple of years after I got into OC, President Reagan's Commission on Organized Crime issued a book, "The Impact: Organized Crime Today," that tried to lay out the basics. A presidential report, a big fat volume, all the experts—and they still got a lot of it wrong. For instance, the report had the McLaughlins as a major presence in Boston—when they hadn't been seen in years. And the commission didn't pay much attention to the bookmakers who were the basis for a lot of mob revenue.

But the report did provide a useful overview of the Irish mob, which can be hard to track because it's so free-form. The commission indicated that, while the Irish mob was generally in retreat, it was growing in a few northeastern cities, including Boston. The report had "Howard Winter"—known to everyone as Howie—running the Irish mob out of an auto repair shop in Winter Hill, although Whitey was even then vying with him for supremacy.

The report also claimed that another of the three most powerful mobs was run by a man it identified as "James Bolger." Bolger. Whitey, of course. Aside from the misspelling, the commission was smart to describe Whitey as on his own, free from Winter Hill. It was telling that, while Angiulo was Mafia and Winter was Winter Hill, Whitey was just Whitey, largely on his own, beholden only to himself, even if he was in with Steve Flemmi. But the names indicated how hard it can be to draw the line between the Irish and the Italians, since Flemmi was with the Irish, despite his Italian descent. (And he had been with the Mafia once, only to be lured away by Whitey.) The report failed to mention the territories in Boston where the different mobs actually operated. Winter Hill was based in Somerville, just over the Cambridge border, and drew its strength from there. Bulger had South Boston, as everybody knew, and his power extended out from there. And the Italians had the North End, a slice of the northern part of the original city, near the water.

In Boston, the Irish weren't entirely independent of the Italians, however. They couldn't afford to be. A bigger organization, with a broader reach, the Italians had the money, and the Irish had to use it to bankroll their heavy loan-sharking operation. So the Mafia was the Irish mob's bank. The Irish borrowed the money at 1 to 2 percent a week, and turned around to shylock it out at 5 or 6 percent to people who had nowhere else to go. And Whitey worked with Winter Hill as necessary, too. The Winter Hill mob controlled the docks along the Boston waterfront and was tight with the Teamsters who operated down there. Anyone who wanted to bring anything onto or off the docks had to pay Howie's people a hefty toll. If anyone wanted to run a business down there, the charge was steeper, a quarter of the profits. But Bulger and Flemmi policed that, and they took their share.

At this point, Angiulo had been arrested, his pork chops cooling, but the Mafia headquarters remained on Prince Street in the North End. That was a festive, light-filled part of downtown, long Italian to the core, but it was finally getting gentrified as ethnic barriers were coming down all over the city. Big as the city was, the Boston Mafia was still subservient to the boys in Providence, chiefly Raymond Patriarca's son Ray Jr., a stubby guy who was the new godfather after his father's death a few years back.

Given the Italians' superior power, why did they put up with the Irish? Why not just wipe out the Irish and have all of Boston to themselves? When I asked Mattioli about that, he just smiled. "It's because the Italians are scared shitless by the Irish, just like everybody else is," he told me. "The Winter Hill mob may not be long on numbers, but they're killers, Tommy." One bullet, that's all it takes for them to solve a problem. That was the idea. If they want you dead, order your casket.

When the Mafia wanted to take somebody out, it often subcontracted the job to Winter Hill, especially to a hit man named John Martorano for the most important jobs. He'd developed a reputation for being lethal and silent. When the Irish wanted to liquidate someone, they did it themselves.

— CHAPTER 5 —

For the first case in our joint effort with the FBI, the feds decided to go after Frank Oreto Sr., an edgy mafioso who'd done fifteen years for the gangland slaying of another Italian mobster, Joe Lanzi, back in 1967. Apparently, Lanzi needed to be taught a lesson. Now Oreto was out of prison and back with the mob like he'd never left, this time running a huge loan-sharking operation out of a nightclub called Fasads in Revere—a tough town along the water just past Logan Airport.

Just like the Irish loan sharks in the presidential commission's report, Oreto was putting out thick wads of Mafia cash onto the street, with a roving gang of thugs to collect the payments due. If you didn't pay up— well, the idea was that you'd never think about not paying up. But if it came to that, they'd definitely hurt you, hurt you in all the most sensitive places, and bad enough that you'd happily pay them more than they asked. But they would never hurt you enough to keep you from paying. If they've lent you money, they don't want you disabled, just like they don't want you dead.

The FBI focused on the loan-sharking, but the feds were aware that Oreto was a contract killer. And they were afraid that he might want to move up in the LCN by derailing the case the FBI had built so painstakingly against Angiulo by knocking off a juror or the judge, or maybe even by blowing up the courthouse. If he was going to try such a thing, the feds wanted wiretaps and bugs in place to let them know about it well in advance. And Oreto was the kind of guy who'd do something crazy like that. The feds thought so, anyway, and they wanted us to take him out of the picture.

Oreto made for a long, heavy, exhausting investigation, a lot more of everything than anything I'd ever faced before. Nothing I'd ever done in Worcester prepared me for it. The feds figured it could last six months, but they were short by six. It wasn't just a matter of getting Oreto; it involved getting his whole network—his leg breakers, his Mafia contacts, his partners, and a lot of others. And, again, it was a test to see if the State Police and FBI could work together. The feds knew everything there was to know about mob investigation; we knew the territory. They had money; we had manpower. But then, there's always a difference between how you draw up the play on the blackboard and how you run it in the game.

———

In the early stages, Nick and I were going to handle it all by ourselves. State Police, FBI. Go to it. I learned quickly what to expect from Nick. You couldn't wait around to get something done; you just had to do it yourself. Clearly there were two different work ethics in play when it came down to the State Police and the FBI. We did most of the street work; they manned the interior jobs, monitoring the recorders. We worked the late hours; them not so much.

An investigation like Oreto is a real grind—there's the months of undercover surveillance to gather the evidence you need to persuade a judge to approve a wiretap, and then there are all the months after that holed up in some listening station monitoring the bugs, and don't ask about the transcribing, which is done by hand and causes cramps and the sort of brain fatigue that can't be cured by sleep. For the first part, I spent a lot of time in Fasads, which is one of the more depressing places I've ever been in. It had a huge dance floor—empty most of the time—with some of those big glittering balls dangling overhead. Hell looks different, I expect, but it probably feels like that.

That was in the main room. There was a bar out back, and I'd usually park myself there, nursing a beer for as long as I could. I'd watch people out of the corner of my eye, and try to look like just another guy in no hurry to get home. The bartender was the suspicious type, and he kept eyeing me, but after a few days he took me for a regular and would set down a Bud Lite for me practically as soon as I walked in.

I saw a lot of Oreto down there. You couldn't miss him. In the bar, behind the counter, all over the place. Short guy—he couldn't have been more than five-six—but he was built like a refrigerator, and he had a cartoonish Fu Manchu mustache and an Italian Afro. He was a wild man. He seemed to have electricity in his veins, and you never knew when he was going to go off. He might be talking to somebody, calm as anything, and then—*zing!*—he'd just lose it. He'd start hopping around, hands going everywhere, and screaming like he was going to kill somebody. He had to be on coke. Nobody is that crazy.

When I wasn't at the bar, I was out in the parking lot, sitting in my car, checking out the people coming and going. If I saw someone suspicious, I'd fire off a few photographs out my rear window, and I'd take down the plate number to run. I'd get the ID, then do a background check. Anyone who didn't seem to be coming in to get laid or drunk—those were the ones who interested me. They were obviously here for Oreto. Some of these players were hard to miss—the loud suits, the man jewelry, the shiny shoes. Others were guys who carried a lot of darkness around with them.

———

A fair amount of the ID checks I ordered on the people at Fasads came back positive, and gradually I could start putting the people together into Oreto's world. I had the money guys, the muscle, the Mafia connections, and a lot more who were hard to classify.

A lot of these guys were straight out of *Goodfellas*, but the one who caught me up was the fellow who rolled up in a Lincoln Town Car. He seemed to be out of a different movie altogether. An imposing character, but smooth, he was dressed for a night out, in a jacket and tie. At first, I thought he was just a rich suburbanite out on the town, but he kept coming back. And he always greeted Oreto warmly, with a smile and a slap on the back, and then a few quiet words. I didn't get it—why would a man like that be so chummy with a guy with a Fu Manchu?

So I ran the plates, and found out that his name was Sid Weiner, pronounced "whiner." He had a few years on him; he lived in a nice part of
Wakefield; and the stunner: he was vice president of Capitol Bank, one of
the largest banks in Boston back then.

What was the vice president of Capitol Bank doing here? I dug into
that for weeks, pulled out bank records, hit the newspaper morgue, and
followed Weiner wherever he went. I'd never tracked anyone before, and I
got very curious to see where he would lead, where *this* would lead.

And finally I had it: Oreto and Weiner were partners in a side operation that skimmed off some of Weiner's own Capitol Bank customers, the
ones that Weiner had pegged as deadbeats. Which made them perfect for
Oreto. When they couldn't make their Capitol payments, Weiner recommended they turn to this other financier he knew, a Mr. Frank Oreto,
who'd be happy to tide them over with a short-term loan. He left out the
part about the interest rate. Weiner then wrote the bank loan off as uncol-
lectable, so Capitol wouldn't expect the money back. But with his posse of
leg breakers, Oreto had a way to collect what Capitol Bank couldn't. Oreto
and Weiner split the proceeds. It was sweet: they got to keep the capital
and the interest, both.

When I brought all this back to Ring and Mattioli, they were thrilled
by the Capitol Bank connection. This was obviously much bigger than
they thought. We put together an affidavit for a judge's permission to
wiretap, and soon we were good to go.

For a listening post, I rented a nasty little one-bedroom apartment
on the top floor of a condominium about a mile away. No AC, broil-
ing in summer, and, without much heat, freezing in winter, it was like a
grubby bachelor pad. I slept over a few times; a bunch of people did, since
we had to monitor the taps pretty much around the clock. There were
three phones tapped, and a bug in the office, which meant four people
to man them, and, since Fasads was open late into the night, long hours.
Sweaty headphones clapped over your ears, hours of messy conversations
in heavy Italian accents long on fuckin' this and fuckin' that—this wasn't
always easy listening. We had to record all the conversations on multiple

machines with multiple cassettes for the different parties: one for the judge, one for the prosecution, one for the defense, one for us, etc. And we had to go by the book, so we could follow an off-case conversation only for a few minutes before shutting it down for a bit, and then tuning back in. Repeat and repeat and repeat. The rule of minimization, they called it. Judges are sensitive to people's privacy, and they should be, but it was a total pain for us. And then there was the transcription.

The feds were supposed to go in with us, and I saw a few agents in there besides Nick. One of them was John Connolly. Seeing him on Oreto, you'd almost think he was Mafia, not fed. He had the chunky ring, the slicked-back hair, the jet-black Italian suit, the glad-to-see-ya smile. He could have been John Gotti's younger brother, but I'll give him this: The guy exuded likability. He used to come in with pizza on the late Sunday shift, and, back then, he was a welcome sight.

First time we met there, he came right up to me and stuck out a hand. "You're Danny's nephew, right? Danny Foley?" He meant my uncle Dan Foley, a longtime state senator from Worcester, who was the Democratic majority leader and Billy Bulger's number two. How he knew, I don't know. But that was Connolly. Always ready to make a connection, and to use one.

"Yeah, that's right."

"I'm pretty close to Billy." He brightened and tapped me on the shoulder, his face shining.

"Nice to meet you, John." I felt like I'd been cleared, accepted into the club. John made you feel that way. He was engaging and disarming at the same time.

Connolly had grown up with the Bulgers in the Old Harbor project in Southie. He'd known Bill Bulger from there—Whitey, too, but he didn't mention that. As he talked, he continued to play up the Billy connection. A lot of Billy this and Billy that. He made it sound like he spent every afternoon lazing about the senate president's office.

That first time, Connolly didn't stay much longer than it took to have that little conversation. Gianturco did his time on the machines, but for the most part I got the feeling that the FBI saw this kind of grunt work as beneath them. The FBI was different, no question. It had that elite mentality, and, when it was doing OC, it had those RICO statutes that only it could enforce. But we had stuff of our own. Only we could enforce the state laws, meaning only we could stop a car for speeding or arrest someone for murder. Ring knew this and wanted our authority to enhance his. On Oreto at one point, we needed to plant a bug in the building he was using. The problem was the lock was a Medeco, which is absolutely impossible to pick. If you don't have a key, forget it. But I saw a janitor use a key to go in, and I knew how I could get a copy of it without coming right out and demanding it. I did what the feds couldn't: I got the plate number of the janitor's car, and ran it by the registry, and registry told me his license was about to expire. Perfect.

The next day, I was in my cruiser, and I followed the janitor out from the apartment building. When he was out on the road, I flipped on the siren and pulled him over. I took his license and registration, strolled back to the cruiser, waited a few beats, then came back and told him that he had a little problem with his license that would take a few minutes. "I'll have to take your keys while I straighten it out," I told him. The Medeco key was on the chain with the car key. Back in the car, I took a photograph of it with a 35-millimeter camera. Pretty sharp focus. I gave the shot to the FBI lab, which duped the key for us, and we were in.

When I showed the feds the key, they just gaped at me.

We finally collected enough evidence of loan-sharking and conspiracy to win indictments of Oreto and Weiner. We grabbed Oreto in the early afternoon. He was sprawled out in his bed, dead asleep, obviously drugged out. He barely knew what was happening when we woke him up and slapped the cuffs on him. But Weiner was staggered. We nabbed him in his big house in the suburbs, and when we cuffed him there in his front hall, with his wife watching, he went dead white.

With the Capitol dimension, the case had a lot of elements and pulled in a couple of dozen people all together. The FBI agents said it was the biggest loan-sharking case they'd ever been in on, anywhere. Gianturco and I and a few others from both the State Police and the FBI handled the arrests. We'd worked together, and we'd gotten the job done. And the Angiulo trial went ahead without incident.

One guy we grabbed was a bruiser with heavy arms and a wide neck. Dan Forte, pronounced "forty." A leg breaker, obviously. He was shacked up with a prostitute in a bad part of Peabody, farther north. I followed him from Fasads a few times, watching him make the rounds of bars and back alleys for his pickups. I had him: dates, times, photographs. I ran him. He had a bit of a rap sheet—no surprise there—but nothing serious. Still, it wasn't going to go well for him when we arrested him in the loan-sharking operation.

But he seemed like a guy who got around, so I had a proposition for him.

"Here's how it is," I told him. "I can send you to prison for probably five or six years. Or maybe we can work something out."

"Like?" he asked, as if he didn't know.

"Help us out with a little information now and again. You know some people that I'd like to know a little more about."

"Aw, fuck, man. Be an informer, that what you mean?"

"Do everything you're doing now is what I'm saying, just pay attention to who, what."

"A wire?"

"Maybe sometimes."

"Fuck," Forte said.

I spelled out a little more about what we had in mind, and where the limits were.

"Don't worry," I wound up. "Nothing will happen. And if it does, I'll always be right outside. No shit. Right there."

"How many years did you say?"

"Five, six."

"Fuck," he repeated.

And so Forte became my first Boston informant. I'd had plenty in Worcester and around there. And there would be plenty more in Boston after Forte. But he showed the way—both as to what you should do with informants and as to what you shouldn't. I knew enough to know you can't just let informants go. You have to watch them, be careful. They can be manipulative and often calculating, but you do end up depending on them, and they on you. To a degree, you're in it together, the two of you moving around in the dark.

— CHAPTER 6 —

The Oreto operation dealt the Italian mob another heavy blow by taking out a major source of money, and by wrecking any hopes that it could scuttle the Angiulo trial.

Lieutenant Dave Mattioli, the head of my OC unit, was happy to see how it turned out. Back at headquarters in Framingham, he took me aside. "So what do you want to work on next?" he asked me.

I was starting to see that after the Prince Street indictments, the Mafia wasn't nearly as much of a threat anymore. And Howie Winter was just completing prison time and decided not to come back to Boston, relocating to Worcester.

That left only one mobster, the only one who was rising while the others were falling. Rising in power, in control, and in reputation. You didn't even have to say the name, because everybody was already thinking it.

"I want to work on Whitey Bulger," I told him. "Him and Flemmi." I'd checked the records. Neither of them had ever even been arrested since 1965. That was about twenty years ago. "Come on," I told Mattioli. "Does anybody really think he's gone straight? Got an office job?" It was almost laughable, the notion of Whitey Bulger pulling down a regular paycheck.

Mattioli had to smile at that. "Let me check with Ring."

I'd gotten to know another trooper, Jimmy White, back when we were on patrol and later on the Oreto investigation, and I loved the guy. He was about the hardest worker I'd ever seen. He could really grind it out. I couldn't imagine trying to get Bulger without Jimmy. For something like that, you need people you can trust with your life, and that was Jimmy for me. He'd been a Gold Gloves boxer when he was younger. Threw some heavy punches, and he must have taken some, too, but there wasn't a scar on him. He'd hold his ground and let fly. The man was as solid as they come.

When I ran the Bulger idea by him, he was ready to start that afternoon. "Perfect," he said. "Let's do it."

A couple of days later, Mattioli invited Jimmy and me into his office at headquarters, and he shut the door. That wasn't good.

"I've run it by Ring," he told us. "And he says no. Can't do Bulger. Can't do Flemmi."

Jimmy and I looked at each other. "Why the hell not?" Jimmy asked.

"Because they're not LCN, and the FBI is only doing LCN."

"Yeah, but Dave," I told him. "Come on. LCN is way down. But Bulger, shit. He's the biggest thing in Boston right now. Maybe ever. You know that. Everybody knows that. Just by himself, he's probably bigger than the whole LCN right now. Add Flemmi—"

He didn't want to hear it. He raised his hands to shut me up. "Guys, I know. But the FBI wants to go after the LCN, OK? So that's it. LCN."

———

So, LCN it was. And the FBI laid out the plan, just like before, with Oreto. This time, the idea was to wipe out the next rank of mafiosi before they could take over. It was like chopping off the head of a snake, the way the FBI explained it. Chop off the head, and you don't have to worry about the rest of the snake. It made sense if you were worried about the LCN in Boston. That wasn't Jimmy and me. As far as we could see, after the Angiulo takedown and the Oreto case, Whitey posed the greater threat. But we were both new to OC and the FBI had been working it a long time. The feds had spent years killing off the Italian mob, and they probably wanted to make sure it stayed dead, and I had to respect that.

This new one was called Operation Jungle Mist—an inside joke that I never got—but instead of going after a single loan shark, this one targeted five wiseguys who were comers in the mob. And these weren't hotheads like Oreto, but serious, methodical, and dangerous killers who knew the feds were all over them, and so the feds were going to proceed very cautiously.

The operation focused on a sub shop called Vanessa's on the ground floor of the Prudential Center by Boylston Street in the Back Bay. It was run by a dark, thickset man named Angelo "Sonny" Mercurio. At the time, he wasn't much, but he was ambitious, and he later decided that if he couldn't rise up in the mob, he'd bring it crashing down. He tipped off the FBI to a big Mafia induction ceremony that was to take place in Medford, in the presence of all the Mafia heavyweights, from Raymond Patriarca Jr.—that chubby son of the towering New England godfather Raymond Patriarca Sr.—on down. The ceremony was like something at the Vatican. On Mercurio's say-so, the FBI sneaked in some recording devices and got the whole thing on blurry videotape: the teary speeches, the pricking of fingers, the blood oaths as four new recruits joined the Family. That tape sent a bunch of mafiosi away for a long time, but it did worse things for the morale of the mafiosi who remained. It was embarrassing to the mob to have its most sacred ceremony on the local evening news, and the butt of a thousand barroom jokes. Lucky for Mercurio, no one fingered him as the rat.

At the time of Operation Jungle Mist, though, we knew Mercurio as an LCN foot soldier with decent prospects. He owned Vanessa's, where he'd have regular get-togethers with some other wiseguys to talk business in the storage room in the back. It was a perfect cover. At that point, I still didn't know Boston all that well, but the Prudential Center—the Pru—was about the last place I'd have picked as a mob hangout. It was like finding the New York mob holed up by the skating rink at Rockefeller Center. But it had the perfect entrance. The wiseguys could park their fat cars on the fifth level belowground, ride up in the service elevator, sneak down a long dark corridor, and come in through a back door, never once showing themselves to the street.

Inside, beside an industrial refrigerator and some racks of bread, all the heavies would sit in a ring of metal chairs and talk business. From the beginning, it was clear that the FBI had come to the right place. When Angiulo went down, it was like a forest had burned, and this was the new growth pushing its way up. Besides Sonny Mercurio, there were Vinny Ferrara, Bobby Carrozza, Joe Russo, and Dennis Lepore. This was summer, and, in the glimpses we got of them, all of them wore the usual open shirts, creased pants, and a lot of jewelry. And guns, for all we knew. All of them were made men, so named because they'd murdered for the mob, and a couple of them—Ferrara and Russo—had strong reputations as capable hit men. If this was poker, they were four face cards, with Mercurio a nine, with ambitions.

To record what went on, working with a few members of the FBI tech team, some of us from state OC went over there late one night. A locksmith picked the lock, and we sneaked in. We put a few mikes in the storage room where the mafiosi met, each mike about the size of a match head. We dropped the wires down to the basement underneath, and outside to a line that could have sent it anywhere in the world, but this time sent it literally straight up—to the fiftieth floor of the Prudential tower that loomed overhead. Up there, two floors down from the very top, we'd set up a listening station in a vacant office with a nice view of the Charles.

For hours on end, we were up in that office, grinding through days, headsets cupped over our ears. It was Oreto all over again. All the wiseguys sounded alike—five gruff Italians barking at one another, lobbing f-bombs.

But that was only half my job. The rest of the time I spent undercover down at ground level. I grew a beard—much to Marguerite's distress—but kept it neatly trimmed, since I was carrying myself as a proper businessman. I kept my hair brushed, shined my shoes, and wore a jacket and tie.

After the FBI's campaign against Angiulo, and ours against Oreto, all the mobsters were on high alert. You could feel it. When it was my shift, I'd hang right by Vanessa's, to see if I could spot anyone. One lunchtime, I was sitting at a table out front, reading the *Globe* over an Italian sub. I had a briefcase by my feet, rigged up with a tiny camera inside, ready to snap away through a pinhole. Suddenly, the door opened and it was Vinny Ferrara, out to have a look around. He's a big, menacing guy, anger all over his face. He saw me sitting there with my newspaper, and I could see his eyes narrow. He walked right up to me, hovered there for a moment, then swung around to stand behind me. I could almost feel his breath on the back of my neck.

He was testing me. Was I going to allow this? How was I going to react? Was I going to go head-to-head with a Mafia hit man? Well, I didn't know what was going to happen, but Ferrara was going to learn that I wasn't going to let anyone breathe on me, whoever he was.

I wheeled around and stared at him—hard. Deep into his black eyes. He stared just as hard back at me. We were really locked in. Finally he gave a little half smile and a tiny nod and broke it off. He stepped around me, made his way to the door, and disappeared once more into the darkness of the sub shop. To this day, I don't know if he decided I was a cop, or if he decided I wasn't, but I am pretty sure he figured he'd sent me a message either way.

It wasn't just Ferrara. They all radiated sweaty, anxious heat. Like Ferrara, the others would sometimes come outside, glance around, then disappear inside again. When they were inside, buried in that storeroom, they assumed they were invisible, which they were—from us. But not from the various informants who came through. And their words were captured in our headsets on the fiftieth floor.

After Oreto, an investigation like this was getting to be pretty straightforward—watch, listen, use informants, build case, indict. It was gutsy to go straight at these gangsters, but nothing unusual for OC work. What got to me came on before any of the gangsters even got on the scene. It was the initial affidavit from the FBI, the one the feds submitted to the court to get permission to do the electronic surveillance at Vanessa's in the first place. As with the request on Oreto, an affidavit like that is intended to convince a judge that there is enough evidence of serious crimes to warrant a tap—and the breach of a subject's First Amendment rights that this entails. Judges take those rights seriously, they look at an affidavit hard, and they count on investigators to tell the absolute truth in it.

This particular affidavit cited a name that caught my attention. James J. "Whitey" Bulger, as the writers always put it in such documents. The affidavit named Bulger as meeting at Vanessa's with all the other wise guys. Interesting. Bulger was meeting at this place, too? Maybe we'd have a shot at him after all.

After I saw that affidavit, I asked Jimmy about it. "Did you see that?" I asked him. "It says Whitey Bulger has been meeting at Vanessa's with these guys."

"Yeah, I noticed that."

"You ever see him around Vanessa's?"

"Shit, no."

"And you'd remember, right?"

Jimmy just looked at me.

"So, how do you figure it?"

He just shrugged. "Can't."

We checked around with a couple of other troopers working the case. Nobody had ever seen Whitey, or heard him, or heard anything about him on all the hours of talk we listened in on. And yet the FBI had claimed that Whitey had been there as a major player before we arrived. This was why the wiretap was so important. I didn't get it. Whitey was cited by the FBI as someone on the inside, and yet there was no indication that he'd ever been one. Jimmy and I talked this one over a lot. Neither of us could come up with a good scenario. Could the FBI have faked all this, put Whitey's name on an affidavit to sell it to the judge? Neither Jimmy or I had any idea—but there was no one to ask. We'd never get a straight answer, and if we tried to get one, nobody who'd know would ever talk to us again. No—far better to keep our mouths shut. We were still the new guys, and new guys don't ask those kinds of questions.

— CHAPTER 7 —

Operation Jungle Mist did not end there. It only began there. When the electronic surveillance was nearly over, we got warrants to search Vanessa's and a few other places for further evidence. One of them was Mercurio's place north of Boston. We brought Mercurio with us when we went over there. Me, Jimmy White, and some FBI agents, one of them John Connolly. Like he had on Oreto, Connolly had been breezing into and out of the Vanessa's surveillance, like someone between appointments. Ring was there, professorial as always, but off a little to the side, as usual. As we were going through his place, Connolly tapped Mercurio on the shoulder and nodded for him to step into another room with him, where it could be just them. Other FBI guys had let me know that Connolly handled the most valuable FBI informants, the "top-echelon" ones, meaning he recruited them and he was the agent they talked to, maybe the only one. He was famous for it. He was like one of the superagents who rep the star athletes. Connolly was cocky about it; he knew it was his claim to fame. The whole thing of being a handler, as it was called, was supposed to be cloaked in mystery, the deepest of FBI secrets, but it was pretty obvious. To begin with, it was why Connolly didn't do any of the hard stuff, why we hardly ever saw him, and why he was always peacocking around.

When Jimmy saw Connolly move in on Mercurio there in his apartment, he could tell that Connolly was giving him the talk. By now I'd made plenty of pitches myself, and I knew how it went. How Mercurio had only two choices—go away for years and years and years, or talk to us from time to time. It seems so easy, when put like that. Jimmy could tell just by the way Connolly took Mercurio aside. For Mercurio, it wasn't all bad news. To be an informer meant that he wouldn't be doing time. But it wasn't something the FBI wanted to advertise; that was why Connolly took him into another room and spoke quietly enough so Jimmy couldn't hear a word.

That wasn't the end of it, though. It was as an informant that Mercurio tipped off the FBI to the induction ceremony, but after that he started to get cocky himself, because he figured out that the FBI wasn't likely to hold him back from pretty much whatever he tried to do. He knew that the feds didn't want to lose him. Not only would they not go after him; they'd make sure that nobody else did either. Mercurio was golden, and all he had to do was shine.

Mercurio had it in for "Cadillac" Frank Salemme, who'd just gotten out of prison and was seeking to move up the ladder in the Mafia. It was a grudge that went back to the 1960s, when Raymond Patriarca Sr. asked Salemme to do him a favor. The hit man Joe "The Animal" Barboza had strayed from the mob's interests, and Patriarca wanted Salemme to straighten him out. Barboza was in custody and unreachable, but his lawyer, John Fitzgerald, wasn't. Salemme rigged up Fitzgerald's car with explosives. When Fitzgerald hit the ignition, the car went sky high. Incredibly, Fitzgerald lost only a leg. Salemme fled to New York, but the FBI was tipped off to his whereabouts, and our friend John Connolly picked him up. Salemme did some serious time, and because Ray Sr. was dead by the time he got out, Salemme wanted to collect on the father's obligation from the son, Ray Jr. He wanted a spot in the Boston leadership, and the chance to take over.

Mercurio feared that Salemme's rise might mean his own fall, and he had the solution. Mercurio put together a crew, and one morning he asked Salemme to come to a meeting with everyone at the International House of Pancakes in Saugus. When Salemme strolled out to his car, Mercurio's gang leaped out at him with machine guns and sprayed him with bullets. Salemme went down screaming. Amazingly, none of the bullets hit anything vital, and somehow he survived.

Salemme never identified his assailants.

There were plenty of rumors, but the FBI never said a word. But I could see the results for myself a few months later. Jimmy and I had been tailing Salemme in a couple of unmarked State Police cars, ready to grab him on a warrant for a scam in California. The idea was just to get into his pockets. Literally—empty his pockets to find any little notes he carried, which can be surprisingly helpful in figuring things out; you get names, phone numbers. I was out with Jimmy and a trooper we sometimes worked with, Ray Stevens. Jimmy and Ray pinched Salemme off from the front, and I pulled up behind so he couldn't back up. We were all in plain clothes, and when we had Frank stopped, we got out of our cars and approached him with our guns out. We were yelling at him—"Get out of the car, Frank! Now! Out of the car!" Salemme opened the door and got out, his hands up, terrified, and braced like we were going to blast him. "No!" he shouted. "Please. Shit—no!" Just quivering with fear.

"We're State Police, Frank," I told him.

"State—?" He grabbed his heart, he was so overwhelmed, and his body went limp for a second. "Oh, shit, man, Jesus. State Police. Oh, thank God. You gave me a hell of a scare there." He had to wait a second to catch his breath. "God. Fuck."

We took him in to the barracks. "I thought you were coming for me," he gasped when we had him inside. He didn't want to be any more specific, but he was too worked up to say anything. During the booking process, Frank showed his wounds like they were medals. He reached down and yanked up his shirt, and I could see purplish scars all over his chest, maybe half a dozen of them. "Look at this! I nearly fucking died. See what those fuckers did to me? You see that? Those pieces of shit." He dropped his shirt again.

From the way he was talking, we knew perfectly well it was a hit, and we knew who'd done it, and he knew we knew. We all knew why, too. The only thing none of us knew was how much the FBI knew about it. But we had a pretty good guess that, since Mercurio was FBI, the feds knew a good deal. By that time, I'd figured out that information like this went into the FBI, but it never came out. The FBI was a black hole, you might say.

— CHAPTER 8 —

When I was working on OC, it was never just one case at a time. It was two, three, and you never knew when the next one was coming in. Like late one Friday afternoon back in October 1986, I was out on the turnpike, headed home after another rough day on Operation Jungle Mist, when I got word that I was wanted at FBI headquarters. I didn't have to ask if they wanted me *now*. I pulled right off at the next exit and doubled back.

At the McCormack Building I was ushered into Jim Ring's office, where I found Mattioli, Ring, Gianturco, and Sergeant Sullivan, a supervisor of ours with the State Police. They'd been talking animatedly, but they went dead silent when I came into the room.

Finally Gianturco spoke. "Sorry about this, Tommy," he said quietly. He patted my shoulder lightly, then he stepped out of the room to leave me alone with my superiors.

"What's going on?" I asked Ring.

Ring gestured for me to take a seat by his desk, while the others drew up chairs, and he settled himself comfortably in the swivel chair behind his desk. Then he leaned back, lit his pipe, and took a long draw. He dropped his match into the ashtray and turned to me. "We need to ask you, Tom. Who've you been talking to?"

"What do you mean?" I couldn't read his eyes. "About what?"

"About Danny Forte, and how you're using him."

"Forte?" I wanted to make sure I had that right. "That source of mine?" He was the leg breaker I'd flipped on the Oreto case. Forte wore a wire for us, and Jimmy and I had followed him and listened in when he made his rounds collecting, and then when he passed the money on to the wiseguys in the North End. He'd proved to be a key player for us, pulling in conversations with the other hoods in the Mafia network. And he'd helped out with Vanessa's, too, since he was in with people like Vinny Ferrara, the heavy who'd tried to stare me down outside the lunch place. Thanks to Forte, we'd made some cases we wouldn't have made otherwise. And whenever it got risky for him, we held up our end of the bargain. Jimmy and I were always right outside, ready to pounce if anybody got suspicious and wanted to pat him down.

"Yes, your informant." Ring narrowed his gaze on me as pipe smoke curled toward the ceiling. The rest of the room went very quiet. "Anybody else know about him?"

"Well, Jimmy."

"Of course," Ring said impatiently. "Anyone else?" He kept his eyes on me.

"Nick," I said, meaning Gianturco. "I left him a copy of all my reports just the other day."

He nodded. Said nothing. No one else in the room said anything either.

At the time, I was surprised that Nick had wanted to see the reports. He'd never asked for them before. He'd said they were "for Washington." And no more. But that qualifies as a full and detailed explanation in the FBI. I kept the records in my office safe. But I wasn't going to be in the office when he wanted to pick them up, so I left them out on my desk. Nick was always late, so I didn't want to wait for him.

"Nick told me Washington needed it in a hurry, and this seemed the fastest way to get it to him."

"I see. Who typed the reports?"

"I did."

"Personally?"

I nodded. "Am I under suspicion of something here? Is there something I don't know?" It was a horrible feeling, something I had never experienced before. I'd always been the one to look hard at other people; I wasn't used to other people looking hard at me.

"Based on what some of our sources deep in LCN are telling us,

Vinny Ferrara has obtained information about Forte's activities that matches your report word for word." This was in the middle of Operation Jungle Mist, when Ferrara was still at large and trying to make a run at taking over the Italian mob. "Can you explain that?"

I was taken aback. Did he really think *I* was tipping off Ferrara? Or giving information to someone else to do it? Why would I ever do that? Why would anyone ever think I would do that? Was it really possible that Nick had taken my reports in order to match them up with the information the FBI informant said Ferrara was getting?

At this point, I thought of Nick as a pretty good friend. We'd gone out together; once we brought our wives along for dinner in the Bay Tower room on top of a Boston high-rise with a great view of the city.

"No, I can't explain that," I told Ring. "But let me ask you. How do you know that somebody in *your* shop didn't leak it? Have you checked here?"

"We have conducted a thorough review, and this was not leaked by anyone at the FBI."

He paused only a moment. "Now, Tommy, did you divulge this information to anyone else?" Ring probed.

I thought some more. The case went back months. Then I remembered. "Yes, one other person. On Dave's instructions"—I turned to Mattioli—"I told Trooper John Naimovich of the State Police."

With that, the attention of everyone in the room shifted a little. It was subtle, but I could feel it move away from me. A tough, burly guy, not far from retirement, Naimovich had all the personality of a nightstick. Few liked him, and that is saying something in the State Police, which is a get-along kind of group. Naimovich would give you a grunt or a look, and think he was being helpful.

I turned to Mattioli. "You remember, right?" Henderson's old Special Services unit was merging with Mattioli's Intelligence Unit to form a new entity called Special Services Section, SSS. So Mattioli needed to bring some of Henderson's people into our investigations. It looked like Naimovich could help us, since he was a gaming expert who knew where all the bookies operated around town. Drive with him, and he'd point to the third floor of some apartment building or a corner gas station or an insurance agency, and he'd say "There. Dickie operated up in a back room there in 1973." Or, "Shit, Fontina was huge in that place till we nailed him in August of 1981. What a prick that guy was." He was always testifying in court as an expert witness. It was incredible. A veteran member of the State Police was under scrutiny, and a useful asset for us was suddenly in danger.

"We'd better get Forte out of there," I told them.

"Agreed," Ring said.

"I'll get started putting him and his woman friend into the Program." Witness Protection Program. I was surprised the FBI hadn't started on that.

"Do that," Ring said.

————

Whoever was leaking the information we had about the LCN most likely wasn't going straight to Ferrara with it. He was going through a middleman. Ring believed that this person was a small-time bookie named Franny McIntyre who paid tribute regularly to Ferrara.

Mattioli checked later, and Naimovich was indeed using McIntyre. It seemed to fit. The only people who had access to all the information given to Ferrara were Gianturco, Naimovich, and me. Even Jimmy didn't have everything. If Nick had been cleared, that left just Naimovich and me. And I knew it wasn't me.

To figure out what was going on, Ring and Mattioli decided to set up a top-secret internal investigation to see what Naimovich was up to. They'd let him carry on as though everything was fine—and then try to catch him in the act. But it doesn't feel too good to send a cop to catch another one. It's like spying on your brother. Plus, a cop knows surveillance, what to look for, when something feels off. If Naimovich knew he was under suspicion, he'd stop dead—and, if he was indeed guilty, he'd tip off the LCN, ruining everything.

The plan was for Mattioli and Sergeant Sullivan to be the inside guys.

They'd keep an eye on Naimovich in his office on the second floor in our Framingham headquarters, watching everything he did, who he saw, what numbers he called. But quietly, without letting Naimovich have any idea.

They'd need others to handle the outside work, which was everywhere Naimovich went when he wasn't in the office. The FBI would put a bug on McIntyre's home phone, but the agents would need help tailing him and keeping track of everyone he saw. Mattioli figured there were only two of us who could handle that. Me and Jimmy. We were on the case already, so we knew what to look for. And I'd gotten to know Naimovich a little from briefing him on where things stood on the Mafia numbers run. And surveillance was what we did.

We didn't really want to do the dirty work on a fellow officer. Nobody would. But that was the job, and we couldn't say no.

Poor lumbering bastard, Naimovich had no idea what was happening to him. The mole was being tracked by other moles. I wasn't going to stick anything on him that wasn't true. But if Naimovich was indirectly leaking information to a thug like Ferrara, breaking the law, and endangering the lives of troopers, we sure weren't going to look the other way.

So we went ahead. Once the phone tap was in place, we rented a small cottage near McIntyre's as a listening post. John Connolly did a few shifts, to keep his hand in, but he was always a man on the go.

Jimmy and I tailed Naimovich when he hit the road, and kept an eye out for anyone coming to his house. It's always better to tail someone in two separate cars, so you can cover more of the options, and Jimmy and I worked well together. Like with Salemme, I'd always known where Jimmy was going to turn before he knew, and vice versa. Sometimes it was like we shared a brain. We'd laugh about it afterward. "I just knew you'd pull over there," he'd tell me.

"Well, you should have told me," I'd laugh. "Because I couldn't decide."

We stuck with the investigation around the clock for a couple of months. We didn't get very much, but we did get something—Naimovich taking small amounts of money from McIntyre. It was nothing like what the FBI was expecting. We did intercept some words he'd told

McIntyre to pass on to Ferrara, warning him to "walk softly in the new-fallen snow." Not the language you'd expect to hear from a state trooper to his informant. He was letting McIntyre know that people were looking into the connection between Ferrara and Forte. So Ferrara had better watch out.

When we were nearly done with the tap, we collected bits of evidence from a few houses we'd searched on the case, and we looked through all the transcripts and our own surveillance logs. Precious little of it supported the core charge from Ring and the FBI: that Naimovich was supplying information about Forte's movements to Vinny Ferrara. The remark about new-fallen snow referred to the interests of the State Police. There was no question that Naimovich was too cozy with the mobsters he was supposed to be investigating, but it was nothing beyond that.

Still, when we brought all the evidence back to the FBI, Ring looked it all through and finally glanced up at me with a look of satisfaction. "Excellent," he said.

Afterward, when we were heading down the hall, I overheard him say to Gianturco, seemingly in passing: "Now we have to take care of *our* problem."

But he said nothing to me about what that problem was.

Little as it was, the evidence was enough for the feds to get Naimovich arrested. It happened early one morning, in a common room at headquarters. Naimovich was having coffee with me and a few other troopers when Mattioli, Ring, Sergeant Sullivan, and the deputy superintendent came in and went right up to Naimovich where he was sitting. "You're under arrest, John," Mattioli said. Then he recited the charges against him, someone put the cuffs on him, and the other officers led him away. There were probably a dozen people in that room, and the place was dead silent as he went. I get sick thinking about it. They took him, hands cuffed behind his back, downstairs to the cell room, where we booked him, placed him in one of the cells, uncuffed him, locked the door, and left him there, sitting on his bed, his head in his hands.

To cut a deal on his sentence for bookmaking, McIntyre turned state's evidence, but he still didn't tell us much that we didn't already know. He acknowledged being Naimovich's informant—no surprise—but he insisted he'd never passed on anything from Naimovich to Ferrara about Forte.

I pressed him hard on this, but the FBI agent I was working with, Vince DelaMontagne, didn't seem to care whether McIntyre had leaked it or not. It was odd, like he was bored with the whole thing.

It didn't make sense. The FBI made it sound like Naimovich had a pipeline to Ferrara. But that pipeline could only go through McIntyre, and the feds' special agent on this, DelaMontagne, didn't care if it did or didn't. But it mattered: If McIntyre hadn't passed any information along, Naimovich couldn't have either. And if Naimovich didn't, then why was he locked up?

At that point, I was still on friendly terms with most of the FBI guys, and every once in a while we'd go out to a bar and knock a few back. One time I told a couple of them straight out that the Naimovich investigation wasn't coming together. "I really don't think Naimovich has anything to do with Forte and Ferrara." I looked across the table at the two agents, waiting for a reaction. This had been a huge deal for the bureau, after all. A rat in the State Police!

Instead, I just got a pair of shrugs—So what else is new?—just like I'd gotten from DelaMontagne. It was like they'd known there was nothing to it all along. The silence told me everything I needed to know.

Now I was getting upset. I went to Mattioli, and I laid it out to him.

"Dave, if Naimovich's broken the law, I want him in prison, same as anybody," I told him. "But only on the evidence, and it's not here."

"I'm sure they have evidence," Mattioli started to say.

But I told him that if there was evidence, I certainly hadn't seen any of it. And I'd spent months on the investigation, including days with McIntyre, who was the only one in a position to know. And he'd said there was nothing to it. "And tell you what, I believe him," I told Mattioli.

"All right," Mattioli said finally. "Let's have a talk with Ring, see what he's got."

The next day, Ring drove in to SSS Framingham barracks. He disappeared into Mattioli's office with Mattioli and Sergeant Sullivan for a closed-door meeting where I wasn't welcome. I waited out in the hall with Jimmy White, and could hear raised voices inside. Maybe a half-hour later, Sergeant Sullivan came out and told me, "Ring's puking up everything!"

Then the door opened, and Mattioli invited me in. Ring was sitting by his desk. For the first time, he looked uncomfortable, like he didn't know how to sit. And he'd finally killed the pipe.

"I want you to tell Tommy what you just told me," Mattioli began.

I took the other seat by Mattioli's desk. Ring didn't look at me, and it took him a few moments to find the words.

"I was just telling Dave that we've determined that Trooper Naimovich was not the source of the information that was passed to Vinny Ferrara."

"Wait—*not* the source?" I repeated, to make sure I understood. "You know this? You're shitting me."

"That is correct. Trooper Naimovich is not the source."

"You're kidding me," I repeated, barely able to contain my fury. "How long have you known that?"

"We developed this information approximately two or three months ago."

I just exploded. "What? Two or three *months*?" That wasn't long after that first meeting, when they lit into me as the suspect, and around the beginning of the time that I started busting my butt on Naimovich. Here he'd let me twist in the wind with the vague allegation that I was behind the leaks, and then set me to nail Naimovich.

"And you had us investigate a trooper who you knew had nothing to do with it?"

"We didn't know that for sure."

"Jesus Christ, Jim, we put our careers on the line over this. We've been trying to do the right thing here, and we've done exactly what you asked. And now you're saying that you straight-out lied to us? That it was all bullshit?"

I let that hang there for a moment. "All right, so who did it? Do you even know?"

He looked down at the floor. "We now have reason to believe that it was"—he paused—"well, that it was a typist in the FBI stenographers' pool."

The words shot by me so fast, I couldn't quite take them in. "A what?" I demanded.

"A steno."

"A steno? What are you trying to tell us, Jim?"

"She was passing Nick's reports to Ferrara, and they had a lot of the same information as was in your reports." Ring had gotten it all 1,000 percent wrong, but he didn't seem too disturbed either. "We may have made a few mistakes on this one. But we got the basics right. Naimovich is a bad cop, and he'll be convicted, believe me."

"Not if the jury learns the truth about your steno he won't."

"They'll get the truth."

"The full truth, Jim. About this. This is coming out. Naimovich is getting a fair trial. If you don't give this to the defense, I will. You follow me?"

"Hey, easy, Tommy. I understand, you're upset. Don't do anything rash. Remember, you could get Nick in serious trouble." He meant Gianturco. "And he's your friend, right?"

I stared at him. "Don't pull that shit, OK? I'm not going to send a guy to jail just to be nice to somebody else. That's not the way it works around here."

He didn't respond, just stood up and started to gather his things.

"So what are you going to do with the steno?" I pressed him. "Tap her phone, see who she's talking to? Or just arrest her?"

He looked a little surprised at the idea. "Arrest her? No. We're going to deal with her administratively. It's better that way."

"Administratively? You're kidding me. After you got our trooper arrested like a common criminal? And you've known for months it wasn't him?" I stood up. I'd had enough of Ring to last me awhile. "And believe me, Naimovich is going to know all about your steno. If you don't give the information to his attorneys, I will."

"OK," Ring said, standing, too. "Thanks for the meeting." And then I left the room.

The FBI knew they had to turn the information over to Naimovich's attorneys, and to the prosecutors from the U.S. Attorney's Office, and they did. The charges against Naimovich were changed to reflect only the violations we picked up on the wiretap. He was not charged with passing the information about Forte to Ferrara. In my opinion it was too little too late.

Another issue loomed over the case instead—the whole question of informants. At Naimovich's trial, the FBI claimed, through the prosecutors from the U.S. Attorney's Office, that we in the State Police had no clear informant policy and that encouraged a certain laxness on Naimovich's part. But the defense believed that with nothing formally in place to restrain him, Naimovich could do whatever he thought right. The question was, without clear rules, where was the line between OK and not OK, and what was the penalty for crossing it? The uncertainty confused the jury, and it didn't help to see the state's two highest law enforcement agencies argue opposite sides of the question. In the end, an obviously baffled jury cleared Naimovich of all charges but the broader criminal conduct relating to McIntyre. On that one, they ended up hung. I could see the life come back to Naimovich when he heard the verdicts. He made a deal with the federal prosecutors to retire in exchange for their not re-trying him on that last charge. So it wasn't a complete exoneration. He'd escape prison, but he was off the force.

When it was over, the State Police undertook to clarify its policy, specifying how informants are to be handled. Chiefly, the handler is required to provide regular reports on the informant's productivity, and underperforming informants are let go, to be prosecuted as criminals if necessary. That policy is still in force today, and it is carefully observed. The FBI, on the other hand, stuck with its existing policy, which was almost no policy at all.

The whole episode really shook me. It was bad enough that I'd briefly been a target, but I hated being co-opted to turn against a fellow officer, even though I was sickened by what his conduct had done to the image of the State Police. I was outraged that the FBI agents would out-and-out lie, putting one of our troopers in the dock for a crime they knew he did not commit, and that they knew full well that one of their stenos was guilty instead but would not prosecute her! It was all too much.

Naimovich's trial finished up sometime after we were done with Operation Jungle Mist in 1988. When the verdict came down, I had a sit-down with Mattioli.

"I'm done here, Dave," I told him. "I'm tired. I need to get away from all this."

"A vacation? Sure, how long?"

"Not a vacation, more like an end. Naimovich really took it out of me, Dave. It revealed some things I never wanted to see. I'll be honest. Working with the FBI is like—well, shit, you know what it's like, I don't even want to say. I need to get my life simple again. I want to see my family, stay clean, clear all this crap out of my head."

He heard me out, and he understood. It had been a hard time for him, too.

"So what do you want to do instead?" Mattioli asked me.

"I want to go back to uniform."

"Where?"

"Someplace around Worcester."

He said OK, he'd arrange it, and days later I was officially transferred back to my old barracks in Holden. I'd be back in my cruiser again, doing what I used to do.

I'd miss working with Jimmy, but that was about all I'd miss.

———

A month or two later, Mattioli surprised people by announcing his resignation from the State Police. The Naimovich affair had weighed on him, too, bringing up the same issues that I'd been fighting myself. He'd always been a steady guy, never one to rant and rave, but the FBI had gotten to him, too. It's too big, too demanding. He didn't have much left to give.

By then I was in Holden, a small town just south of Worcester, and it was like I had never left my old life, before I went to OC. Once more, there was a clear line between right and wrong; you didn't have to work through layers of bureaucracy. It was good to be back out on the road.

After I was in Holden for nearly a year, I took the test to make corporal, and passed, so I was bumped up one grade. I was going up the ladder, doing it right. I loved it.

And it wouldn't last.

PART TWO

Getting Whitey

— CHAPTER 9 —

In October 1990, I got a call from Colonel Charles Henderson, the new super-intendent of the entire State Police. He said he had a problem, and he needed my help.

"And what's that?"

"It's about my old unit," he said. The Special Services Section that had been created when Henderson's original OC group had merged with Mattioli's version, the Intelligence Unit that I'd been part of. "It's been falling apart, and I need to pull it back together."

I'd heard that there'd been some lingering tension between Henderson's people and Mattioli's, like what went on with Naimovich, and that morale had suffered. The SSS used to be an elite unit and a choice assignment, but now it was having trouble attracting the people Henderson needed to make it work.

"It needs a new commander, somebody experienced who can pull the thing back together." He paused for a second. "I'd like you to do that for me," he said.

"Wait—me?" I'd been out of it so long, I had trouble picturing this.

"You'd be perfect."

Still, I was thinking: hell no. I was really happy with what I was doing, I loved being close to home, and I was sick of all the BS with the FBI.

"I'm sorry, Colonel, but I'm afraid I am going to have to decline," I told him.

There was silence on the line for a moment. "Tommy, you don't understand," Colonel Henderson corrected me. "You can't decline. This is happening. We need you to do this."

"Oh." It was an order. A knot formed in my stomach. "I see. OK. Right."

"Good. Now the question is: what would you like to do?"

I didn't want to go back. But when I started to think about what I might like to do at SSS, my thoughts returned to where they'd been a few years before when Mattioli asked me the same question. It was the only thing that made sense.

"I'd like to get Whitey Bulger," I told him. "Him and Steve Flemmi."

There was a long pause on the line while Henderson chewed on that. "Well," he said finally. "That's ambitious."

"Sir. It's past time."

"That is true enough."

"So—that's OK with you, Colonel? Bulger and Flemmi? You'll back me on that?"

"Yes," he said. "We have a deal. Do it."

— CHAPTER 10 —

In 1990, Whitey Bulger had been at large in and around Boston for twenty-five years. Virtually alone among serious criminals, he had never served a day in jail during that whole period. He'd been subject to a State Police investigation back in 1983, but that was abandoned after several attempts to perform electronic surveillance on him were compromised, often within hours after the bugs were put in place. To some people, this just enlarged the legend of Whitey Bulger, as if he had almost supernatural powers to detect threats to him and his operation. To others, though, it was simply proof that he was very well connected, and that he had cultivated a law enforcement mole, or possibly several moles, who were in a position to know what was coming, and were inclined to tell him.

Bulger's activities were all pretty much standard mob stuff, just more of it. Tons more. And unlike most mobsters, Whitey operated pretty much alone. He worked only with Flemmi and sometimes a young hood named Kevin Weeks. And it was always Whitey who made the decisions. Also, he kept his own counsel. Nobody ever told him what to do about anything. Other mobsters had their women, their bling, and their corner tables at name restaurants. Whitey was known to hang out in Southie, but he was rarely seen, and few people in law enforcement even knew what he looked like. When I got on his case, there were only about half a dozen photographs of him that were at all current, usually grainy telephoto shots of him in a Red Sox cap, with dark aviator glasses covering his eyes, taken from hundreds of feet away. I could tell the basics: five-ten, thinning hair, upturned nose, killer eyes. But I couldn't be sure I'd recognize him on the sidewalk, or in a car.

He'd read those books on military strategy in prison, and informants told us he had devoured a lot more true-crime books since then. And it showed. He never lost his focus, always planned ahead, and kept it simple. He left no incriminating papers around; kept everything in his head; talked only on pay phones, and then said little; even in person, he kept the conversation very brief, and let his ice-cold eyes say the rest; and he lived out of a suitcase, ready to jump the moment things got hot. No records, no bank accounts, no place of residence. When he was younger, he'd had a bunch of girlfriends—and, according to one informant, a taste for watching nude girls have sex behind a two-way mirror. But now he'd narrowed his women to just two—the former dental hygienist Cathy Greig, and Theresa Stanley, a mother of four who'd worked at the Massachusetts Convention Center that was home to many appointments of Billy Bulger. Both of them were much younger than Whitey, who knew the game. Eventually, of course, he took off with Greig, after dumping Stanley. Greig always knew about Stanley; Stanley had not known about Greig.

Whitey was in his early sixties by the time we went after him, but the photos showed that he could still rip you apart. Every day, he hit the weights, and he had developed the sort of build—thick shoulders, powerful arms, heavy chest—that seemed designed for strangling people with his bare hands. Despite the muscles, it was the eyes everybody remembered. Ice-blue, under clenched eyebrows, they could stop your heart; no one who saw them ever forgot them. Them and a tight, angry mouth that was always ready with obscenities. If the edges of his mouth ever turned up, it wasn't a smile.

The press may have called him a vicious mobster, and we certainly thought of him that way. But because he'd never been arrested, people could think of him however they wanted, and a lot of people around town made him out to be a comic-book villain, or even a folk hero. There were stories about how he helped old ladies cross the street and punished bullies. Maybe if his criminal activities had been confined to gaming and a few drugs on the side, sure. But they weren't. The guy was a murderer, and it was the murders that set him apart. It wasn't his way of thrusting a gun in the victim's face to fill the head with lead. Nor was it the arsenal of guns he had—even though the count approached a hundred, with dozens of submachine guns and automatic rifles in the mix, enough to arm a small battalion.

He used them plenty, and often close-up. But he loved to kill with his bare hands. To strangle people, bringing his fingers around the neck, his thumbs feeling for the windpipe, while his eyes bulged and reddened, his face turned savage, and his chest heaved from the effort. It's not easy to snap someone's windpipe with your bare hands, especially if your victim is fighting for their life. Guns are much easier, but less intimate. With one young woman he strangled, he lurched at her, knocked her back onto the floor, hooking his legs under her, and sprawled forward onto her, chest to chest, as he reached for her neck.

In those days before DNA analysis, dental records and fingerprints were about the only ways to positively identify a body. So, to disguise the victim's identity, when he'd finished the kill, he'd jerk the victim's mouth open wide, then insert a pair of pliers to yank the teeth out one by one while the blood welled up. He'd drop the teeth into a bag to dispose of separately. The blood must have been everywhere.

When he was done with the dead person's teeth, he'd move on to the hands. Whitey would take an ax and splay the hands open flat against the floor, and then he'd bring down the ax and chop off all the fingertips. They'd go into the bag, as well. The bag would go into someone's trash. And the body—it would be hauled off somewhere to a shallow grave where it would be wished away.

Some of this we knew then, and the rest we learned later. But we knew enough then to realize that, formidable as Whitey Bulger was as a mobster, "mobster" didn't begin to describe him. Habitual murderer was closer, but psychopath was it.

This made our intentions simple. Stop him.

———

Like everybody else, I'd known enough about Whitey to give me a vague im-pression but few details. It wasn't until I joined the Intelligence Unit back in 1984 that I got a fuller idea. The IU had put together detailed files on hundreds if not thousands of gangsters of potential interest, many of them with names like Bobby the Greaser, Shawn T. "Rooster" Austin, and "Sonny Boy" Rizzo. The files were all stored in a thick block of filing cabinets in the State Police's main office in Framingham. The clips and reports went back all the way to the 1930s, many of them curled and yellowing, with pencil notations and smudged typewriting. Not too many people went down into the basement, but I did. From my first days with Mattioli back in 1984, every few nights I would bring home a dozen or two of the files to pore over.

Whitey's wasn't the thickest. That honor went to Angiulo, since as a Mafia chief he'd been so public, and he was at it for such a long time. But the material on Whitey was plentiful—police reports, informant interviews, military records, newspaper clippings, court records from the early days. I spent plenty of time on other mobsters in the LCN and Winter Hill, trying to see the connections, the bloodlines. But I kept coming back to Whitey. He was different. Unlike so many of the others, he started up on his own. He had no brothers in the business; didn't learn from his father; and created his own organization. He had Flemmi, yes, but he himself was always a mob of one. A survivor, that's what he was. Doing whatever it took. It was like with the bank robbers he organized, or his being the bodyguard for Donny Killeen, only to split when things got hot. Whitey was always about Whitey.

The people in the LCN were more colorful, but they were organization men. The Winter Hill people were just killers, but with an eye out for a buck. But Whitey's mob was a much looser outfit that he shaped and reshaped as necessary. In that sense, it was brilliant. Small enough to be reliable and absolutely trustworthy, answerable only to him, flexible enough that it could take on almost any job, and terrifying enough that those who encountered it did what they were told.

What was he after? I thought about that a lot. You have to if you're going to have a chance at catching someone like him. You have to know where he's likely to go, so you can be there first. Like most mobsters, he wanted power and control, and the money that those things can bring. That was a given. In this, he was basically like his brother in the statehouse, although his brother maintained a certain respectability. That's understandable, after his impoverished childhood. Who wouldn't want security? But he had that other thing, the blood lust, that loomed over everything else, the desire to be the one who decides if others live or die, and the thrill of being the one to make it happen, either way. For him, control was total.

He was disciplined, like with the regular weight lifting. He'd get in on other people's drug deals, but not allow anyone in his circle to touch them. He never smoked, rarely drank, and watched his weight. Other wiseguys had their fast women, big cars, lavish houses, and jewelry, but not Whitey. He had those girlfriends, and kept two, to make sure that neither took over.

Start to finish, throughout the investigation Whitey gave us almost nothing. He was like air. You know he's there, but you can never see him. One of our informants said that Whitey spent 98 percent of his time on business and 2 percent on pleasure, which is the reverse of most criminals. Like those World War II generals, he didn't act without thinking about the consequences. Would the victim rat him out? Where would he hide the body? Who might talk? How can any talkers be silenced? What then?

He never spoke about business in an enclosed space. In his car, the interior panels and floor mats were touch-sensitive, so they'd give off a warning signal if anyone tried to plant a bug. We learned that the hard way. He once juiced up a Chevy Malibu to be his getaway car. It could do 160, and then release a billowing fog of oily smoke and an oil slick to blind any pursuers and send them spinning off the road. That was the mentality.

I spent weeks poring over his file. There were bits here, bits there, but nothing that really added up. I'd try to put the files into order, at least in my head so I could get a read on the guy, and how he got that way. I pored over the few mug shots from long ago, and some surveillance photos taken since then, the early ones showing a cool-guy smugness, the later ones burning with anger. In the end, I realized the files would only take me so far.

— CHAPTER 11 —

When I took over SSS in 1990, we were going after Whitey. Him and Flemmi. Sadly, by then, Jimmy White had left the unit. That was a great loss for me; he was the best partner I'd ever had. But he'd had it after Naimovich, too. But I pulled together a handful of the troopers working on OC, and they'd form my core group for the first phase of the investigation. I'd worked with some of them before, and others I had merely heard about. They all threw themselves into the effort. Everybody did a bit of everything. Big John Tutungian would be our affiant primarily, writing all the affidavits we put before a judge to get permission to tap a phone or search a house. He was also a court-recognized expert in the gaming business, and that would be a key piece of knowledge for what we were trying to do. Hanko and I did most the hookups, the electronic surveillance. At first, I probably knew more than he did, since he'd only recently gotten training, and I'd been doing it for a while by then. But he caught on quickly, and we soon thought of ourselves as reverse exterminators, planting bugs everywhere—up telephone poles, behind walls, in cars, all over the place. Patty Gillen and Gale MacAulay handled a lot of the street surveillance. They were my eyes and ears out there. A pair of tough, enterprising women, they could follow anyone most anywhere without getting made. On a case like this, they had an advantage: mobsters tend to be old-school and never imagine that they are being followed by a woman, let alone two of them. Plus, with Patty only a little over five feet, and Gale a little under six, they made an unlikely pair of state troopers. And finally, we had Mike Scanlan, or Sly as we called him, since he looked like Sylvester Stallone. He was Mr. Steady, a guy who could do a little of everything and could always be counted on. These guys never dreamed they'd be called on to bring down Bulger, but they didn't flinch.

One reason the investigation of Bulger back in 1983 had failed was that it was too ambitious, and the investigators were too impatient. They had gone straight after Bulger, right from the start. No way. Bulger had too many spies around for that. Once he figured out he was being targeted, he disappeared, never to resurface, and that killed the investigation. The troopers had used up all their ammo; they had no bullets left. Our approach would be slower, but more methodical. We'd start at the bottom and work our way up, level by level, until we got to the top.

The thing was that Bulger may not have had all the Mafia foot soldiers, but he was sitting on a pyramid all the same. But it wasn't based on power, like the Mafia; it was based on revenue. Bulger drew his funds from the bottom. To get to him at the top, we had to follow the money. That was the idea. As in any business, the money flowed from the bottom to the top. The money would reveal him like heat to thermal goggles. You can't shoot at what you can't see. But he did have a need for money, a constant need for money, a flow that could be tracked.

While Whitey's business ran on money just like anybody else's, it drew from an unusual array of sources, since they were all mob-related—bookmaking, racketeering, loan-sharking, drug deals, extortion. Of all the revenue sources, we figured that the bookmaking funds would be easiest to follow. Unlike the others, bookmaking was steady, but it was also a pretty decent piece of change, probably $2 million a year for Whitey when all was said and done. Still, it's just dollars in, dollars out, all noted on a ledger. It wasn't a secret onetime thing like a truck hijacking, or a huge marijuana deal, or some big scam. The bookies were the back door, but they'd offer a way in.

Also, with us starting at the bottom, Whitey probably wouldn't have any idea. We'd go after the dozens of penny-ante bookmaking operations around town, and he'd never know. Any one of them didn't make that much, not by mob standards. Maybe half a million a year, tops. It would be kicking back a grand a week to higher-ups for "protection," but "shakedown" is a better word. Pennies, really, in mob terms. But if you had enough of them, that's how it got to be serious money. Years back, Henderson's Special Services had gone after the mob bookies, but not any higher. We'd *start* with the bookies, and go up from there. Bookies are never stand-alone operations. They're more like franchises, who have to kick some money back to the local office. But it kept going up from there.

Bookmaking wasn't a major crime, but an investigation would provide a look inside his organization, and then maybe we'd see the real serious stuff. If we only got him on bookmaking, Whitey would do five or six years tops. But it would put him behind bars, and that was the point. We didn't need to send Bulger away forever; we just needed to get him into prison, so the jackals could come. He wouldn't be invisible anymore, and he certainly wouldn't be untouchable, let alone omnipotent. He'd be just another convict shuffling around. Seeing him brought low, other mobsters facing stiff sentences might want to shave off a little time by telling us a few details about Whitey that he wouldn't want us to know.

For all the talk of loyalty in the mob, it's more like every man for himself, especially in the Irish mob. The Mafia mobsters tended to serve their sentences quietly. But Whitey would rat out anyone to save himself some time, and I was guessing his pals would think the same. I didn't think Flemmi would make any exceptions. If we could get Whitey at all, we'd get him for good. That was the idea.

————

When you work on a case like this, you need help from the local DA. The DAs kick in some of the funding during investigations, and they'll help you with the legal stuff for court later on. Scott Harshbarger had been the local DA, but he'd left to be the state attorney general; and Tom Reilly, Harshbarger's assistant DA, took over. Before I got started, I went to see Reilly and made sure he was on board.

I always liked Reilly. Slender, intense, he was always a big backer of ours. And he was now when I pitched him on Whitey.

"Do it," he said, "I'll get you whatever you need. And I'll be behind you every step of the way."

"Even with"—I paused, trying to find the right word—"the politics?"

I meant Billy Bulger, of course. He had a hand in Reilly's budget, as well as in the State Police's. Everybody knew: don't cross Billy Bulger.

"Politics?" Reilly said lightly. "What politics?"

I loved the guy.

To go after Whitey, I'd have to work with the FBI, and after Naimovich, I had some misgivings about that. But Henderson was confident I could handle it. I still had plenty of friends over there and many of them felt bad about how we were treated on Naimovich. And I still got along reasonably well with the U.S. Attorney's Office, which would be likely to prosecute our cases. Besides, Henderson needed to show that we could all get along— local, state, and federal. Everybody in it together, and us not the least of them.

And Ring was gone. After the Naimovich case, he was replaced by Ed Quinn. A legendary figure, Quinn was the one who had brought in Angiulo, one of the most impressive collars in the history of the Boston Mafia. Genial but commanding, he knew everything there was to know about Boston OC. I had a world of respect for him. He had the reputation of being Mr. Integrity, which sounded good to me, and he held himself like a marine, straight up, smooth. It was a big step up from Ring. Still one thing worried me. Quinn once told a friend that he wished I was more than a corporal. To my way of thinking, we were basically equal in rank, since we were both supervisors of OC units. He ran the FBI's for the Boston office. And I ran ours for the State Police. That wasn't good enough for him?

The deal was that Bulger would be our investigation, but we were supposed to coordinate everything with the feds. If that seems contradictory, it's because it was. We worked with the FBI, but the feds worked with us only if they chose to. Still, I didn't think that would be a problem. At that point, I was focused only on getting the job done.

While the FBI had its offices in that high-rise downtown, we set up shop in a grungy corner of our Framingham barracks with almost no money. That bugged people a little. And while the feds tended to keep regular hours, all of my people were real grinds who'd go late into the night, work on weekends and holidays, doing whatever it took. To us, getting Whitey wasn't a job. It was a mission.

Bookmaking is basically just betting, usually on sports. Now there is the Internet, but back then, if you wanted to bet on a game, you'd have go to a bookie, who'd tell you the line—the favorite, the underdog, and by how much—on the game you were interested in, and you'd place your bet. If the Patriots were favored to win by six points, they'd have to win by at least seven for you to win your bet. If the bets got too big on one side of a game, the bookies would have to "lay off" the risk with a higher-up, with bigger reserves, which could get expensive. So the line is critical: you want to find that exact balance point where half the bets go to one side, and half to the other. Usually the line came from Las Vegas, but there were some sharp people around town with better ones. The bookies were everywhere in the city, but they were concentrated more heavily in the tougher parts of town like Charlestown, the North End, and Southie, where the mob tended to be most heavily entrenched.

A bookie would rent an apartment for an office, the line was set, and then the bets came in by phone, sometimes by fax. The bookie would record them all in his book until game time. The losers would pay him; he would pay the winners. And then he'd kick out his protection money, called rent. Theoretically the money was to protect him from other hoods, but actually it was to protect him from his protector, who could otherwise make his life miserable, or short.

While we cared about the bookies, we wanted to get the people the bookies paid off. The idea was to trace these "protectors" back to their homes, where we could bug their phones and search their rooms, and figure out who *they* owed. Home was where they kept the records of their business, and where they made the calls. They thought it was safe there.

We went after the bookies hard. Hanko and I did the hookups. I'd gone to school for it myself by then, and Hanko had just gotten basic training. Between the two of us, we got pretty good. With Tutungian cranking out the affidavits needed for court permission, we went way beyond phones and offices to intercepting beepers and bugging cars, and we even got a line into fax machines, so that every sheet that went into or out of a bookie joint produced a duplicate for us. Nobody had ever done that in Massachusetts before, and I'm sure the bookies had no idea, because they laid out everything on those pages. We'd set up a wire room upstairs at our office as a listening post for monitoring all the bugs. Maybe twenty feet across, it had a long shelf along one side, and a couple of windows that looked out onto the dark parking lot. There were probably half a dozen stations there where troopers could listen in through headphones clapped over their ears.

And we had a handful of informants, low-end bookies mostly, sniffing around for us, letting us know what was going down. Tutungian had a talent for informants. He knew when to play nice and when to get firm. But being an informant wrangler is never easy, and you always had to worry about what Whitey might do if he figured out that one of his people had flipped.

To start, we targeted "Fat Vinny" Roberto. Fat he was. At least four hundred pounds, just a mammoth human being, and an unmistakable presence on the sidewalk. He was an LCN functionary whose primary job was to collect payments from bookies to keep the bullets and beatings away. It was perfect for us: Roberto worked for the Mafia, *and* for Bulger through Flemmi. He was a bridge between the two reigning mobs in the city. We watched him in his big Lincoln, cruising between Whitey's operation and the LCN.

Fat Vinny made a big target, and Patty and Gale were all over him as he went on his rounds, starting at his home in Framingham and staying on him all day through Boston and the closer suburbs before he made his way back home late that night.

One thing about Vinny. Because of his weight, he had terrible sleep apnea and never got a good night's sleep, so he was prone to drifting off, even in the middle of conversations. We knew because we'd tapped his car phone, and we were always listening in. One afternoon we tapped into a phone conversation, and we could tell he'd pulled up to the Allston tolls because he greeted the toll taker with a hello, and there was a hi back. And then we heard—zzzzzzz. Fat Vinny was snoring to beat the band. No letters in the alphabet can capture it. Then we heard the toll collector go:

"Hey, buddy, here's your change. Hey—wake up!" Then the guy must have stepped out of his booth to shake him, because Fat Vinny lurched awake. "Oh, Jesus, sorry," he said, snuffling, and then motored on through.

We had a good laugh over that one.

Fat Vinny was a big enough deal, with enough action, that both the LCN and Whitey wanted in. He didn't pay off Whitey directly. Hardly anybody did. Still, Vinny was clearly a player who was a big step up from the street-level bookies. From our surveillance, we discovered that he paid his tribute to Whitey through Burton "Chico" Krantz, who was probably the biggest bookmaker on the East Coast. By Boston standards, Krantz was the ultimate. I'd known about him for years; a lot of us in OC had. He lived in a big house in Newton, one of the plush suburbs, with all the ophthalmologists and stock analysts. He was a big chunk of a guy with wispy comb-over hair that he liked to tuck under a wide-brimmed Stetson. He was king of all he did, in his own mind anyway. His code name among other bookies was "The President." Jimmy the Greek once interviewed him on TV before a Super Bowl game. A successful gambler himself, Chico was so rich that he once bet $1 million on a Super Bowl game—and then fell asleep before it was over. He woke up to find out he'd lost. Knowing Chico, I bet that he didn't take too long to get back to sleep. Roberto may not have gotten anywhere near Whitey, but Chico got closer. He got to another associate, George Kaufman; and Kaufman got to Flemmi; and Flemmi got to Whitey. He was three steps away, and for our purposes, that was close enough.

When Big Vinny paid off Chico, he got something important back—access to Chico's "lines," meaning his betting lines, which were much better than the ones coming out of Las Vegas, and addressed the layoff, the problem of too many bets coming in on the same side. That made them a little tighter, and Patty and Gale saw Big Vinny pull into Chico's driveway a few times. We heard all the talk on Big Vinny's phone. Chico knew not to talk on his own phone, but he couldn't control what Big Vinny did on the other end.

When Patty and Gale followed Roberto, they saw him going to see a couple of guys we identified as Charlie Quintana, a consigliere who was up pretty high in Providence, which was the New England Mafia head-quarters; and "Sonny Boy" Rizzo, a foot soldier in Revere. If we had him with Chico on one side, and these guys on the other, there was no question he was working both sides of the street, Whitey and the LCN. We'd look at both, absolutely. But where to place the emphasis?

I didn't think there was any doubt, but I had to sit down with Colonel Henderson and DA Tom Reilly and make sure they were with us. We met in the back room of a little restaurant in Watertown, and, on a napkin, I diagrammed where we were.

"We're at a crossroads here," I said pointing with a knife at a box in which I'd written BV for "Big Vinny." Above it was W for "Whitey" on one side and the LCN on the other. I slashed up to the W, and up to the LCN. "We can go this way or that way. We want Whitey, but I need your OK." It wasn't easy for any of us but it was particularly hard for them. We all wanted to get Whitey. But they had other things to consider, like Billy Bulger and the fact that the FBI would much rather go in the opposite direction. As I learned with Oreto and Vanessa's, they were built to take on the Mafia. To them, anything else seemed beside the point. They'd help with LCN, but who knew what they'd do with Whitey? Then again, they hadn't done much for us on Whitey so far.

"We're looking for the green light. Can we go ahead on Bulger?"

They looked at each other, and then both told me the same thing. "Yes, absolutely. Don't worry. We'll take care of the rest."

Looking back, I think that the decision was a lot easier than it seemed at the time. Why? Because they never thought we'd ever get anywhere on Bulger since no one ever had. We'd be just another dead car in the junk-yard. But they still had the guts to go along.

And we plowed ahead. We pushed the investigation to the next gear. The plan had always been to get into the bookies' homes to get the full story. Bookies never figured to be hit at home, because they never had been, so that's where they kept the good stuff.

Tutungian worked with Tom Reilly's office to crank out the affidavits that won us a slew of warrants. To execute them all, I had to organize a small army of troopers, each group headed by one of my people, to fan out across the city and hit as many of the houses as we could at once, before word got out.

One of the houses was Krantz's. Nobody had ever done that to him before, and he didn't think it was possible. He was vacationing in Florida at the time, and he was stunned when he heard it. Tutungian, Hanko, and some other troopers worked on that one, and they moved quickly to clean him out. They pulled out piles of detailed records and other material, including a couple of security deposit keys.

There was no tag showing which bank they were for. But each key is distinctive. When the troopers were done and had brought all the documents back to our headquarters, we took a sharp photograph of the two keys and then faxed the pictures around to various banks in the city. Almost everywhere, the answer came back negative, of course. But we scored two hits: Dedham Savings Bank, and U.S. Bank and Trust in Chestnut Hill.

While I rushed to secure search warrants, I sent troopers over to the two banks, and told them to keep everyone well away from those boxes until a court gave us clearance to pull them. Scanlan was in Dedham and soon got me on his cell. "Guess who's here?"

I had no idea.

"Michael."

Michael Krantz, Chico's son.

"And he's got this huge duffel bag with him." Scanlan didn't have to say what that was for. Bingo. If Michael Krantz was there with a duffel bag, we'd come to the right place. When the court moved, I brought the warrant to Dedham, a manager led us to the safe-deposit box, and we opened it up. It was thick with solid bricks of cash. The manager blanched. He told us he'd never seen so much money in his life.

I had the tellers count it, so my troopers wouldn't face any questions about any discrepancies later. It was $1.1 million. I had the money transferred to another safe-deposit box, to which we held the key. The money would stay right there until the courts declared that it had been forfeited. Then we'd collect it with U.S. Marshals present. With that kind of money, you can't be too careful.

We repeated the exercise in Chestnut Hill. This time, it was another $1 million in cash.

Hard to explain money like that.

While Chico was still at his winter place in Florida, his lawyer, Richie Egbert, called with a deal. If we didn't arrest Chico, he would fly back and come to the barracks in Framingham on his own for the standard fingerprints and mug shots. (The court would let him out on bail because he wasn't considered a flight risk.) Sure enough, he showed up a short time later—without Egbert. That was a surprise. Egbert handled a lot of other mob figures, including Steve Flemmi, and Chico may have figured he didn't want to say anything in front of Egbert that might get back to Flemmi. Like most gangsters, Chico had reason to be terrified of Flemmi and Bulger. It quickly became clear that Chico was hoping to swing a deal to get all his cash back, but that was a lost cause. Mobsters often think they can use their personal charm to get more information out of you than you can get out of them. He wanted to scope out the charges we had against him. I wouldn't play. I hinted that we had him for plenty more than the ones he was there for, but I wasn't going to say anything else. Not without his attorney there, anyway.

"Don't worry about any attorney," he told me.

"Wait—are you waiving your right to have an attorney here?"

"Those guys, they're fucking rip-offs! They just want to make sure we don't cooperate, because that way's more money for them."

I had to hold it there a moment, and check with the assistant DA and then with the federal Strike Force chief, to make sure it was OK for me to go ahead. It was.

"All right, Chico, we've got you for serious time here. Money laundering—that's a federal crime, to be served in federal prison." Chico was a smart guy, but he was weak, a feathery little guy with a booming voice that's about all you need to know about Chico. It was my guess that he'd gotten used to the soft life in the suburbs—I didn't think he could handle a day in prison, let alone five or ten years. This got his attention.

"But listen, we know what you do, and who you work for and have worked for, for a long time. You with me?"

It was clear from the look on his face that he was.

I waited a moment to say what he knew was coming next. "If you want to work with us, maybe we'd be able to help you out a little bit on this thing."

"They're assholes." He didn't have to say who. "They've been stealing from me for fucking forever. I want to get them . . . I do." Then he paused a moment, and the look on his face changed. "But I don't want to testify. I'm sorry, but I—I can't do that. Shit man, I just can't."

I told him we'd leave it there for now. He should think about it, and we'd think about it. And then we'd see what we could work out.

A few days later we met again, at the Sheraton Tara over the turnpike in Newton. He came alone. He'd obviously had a rough night, and he looked rumpled. He'd spent his life on top of the mountain, and now he was looking down into the abyss. "OK," he told me. "I don't want to testify. I don't want to go public, OK? But I'll cooperate with you."

"You'll tell us all about your operation?"

He nodded.

"And about the people you deal with?"

He nodded again.

"All of them?"

This time, he just looked at me. No nod.

He knew who, but neither of us wanted to give up the names.

"Chico, it's got to be everyone, or no deal. You can't pick and choose."

"OK," he said finally. "Everyone."

He didn't want to talk to us anywhere near Boston, though. Between Whitey's people and the LCN, there were spies everywhere. He'd feel much safer talking to us in Florida, and I understood that. We had him in the fold, had taken possession of his passport, and had seized his money. So the court was willing to let him go down there. We met him a week later.

It was complicated with him, though. He had a number of codefendants on the case we were bringing against him, and by law we can't be privy to any information about any common defense strategy. And if Chico was getting close to any of that, we were supposed to run it by the U.S. attorney. This was delicate stuff, and nothing we'd dealt with before, so I brought in a new guy, a canny veteran named Pat Greaney, to deal with it. Half Lithuanian and half Irish, he was big and hulking, and he was a rock.

Pat and I spent three days with Chico in Florida, and maybe it was the sun, or maybe it was the security, but Chico seemed much more relaxed than he had in Boston, and he gave us just about everything we wanted. Much of it had to do with the financial arrangements with Flemmi and Bulger. He rarely talked to Bulger directly, probably no more than a few times a decade. Instead, he talked to Flemmi, and Flemmi talked to Whitey. But he could lay out the basic structure of Whitey's operation and establish Whitey at the top.

And he told us about Whitey himself. He told us about how Whitey had murdered Louie Litif, a bookie who had been a friend of Chico's. Litif didn't have the best reputation, and he was rumored to have killed someone over a card game, but Whitey had it in for Litif for failing to clear the kill with him first. He shot Litif in the head, stuffed him into a garbage bag, and dumped the corpse into the back of an abandoned Lincoln downtown. Whitey joked afterward that Litif, who was known as a flashy dresser who matched his underwear to his clothes, was now "color coordinated," since he was wearing green boxer shorts while wrapped in a green garbage bag.

Chico told us about Whitey's violent side, the way he lashed out at people for no reason, and how terrified he himself was of Whitey but how much he hated him, too. Chico hated the fear; the endless shakedowns from Whitey, always for more and more money; the threats. Whitey tortured another bookmaker friend by searing his skin with bleach. It was all important material for us, confirmation of what we had always assumed to be true. But if Krantz wouldn't testify, it wouldn't help generate the indictments we were after. Still, it would help us win probable cause to get in more bugs and do more searches, to keep on climbing up the ladder in the hope that someday we'd reach the top.

But things were looking up. We'd barely been at it half a year, but we could already see the outlines of the money trail. It went from our bookies to "Fat Vinny" Roberto to Chico Krantz to Steve Flemmi and Whitey

Bulger. It was hazy, sure, but we knew it was out there. All the guys in the investigative unit could see it. If we could just get the details to fill out the full picture, Whitey was going down.

I was starting to wonder about the FBI, though. The feds hadn't done much to help us with the Roberto investigation, implying that he was a nobody and who cared. But Quinn didn't seem too interested in Chico either when I let him know how things stood. It wasn't as if he ever said no, don't do that, it's much better if you do this. He didn't say much of anything. So we went our own way and figured the FBI was busy with other things.

On some of the mob intercepts, and from Krantz, we'd been hearing about a mob gofer named George Kaufman. He was another Fat Vinny, handling bookies for Whitey and Flemmi all around the city. And, like the real Fat Vinny, he seemed to assume no one was on to him. Like most mobsters, he was careful on the phone, but he gave away enough so we could tell where the big meetings were happening around town, and who was likely to attend. One of the bookies was Joey Yerardi. Boston is a small place, and Tutungian remembered growing up with Yerardi in Newton, not far from where Chico lived now. He might have turned into a thug, but Tutungian remembered him as a decent kid back then.

Kaufman and Yerardi got around. They spent a fair amount of time with Stevie Flemmi, and with Frank Salemme, who was obviously looking to move up in the Mafia. That made me perk up—another pairing of the Irish and the Italian mob, and at a very high level. Flemmi was with Whitey, after all, and Salemme was LCN, blessed by Ray Patriarca Jr.

Here again those files in the basement in Framingham were useful. Someone else had been in on that plot to blow up Fitzgerald. Steve Flemmi. He'd fled the state after the explosion, and not returned until things cooled down. He was never held responsible for the bombing, but would have been if Salemme had given Flemmi up. And he would have saved himself some serious prison time if he had. But he hadn't, instead keeping silent for fifteen years. A favor like that is worth a lot, and Salemme was pressing to collect. The word was that he wanted a good spot in the organization from Ray Jr., with the idea of taking it over. That was probably what had gotten Mercurio so exercised, since he wanted the same thing. And it looked like Frank was holding out for a good piece of Whitey's operation, too. That would increase his standing with the LCN.

Off Kaufman's phone, we found out where Salemme, Flemmi, and a few other mobsters were meeting to hash all this out in a war council: at a gas station in Brookline called Guzzi's Sunoco.

"Beautiful," Greaney told me with a huge smile, when we figured this out. I had to agree.

We used the information from the intercepts and the Krantz interview to get permission to tap the phones at Guzzi's Sunoco station. Mobsters like Salemme, Kaufman, Yerardi, Flemmi, and Salemme's number two, Bobby DeLuca—they'd meet there to plot their next move. The conversations were pretty empty, like this one between Kaufman and DeLuca that Patty jotted down.

Kaufman: Guzzi's.
DeLuca: Hey, Guzz, what's up?
Kaufman: Hey, what's up?
Deluca: What are you doin'?
Kaufman: Nothin' much, lookin' to buy some fuckin' uh, uh, what do you call it?
DeLuca: Tickets?
Kaufman: Tickets, yeah.
DeLuca: That's all right.
Kaufman: Look how easy it is, huh?

It was a safe bet that these "tickets" weren't to the Red Sox. Wary of phone taps, the mobsters liked to speak in code, although some of the code got so confusing that they had trouble following it themselves. A few times, they even shifted into pig Latin. Really.

We were only few weeks into it when an agent in the FBI's Providence office, a straight shooter named Tim Sullivan, called to give me a heads-up. "I just want to tell you I'm working Salemme, too," he told me. "I know you've got something going on him up there."

I'd kept Quinn informed about what we were up to and how our own investigation had veered over to Salemme. As usual, Quinn didn't say much in response beyond OK. Basically, he sounded bored with the whole thing. But he'd passed word on to Sullivan, and that was something.

"I'm going at it from a different angle," Sullivan went on. "A Rhode Island mobster named Robert DeLuca. Know him?"

"Of course," I said. We'd been hearing his name on a lot of the Guzzi's intercepts, He was down with Salemme. "You getting anything?"

"Yeah, Salemme and DeLuca talk every day, and then meet a lot, too. We've been getting great stuff. We're going for a title three." That's fed talk for a wiretap.

"Interesting," I told him. Obviously, Salemme was busy on the LCN, too.

I filled him in on how the Whitey investigation was going.

"That's great," he told me. "But we don't want to get in each other's way."

"Absolutely. We'll do ours, you do yours."

"So I'll tell my guys to stay away from what you're doing up there in Boston."

"And I'll do the same for you down there in Providence."

"Perfect."

It was a nice call, the first time in a while I'd gotten a good feeling about the FBI. This was the way it was supposed to go. Two law enforcement agencies working together, each showing respect and consideration for the other.

Just to be on the safe side, I thought it would be smart to nail down the arrangement, so all the parties would know exactly what was happening. Neither of us wanted the different agencies to converge on the same target. Sullivan agreed we should meet to get it all straight. He called up Ed Quinn and asked him to meet us and the Rhode Island state police halfway to Providence at a little culinary college called Johnson and Wales. As head of the Boston office's OC section, Quinn was in charge of all of New England, so he needed to know the deal between Sullivan and me.

So Quinn showed up at the meeting. And we went through it, Sullivan and I, just the way we had on the phone. Sullivan could do whatever he wanted in Providence, but he'd stay out of Boston. We'd do what we needed in Boston, but we'd stay out of Providence. The FBI agents in Providence have always tended to view Boston as a satellite city of Providence, since the New England mob was headquartered down there. So I made it crystal clear. "The dividing line's the border between Mass and Rhody," I said. "You should stay on your side, and we'll stay on ours. If we're following someone down toward Providence, we'll hand them off to you. If you're following someone up to Boston, hand them off to us. That way, nobody gets in anybody else's way. Everybody got that?"

"It's fine with us," Sullivan said. "Makes perfect sense."

We all shook on it. Done.

Several days later, we found out that there was a failed attempt at getting a bug into DeLuca's car. The feds had Rhode Island troopers pull him over, and then impound his vehicle on a ruse. DeLuca wasn't fooled.

Well, that was too bad, I thought, but that's on them. It shouldn't affect us.

A day or two later, Hanko and Tutungian were back at Guzzi's. They had the place staked out and were driving by to see who was there. I got a call from them. "Problems, Tommy. Looks like a couple of FBI agents are parked outside Guzzi's."

"You're shitting me. Who are they?"

"I don't know, but they sure look FBI."

Just then, the bugged phones inside Guzzi's went nuts, like we'd put a bat to a beehive, and the bees were everywhere. "Shit! Shit!" somebody started screaming into the phone. "There's someone outside. Yeah, right outside. Yeah, in a car. Two of them! It's like fucking FBI! Those fuckers! Quick—getouttahere!" Total panic. What was going on? Hanko and Tutungian drove by Guzzi's, and it was ridiculous. Two men were indeed sitting in a car right across from the gas station, and they could not have looked more FBI—male, early forties, close-cropped hair, sunglasses. You could practically hear the theme song playing from the old TV show *The FBI*. It was that obvious.

How was that possible? I called Quinn right up and asked him about the agents outside Guzzi's. "They're in a white Pontiac with Rhode Island plates."

"I don't know," he said, only slightly interested. "Why do you ask?"

"I told you the other day. We've got the phones tapped at the station. It's a mob hangout. Salemme's in there, remember? We've got the phones tapped and now all the mobsters inside are going ape because there's a car outside with a couple of FBI agents in it."

"Hang on. I'll check to see what's going on."

He called me back. "Yeah, that's a couple of our guys from Providence. Don't worry, we've told them to move out."

"From Providence? You're kidding me. Eddie, we talked about this. Providence stays out of Boston. Boston stays out of Providence."

"Well, our agents didn't know."

"Didn't you tell them?"

"We've got a lot of agents here. I can't know what each one is doing."

"Well, what the hell *are* they doing there?"

"Don't worry, Tommy," Quinn replied, ignoring the question. "They've left the area."

"Now," I told him, and ended the call.

What was it—simple incompetence, or something else? Were they trying to wreck our surveillance, or could they just not help themselves? It was a question I would ask myself again.

———

The mobsters left Guzzi's after that, but they didn't go far. Just down the street to a Greek diner called the Busy Bee. But that posed a problem. There were about a dozen booths inside, with a fairly steady stream of diners filling them. Our mobsters would come in regularly for lunch, and they usually ended up in one of two booths, but not always. We'd rigged up a napkin holder with a tiny mike—but where to put it? We couldn't bug all of the tables; nor could we bug the whole the room and hope to pick out their voices. So what to do? The best we could think to do was to place the modified napkin holder in one of the favorite booths, and try to steer the mobsters there by filling up most of the other ones with members of my team like Hanko, Patty, Gale, and sometimes me. Once or twice I ended up just one booth over from Flemmi and Salemme and a few other wiseguys. That was a first for me. I didn't want to eye them, for obvious reasons, but I picked up on the outsized quality of these guys, the way they were big regardless of the size they actually were.

It was a little like playing Mob Lottery. We'd bet on a booth and hope to score. And we did, more often than not.

But then a waitress was wiping a table down one day before we had a chance to remove the bugged napkin holder. She started refilling the napkins, saw some wires coming out, and started screaming, "There's a bomb! There's a bomb!" The owner raced over, grabbed the "bomb" from her, flung it out the back door, and called 911. Tutungian and Hanko heard all this through the bug, which they'd been monitoring from a mock electric truck outside, and they could see everybody come running out in a panic.

"Tommy, they're going crazy at the Busy Bee," Tutungian shouted into the phone. "They think there's a bomb."

"Well, go in there and grab it. Right away."

They charged in, told the owner they were police, and said they'd handle everything. The terrified owner pointed to the back parking lot, and then watched in astonishment as Tutungian calmly collected the device and continued to stride right on out the parking lot entrance.

It was a funny story, one of those goofy things that happen in this line of work, and we had a few chuckles over it. So I was startled to see an account about the "bomb" incident in a *Boston Globe* column by Mike Barnicle a few weeks later. Barnicle didn't identify the restaurant, but for my purposes he didn't need to. Barnicle was known to be close to John Connolly, along with some other agents, and it was clear that he was being good to the hands that fed him. Still, so few people knew about the incident. I couldn't imagine how Connolly had found out about it, if he was indeed the source.

Fortunately, these mobsters didn't read Barnicle's column, because they continued to meet at the Busy Bee for lunch just like before. And we quickly had a working bug back in there, too. This time, though,

Tutungian and I noticed something as we listened in. While Salemme, DeLuca, Yerardi, and the others all spoke as freely as ever, one did not. Steve Flemmi. We knew he was there. But now he scarcely said a word. Lunch after lunch.

––––––

Making the arrangements got cute. When Salemme's number two called up, they played a game. DeLuca would ask when Salemme was going to be "busy," and Salemme would say he'd be "busy" at two o'clock. Then De-Luca would say, "OK, see ya then." Tutungian and I were usually the ones listening, and we had to laugh. So we'd get "busy" down at the Busy Bee at two o'clock, too.

Still, we picked up plenty of useful stuff, like when Kaufman and Ye-rardi roped in Anthony "Spitzy" Gambale, an established bookie and loan shark in Revere I'd first stumbled across in 1987. And it was fun to hear Stevie Flemmi complain about being called "the Rifleman" in a *Globe* story.

Flemmi: You read the fuckin' paper?
Kaufman: Huh?
Flemmi: Read the paper?
Kaufman: Yeah, I'd like to know what it said.
Flemmi: Oh, you couldn't read it?
Kaufman: I read the whole fucking thing five times.
Flemmi: Yeah.
Kaufman: Didn't make no sense to me.
Flemmi: Yeah, I know it. The fuckin', all they do is keep it, just keep
     fucking injecting our name in there.
Kaufman: That's right.
Flemmi: Ridiculous, it's fuckin' . . .
Kaufman: Now that's the first time they put in the "Rifleman," you
     know what I mean?
Flemmi: Yeah. The Rifleman, yeah.
Kaufman: Yeah. That's . . .

Flemmi: At least they can't fuckin' say I got the nickname hiding
     behind a fuckin' trash barrel.
Kaufman: That's right.
Flemmi: I was shooting at somebody.

Gradually, the calls started to mention "a trim" or "getting a cut" or "talking to Curly." And we started to wonder: why all the talk of haircuts? So we listened some more, and we heard the name Clemente of Clemente's Coiffeur being drawn into the conversation, and we realized the gang had moved the meeting spot from the Bee down the street to Clemente's Coiffeur. Tutungian did the affidavit, a judge gave his OK, and we started planting the bugs the next night. This one needed a return visit to finish up, but when we came by the shop the next afternoon, it was empty. No lights, no business, nothing. A handwritten note on the door said the salon was "closed for business." We learned later that Clemente himself had returned to his native Italy.

"Somebody's on to us," Tutungian said when I told him the news. "No other fucking way, Tommy. This is no coincidence, I'll tell you that. We put in a bug on Wednesday night, and the place shuts down on Thursday morning? Somebody tipped him, that's all there is to it." He looked at me. "You tell anyone?"

"Yeah," I admitted.

"Who?"

"FBI."

Tutungian just shook his head.

———

It was December 1991 when I went to that FBI Christmas party at Joe Tecce's restaurant, the one where Connolly brought in the booze from Whitey. Sly Scanlan was with me, and he told me I should have a word with Ed Troy, a good cop, who was now an undercover narc. Stocky and strong, he practically lived undercover. But he'd surfaced for the party, and Scanlan thought he might be able to help us. So we went off into a corner together, and he told me he was working an undercover drug investigation in Chelsea, a tough town just north of Boston. He told me he'd come into contact with a bookie named Sam Berkowitz.

"Berkowitz?" I said. Then, a little quieter: "Jeez, we're working on him." Berkowitz was a big-time bookie with heavy mob connections. A shifty figure even by mob standards, Berkowitz was one of the FBI informants who'd helped bring down the Angiulo regime. That was an open secret. It had been in the papers, and he'd received a presidential pardon for his service to the nation. Now that the applause had died down, he'd gone back to his mob ways. He ran a mean little bar called the Pub and Grub in Chelsea, where he ran numbers—the mob version of Lotto—and Salemme and Flemmi wanted to get him to manage the numbers for them, since he was so good at it. But they weren't asking in a nice way. They were squeezing him. This was Flemmi's way of helping Salemme out.

— CHAPTER 12 —

Troy told me he'd been placing some bets with Berkowitz as part of his undercover work.

"Yeah?"

He nodded.

"Well, we want to hit him with a search warrant for his gaming stuff. Do you think you could help us out a little on that—maybe get us some information for the affidavit?"

"Sure, Tommy. No problem," he told me.

"And we'll keep it real quiet, don't worry."

We thought that maybe Berkowitz would tell us everything about Salemme. We had his cell tapped, and he was always on it. We figured the moment we hit Berkowitz with the search warrant, Berkowitz would call and give Salemme an earful, and we'd know how Salemme fitted into the Boston rackets, and maybe we'd get something on Flemmi, too.

Next day, I told Quinn we were going to do a search warrant on Berkowitz. I'd just as soon have skipped that step, but Henderson had made it clear that he expected me to coordinate all our efforts with the FBI.

"Thanks for the heads-up," Quinn told me.

I didn't say anything about Troy, didn't even let Quinn know we had an undercover trooper in there.

The very next day, Troy called me up, hot as anything. "Shit, Tommy, you know what Berkowitz just told me? He told me to *watch out*. An FBI agent had told him that the State Police were on him. He said he couldn't take any action for a while. It was too hot. He had to shut down. '*Shut down*,' Tommy. That's what he said. Because some trooper was on him."

"Oh, Jesus." I didn't go into it with Troy, and I didn't have to. He was plenty smart to know the score.

"Ed, listen." Where to begin? "Christ almighty. Let me deal with this, OK?"

"Whatever you have to do."

When I hung up, I wanted to grind the receiver into its cradle.

This time, there could be no evasions, no I-didn't-knows. So I called Quinn up, and I ran through what had just happened with Troy. I wasn't loud; loud doesn't work. But I was forceful. There was nothing but silence on the other end of the phone.

"Eddie, Jesus," I wound up. "What are you trying to do, get my guy killed?"

"Hey, come on. I didn't know you had an undercover trooper in there."

"How can you guys keep doing this? This is bullshit, Eddie!

"Hey, calm down." He went quieter himself. "We need to talk about this, but not on the phone."

He asked me to come in and take a ride with him. We'd talk in the car.

I waited for him in front of the McCormack Building downtown. I was in civilian clothes, with a parka for warmth. He came out in a long topcoat and leather gloves.

He climbed in without a word, shut the door, and pulled on his seat belt. I took us on a jagged loop around the financial district, by the waterfront, and about the North End.

"Eddie, I thought we had an understanding here," I began. "We can't go the way you're going. You can't mess with our people like this. I mean, Jesus Christ. Our guy goes undercover, and you out him? What are you thinking?" There's a phrase for that, not that I told him: obstruction of justice.

"Take it easy, Tom."

I was raising my voice this time. Not much, but I couldn't help it. I was getting loud enough for him to play the calm and reasonable grown-up—and make me the kid who can't control himself.

"Eddie, I'll take it easy when it's easy to take. This is serious, all right? So I'm going to take it seriously."

"Listen, this was a mistake, OK? It happens. And no one was hurt."

To him, it was Guzzi's all over again. "A rookie agent made a mistake, all right? That's all it was. Said something he shouldn't have. It happens. Nobody got hurt."

"Not yet."

Two boneheads at Guzzi's, one here on Berkowitz. Different lies for different times. The agents at Guzzi's existed, but they sure weren't there by mistake. This idiot didn't exist—no one is that stupid. Berkowitz was tipped off, all right, but not by any rookie agent.

Quinn slapped my thigh. "But I've had him transferred so it won't happen again, believe me." He paused a moment. "And as far as I'm concerned, that's the end of it."

I ran through it all in my head. Clemente's, Guzzi's, Busy Bee, Barnicle's column, and now this. The pattern was clear, but still nobody at the FBI would listen to me, or do a damn thing about it. It was like none of it ever happened. We were just a bunch of children, and it didn't much matter what happened to us.

I'd had it with Quinn, but this was no time to take him on. I just needed to keep pushing forward and hope to stay ahead of the dangers that seemed to be looming up all around us.

We were in the North End by now, not far from the Mafia headquarters on Prince Street where Eddie made his name. I saw his eyes turn to the building as we went past, but he said nothing. When I dropped him off, he just got out of the car and closed the door behind him. Gently, like he didn't want to break anything.

"Bye, Tom," he said.

Years later, the Department of Justice's Office of Professional Responsibility looked into the Troy matter. When Quinn was asked about it, he told investigators that he didn't recall any such incident involving anyone named Ed Troy and Sam Berkowitz.

————

For an aspiring Mafia boss, Salemme was unusual in that he didn't live in the North End like all the others; but way out in horse country, in Sharon, and he hung out as much with Irish mobsters like Flemmi as with Italians. Salemme's ascent didn't come easy either. Before too long his chief enforcer, a bank robber named Richie Devlin, got wiped out when he stepped out of a restaurant in East Boston, and then another loyalist named Cucinotta got wasted in Cranston, Rhode Island. But Salemme gave as good as he got. We got reports that a mid-level mobster, Bobby Donati, was found beaten and stabbed to death in Revere; and Barry Lazerini was bludgeoned to death in the living room of his Plymouth home. Frank Salemme Jr. was a suspect in the murders. He was known to be vicious, would do anything to please his father, and was said to be moving up in the mob, too. But for Frank Sr., there were definitely openings in the leadership. Raymond Patriarca Jr. was finally heading to prison after the taping of the induction ceremony, and Vinny Ferrara and the rest of the crew at Vanessa's were going away, too. And it sure didn't hurt that Salemme could call Flemmi and Bulger his good friends.

No question, Salemme was preparing to claim his prize as Mafia boss for all of New England, and other mobsters in other parts of the country knew it. We figured out that Natale "Big Chris" Richichi, a powerful, heavily bejeweled mafioso from Las Vegas, had taken note. Richichi represented the New York OC families in Las Vegas. As a favor to Rhode Island wiseguy wannabe, Ken Guarino, he agreed to fly in to see Salemme for a sit-down to try to hammer out a deal on some peep show machines that Richichi's people wanted to bring into the Combat Zone, the red-light district that Salemme controlled. The FBI had learned about the meeting, but not where it would happen or when—so the feds needed to draw on our existing taps to figure that out. By then, we'd pretty much bugged every aspect of Salemme's life, just as we'd done Fat Vinny's, including his cell, and Salemme lived on his cell.

This was just days after I took Quinn for a drive. For a few months he'd been knocking me about our taps, saying that the mobsters don't say anything on their phones anymore, so why bother with any of that stuff? Well, right now the feds needed it. They needed help getting information together for an application for a bug for the Richichi-Salemme meeting room. I was leery, of course. I was more than frustrated with the FBI, but I still had to work with them. That was my deal with Colonel Henderson, and I was going to stick to it. We got the wiretap information the FBI wanted from Salemme's cell phone. The meeting would be at the Hilton at Logan Airport, and we got when. All the feds had to do was watch Richichi and Salemme and the others check in, drop a bug into their room, and then commandeer the next room as a listening post. It was perfect. The mobsters hadn't a clue.

For the meeting, Salemme came with his new friend Bobby DeLuca, and Richichi showed up with Ken Guarino. For a high-level meeting like that, the two sides have to be even. It's about respect, about power. When the two principals had settled down and gotten comfortable with each other, they dismissed their seconds and then carried on alone, one-on-one, well into the evening. Salemme was usually blunt and dismissive of other mobsters, now that he was moving up the ladder. But you could hear a new deference in Salemme's voice with this king of the casinos. Richichi heaped on the sugar right back. After they worked out the issue of the Combat Zone peep shows, Richichi offered Salemme some advice about how to set up a mob family of his own. You need loyalty, he told Salemme. Loyal soldiers, Frank. You get what I'm saying to you? No jerks. Salemme assured Richichi that he was confident of the loyalty of the men he had around him, and that he had powerful people on his side, too.

And then he mentioned a name that got my attention. Bulger. We almost never heard it. None of the other low-level mobsters had dared mention him, for fear that it would show up on some transcript, and they'd get dead. Whitey inspired that kind of fear. He dictated silence. Big, loud, brash, Salemme demanded to be noticed (that was probably why we had him bugged six ways till Sunday), and he was loose (why Bulger steered clear of him).

It came up when Richichi, a capo in the Gambino family under John Gotti, offered Salemme some fraternal advice. Don't forget about protection, he told Frank. You'll need it, believe me. And don't stint. You're the boss; people will come for you.

You have protection? Richichi asked Salemme.

"I got that crew from South Boston, some kids from South Boston,"

Salemme told him. "Bulger and Flemmi." Obviously, it was just braggado-cio. Calling Bulger and Flemmi "some kids from South Boston" was like calling the navy SEALs a bunch of dog paddlers. Salemme's thought he'd look big by making Bulger and Flemmi look small. If he called them what they really were, Richichi would wonder why he was dealing with Frank and not with Whitey and Stevie directly.

Flemmi had been the one to bring in Whitey; Whitey would never had gone in otherwise. But Flemmi had that debt to Salemme, just as the Patriarcas did, and this was another way to pay it off. But he also paid in exposure. We learned a lot more about Flemmi from Salemme than we ever did any other way. And we got more on Whitey, too.

I kept my word with Henderson and kept Quinn in the loop as our investigation of Salemme went along. I told Quinn how Salemme was expanding his operation, making Bobby DeLuca his number two and re-lying on him to pick the wiseguys to fill out his team. DeLuca was pulling them from Providence, since Salemme didn't trust anyone in Boston. But we were having trouble dealing with some of the code names—Shanks; The Saint. Who the hell were these people? I told Quinn we needed some help, and he said that he had an agent, Shay, who went way back with the mob down there, and who'd be good at working out all the names. Shay was in the hospital just then, but he'd be able to listen to the tapes while he was lying in his bed. "Might give him something to do," Quinn said. A Providence agent, Suddes, would take Shay the tapes if I would bring them just across the Rhode Island border on Route 146.

I made copies of the tapes as Quinn asked, and on New Year's Day 1992 I drove them down to Suddes to pass on to Shay. That was the plan anyway. The next day the cell phone of Salemme's that had produced oceans of great stuff for weeks went dead.

Once again, I was bullshit, and had to struggle to keep from getting pretty loud on this one. Who were they trying to kid? It was the same thing all over again. FBI. No question. FBI. They were the only ones who knew. And this time, I could think why. We didn't have just the mobsters on the tapes; we also had FBI informants. Everybody is protective of in-formants, but the FBI is more so than everybody else. The more people know, the bigger the danger. Makes sense. But the FBI didn't ever want anyone to know a word about anyone. It was the sort of thing that had caused Gianturco to turn to stone back when we worked together. Ring had been the same way. They valued their informants over our investigation into Whitey.

A few days later, I told Quinn what happened.

"Really," he said, like he couldn't have been less interested.

I knew the FBI was behind it, but again, no proof. So I let it go. I had to.

We'd been going full out, and we crashed through the holidays and into the New Year, but it was getting hard on all of us. Early that January 1992, I went back to headquarters as usual and mounted the stairs to the wire room on the third floor. The whole unit was still up there—Patty and Gale, Tutungian, Hanko, Scanlan, and another guy who'd been helping out, John Cahill. It had been barely a year, but we had grown into a tight unit. We'd all been working brutal hours, but it sometimes seemed like we weren't getting anywhere. Nerves were starting to fray. People were starting to snap at each other. And now, as soon as I came into the room, I saw everyone pull off the headphones and turn toward me.

This was the State Police, almost a military operation. No one was going to question my leadership, or my authority. But I could tell everyone was bummed. How many setbacks were we supposed to take? Were we ever going to get Whitey behind bars? We had plenty of wiretaps going, and we had lots of investigative angles to work, but it wasn't going the way any of us wanted. We were up against something much bigger than ourselves. It was like sensing danger in the dark. We couldn't see it, but we could feel it. "Guys, listen," I told everyone that night. "We've just got to keep going. This is hard. There's a lot of shit to get through. But the only way is to keep putting one foot in front of the other." I looked around the room—at Patty and Gale, Big John, Sly, and the rest. Their faces were tipped down a little, but I could tell they were listening. "And we're getting places. It may not look like it but we are." I touched on our

accomplishments, with the bookies, Chico, the results of the search warrants, the Busy Bee intercepts, and now with Salemme's cell. "Things like
this are never going to be easy. There are going to be bad days, bad weeks,
maybe bad months. But we have to believe in what we're doing, and to
persevere. We're building a case here. Brick by brick. That's all we can do.
One brick at a time."

We had to keep on going because we had to. That's what it came down
to. I didn't want to be in this situation anymore than they did. Unlike
them, I had some say over it. But only in theory. In fact, I was just as stuck
as they were. We were after Whitey, but it seemed like the FBI was after us
just as hard. That was on everybody's mind that night, not that anybody
came out with it. And we had to hope that we could catch one before any
of us got caught by the other.

— CHAPTER 13 —

In January 1992, we had enough evidence to bang out some search warrants for some of the bookies and a few higher-ups in the Flemmi-Bulger empire. It was like the night we hit Chico's place, but there was more to it. More important mobsters, over a wider range. I'd been itching to be part of it; these sorts of harvests are the thrill of an investigation. But Marguerite had to be in the hospital for a few days for an operation, and I needed to be with her. Tutungian and others would handle it. The biggest find was something Tutungian and Scanlan pulled out of the back of the gofer George Kaufman's bedroom closet: a stack of money, a few guns, and some face masks, the kind you wear for disguise. Kaufman was there for that, and it looked like he was going to fall over.

They were still going through the house when Steve Flemmi came in. The guys told me he just breezed in, didn't even knock. We'd all seen him dozens of times before. Flemmi's looks are never going to stop anyone, but he's a person to be taken seriously all the same. In a situation like that, he wouldn't have minded scrounging a little information from my guys if he could, but he was really there to give Kaufman a reminder that he was on to him, and don't even think about letting down your hair with the State Police.

Maybe half an hour later, after Tutungian and Scanlan had left the house, Richard Egbert called me on my cell at the hospital. Egbert was Kaufman's lawyer as well as Salemme's, Flemmi's, and Chico's. Like I say, he did them all. He didn't care that I was at my wife's bedside. He lit right into me. "Your troopers didn't leave me an inventory of what they took from Kaufman!" he shouted.

"Rich, they don't have to," I told him. "There's no legal obligation. It's just a courtesy."

"Well, the FBI does it."

"So? We're not the FBI, and this is a state search warrant."

After we put together a list for court, I got him a copy. Then he returned the favor by hitting me with the charge that Tutungian and I had stolen $20,000 from Kaufman's closet. Never mind that I wasn't even there, or that there never was $20,000. The point was to discredit any testimony from either of us later, as he could say I was under investigation for theft. And he did exactly that.

————

At that point, Chico Krantz was the best we had against Salemme, Whitey, and Flemmi. By agreement, he was never going to testify, but he was going to tell us everything he knew. We'd had that one terrific three-day session with him down at his place in Florida. But since then, Chico was becoming very hard to find. We learned from our wiretaps that Chico had returned to the gaming business like all was forgiven.

So we whacked him with a second search warrant, and learned everything about the new enterprise. We discovered that this time he must have been short on manpower, because he'd brought his wife, Jackie, into the game, too. She was his courier, lugging heavy bags of gaming money around to deposit in various banks.

None of this improved his situation. What Chico had done would win him serious time and garner a fair amount for his wife, too.

Obviously, Chico and I needed to have a heart-to-heart. Pat Greaney came along when I met him in the parking lot of the IHOP in West Roxbury, not far from his house. He took off his Stetson as he climbed into the front seat of my car. Pat was sitting in the back. In a situation like that, we always try to give the guy something to eat, to take some of the stress out. Pat had bought him a muffin and some coffee, and he handed them to Chico, who took them greedily.

When he'd had a few bites of the muffin, I told him we knew about Jackie. "She's got problems now, too, Chico," I told him. "Just like you do."

While he was still digesting that, I handed him a draft indictment prepared by Fred Wyshak in the U.S. Attorney's Office.

I watched his face fall as he read it.

"What the fuck, Tommy? You gonna indict both of us?"

"We could," I told him. "All depends on what you want to do."

I told him that my earlier offer—no trial appearance—was off the table since these charges were much more serious. "We've got you for money laundering, Chico." I told him. "These are federal charges—serious time." I paused, knowing I was getting to the heavy part. "Jackie, too!"

The new deal? He'd have to testify at trial, but we'd see to it that he was placed in the Witness Protection Program if he wanted.

"But you've got all my money." He meant that $2.3 million we'd seized.

"And we're not giving it back, if that's what you're thinking." With the court's permission, we'd use it to fund the investigation, which is customary procedure.

"I earned that!"

"Chico, you obtained it illegally, and that's the end of it."

"Fuck," he said again.

"That's our offer, Chico. Testify, and you and Jackie can disappear into the program. No prison time. But you've got to tell the whole truth. You got that? You lie, or leave stuff out, and you're both going to rot in prison. You're looking at twenty years easy, and she's probably going to do ten."

Chico looked a pale yellow, or maybe it was just the light under the IHOP lamps. He chewed on his muffin, staring blankly out the windshield.

"OK," he said. "I'll do it. I'll testify."

As he left the car, he asked me for a favor. "Can I bring a couple of these muffins back to Jackie?"

Pat handed him a couple of warm ones from the bag.

———

Over the next few months, he filled us in a little more about our operation, and we used that information to secure more wiretaps on the bookies in his network. Things were progressing. Slowly, we were spreading out and working our way up, just as I had always hoped. The picture puzzle of Whitey's bookmaking network was being filled in, one piece at a time. We had all the low-level bookies, stuff from the Fat Vinny taps, and plenty more on Yerardi and DeLuca. We'd flipped Chico, we'd gotten a ton of organizational material from Busy Bee before it shut down, and we had hundreds of Salemme intercepts at the Hilton and countless other places that gave us some glimpses of Whitey's operation itself.

I kept telling my guys, "It's working, We're getting there." I needed to keep their spirits up because the work was such a bitch.

But they weren't the only ones getting the message. I was starting to hear back from the FBI, too. And this time it wasn't that mysterious stuff started to happen, stuff that compromised some operation of ours and oops, sorry, we had no idea. That was stuff around the edges, stuff that was hard to pin down. Now I started hearing rumors, notions, ideas. It was hard to know what to call them. Nebulous as they were, they were all vaguely menacing. And they never came from anyone who was in a position to know any specifics, so I could never press people. What I heard was, "You guys have a problem, too." I must have heard that from several agents. But they'd say this to me casually, as if they were letting me know that it might rain. "You guys have a problem, too."

I thought about that a lot. "A problem." What kind of problem? No one would ever say. But I knew what they were hinting at. It was Naimovich all over again. That's how the FBI responds to any threat. They don't hit you with anything specific. They just blow smoke in your face.

I kept telling them: Look, if we have a problem tell me what it is so I can do something about it. I'm not going to get defensive; I'm going to fix it. And then there was that last word, which not everyone added, but a lot did. That last word said everything. "Too." This was as close to an admission of guilt as you'll ever get from the FBI, and it is all the more revealing for being accidental. It just slips out.

They had a problem. I knew that. They were killing off our investigation into the criminal activities of Whitey Bulger, an investigation that was supposed to be joint. Quinn had always made it sound like every compromised wiretap, every blown stakeout, was just a blunder. A rookie agent, a piece of miscommunication. Well, I could accept that once, maybe twice. But half a dozen times over a matter of months?

But why? I thought about that one a lot, believe me. Why would the highest law enforcement agency in the country, and possibly the best one in the world, side with Whitey Bulger over us? How could it possibly be that keeping Whitey Bulger safe and in business was the higher priority? From what we knew—and what they had to know, too—Whitey Bulger was a multiple murderer, a drug dealer, an extortionist, a terrorist, a racketeer, and any number of other things. Why pick him? We had ideas, of course. We always had ideas. But it remained a matter of speculation, not fact. One thing that was not a fact was the idea that we in the SSS of the State Police had "a problem." Sure, we had problems—money, morale, equipment—but we did not have a problem the way the FBI had a problem. And we certainly did not have a problem, *too.*

— CHAPTER 14 —

If we did have a problem, it was the FBI. But it only started there. As our investigation advanced, it spread to another level in the hierarchy of the Department of Justice. The DOJ was the FBI's home in the government, so the attorney general was the ultimate boss of the Bureau. In fact, ever since J. Edgar Hoover used to gather information on his potential enemies in the government in order to protect the Bureau's independence, the FBI has operated at a safe remove from almost any governmental oversight. And its reputation as an agency that will use your secrets against you has served it well to give it power well beyond its station.

The United States Attorney's Office, or USAO, is a little-known agency that operates as a federal prosecutor's office. In Boston during most of our investigation, it was located in the large and ornate federal courthouse in Post Office Square downtown. It was a big deal. There were probably a hundred attorneys working out of there, overseen by the U.S. attorney, one of maybe fifty across the country, all of them appointed by the president. Their job is largely to prosecute the cases the FBI investigates. Supposedly, the USAO directs the action, picking the targets, and the FBI follows through. But, from what I could see of the USAO, the power went the other way. The FBI chose the targets, and the USAO went along.

One organization that was left out of the process was ours. Too much of the time, whatever we said, the FBI and the USAO closed ranks against us. Their message was: what could you possibly know that we don't? And, beyond that: who are you to question our judgment? When we started bringing the case to the federal level in 1993, the U.S. attorney was a Clinton appointee, Donald Stern, but we rarely dealt directly with him. Much more often, an assistant U.S. attorney would handle it. There were dozens of them, and they didn't all think alike. One of the few who saw the world our way was Fred Wyshak. Wyshak monitored the progress we were making prior to bringing our case to the feds. He'd investigated organized crime in New York, so he knew his way around. He was aggressive and liked the challenge. He would be my alter ego on the prosecutorial side, pushing for convictions as our unit pushed for arrests. Gentle and soft-spoken, Wyshak had a hangdog look, but it didn't really fit him. Deep down, he had a fire that I was happy to have on our side.

"So what's all this about?" he asked when I met with him to brief him on our case.

"Whitey," I told him. "We're going after him. You should know that."

We were sitting in Fred's office, with a view of the square. He didn't say anything for a long moment. "Well," he said finally. "OK then."

He put together indictments of Chico for money laundering and a few other things. Unlike all the other assistant attorneys, he asked nothing about our problems with the FBI, which he must have heard about. He didn't care about our struggles with the USAO, which were just developing either. He was just one of those guys who go into law enforcement to bring out the truth. Fred Wyshak was the best. We could never have gotten anywhere without him.

———

By the time 1993 rolled around, we felt we'd turned the corner on the Whitey investigation and were starting to feel better about things. On some of the intercepts, we'd picked up word about Peter Fiumara, who owned a strip joint in Revere called the Sports Page. To boost his profits, Fiumara put any extra cash out for loan-sharking through Kaufman's pal Joey Yerardi. Fiumara handled a lot of bookies for Whitey and Flemmi, and he did it in a big way, and in April 1993, we were all set to indict him. Wyshak drew up the indictment.

Just one problem. I knew how the FBI felt about its informants, and I had been told years earlier that Fiumara was an informant of Ed Quinn's. I did not know if this was still the case. We might have let it go, but Fiumara was a heavy, and we were pretty sure he had a lot to tell us about Whitey's operation.

I called Quinn and laid it out for him. "We're going to indict Fiumara." At this point, I'd given up asking. I wanted to give Ed the opportunity to talk to me about Fiumara if he needed to.

Quinn's voice was chilly, but he didn't say a word about Fiumara, and we went on with our plans.

The FBI can't stop an indictment, since it has no prosecutorial author-ity. But the USAO can, and the FBI can get the USAO to want to. A few weeks after I spoke to Quinn I got a call from Fred Wyshak.

"Tommy," he said. "A heads-up. We're not going to indict Fiumara."

"Shit—why not?"

"Farmer." Jim Farmer was the head of the USAO's organized crime strike force, and reported directly to the U.S. attorney, Donald Stern. I doubt that Farmer did or said anything important without running it by Stern. "He says there's not enough there."

I could hear the doubt in Wyshak's voice. "Do you?"

"Yes. Absolutely."

"The guy is a shylock who's in with Whitey Bulger," I reminded him. "About as cut-and-dried a RICO charge as you're going to see."

"I'm with you there, Tommy. I tried to tell him, but, well, you know."

"You know why, don't you?"

"I can guess."

"You guessed right."

Wyshak went right back to Farmer and confronted him, demanding to know if Fiumara was informing for the FBI.

"Absolutely not," Farmer told him. "Who told you that?"

"Foley."

"He's full of it," Farmer told him.

Wyshak can be pretty persistent, so he went right at it. He asked Farmer straight out which was more important, protecting an FBI informant or getting Whitey Bulger.

Farmer just walked away. "Sorry, Fred. It's out of my hands. If Foley has a problem, he should take it up with Ed Quinn."

Wyshak and I were getting seriously pissed off, and I thought I'd better try to smooth things over with Farmer. The USAO was going to be bringing our cases and we needed them on our side. Farmer told me what he told Wyshak: take it up with Quinn. The runaround. But Quinn didn't have the authority to stop the indictment—only the USAO did. Why should I talk to Quinn?

Wyshak has a long fuse, but he can blow, and this impasse infuriated him. The FBI was blocking a legitimate case to save its informant? Where were the priorities? Is the Department of Justice getting out of the justice business? Fred wrote a scorching letter to his superiors at the Department of Justice in Washington, demanding reconsideration of the Fiumara indictment. It went on for several pages. I was impressed when I read it. But everyone at the DOJ who read it saw it the same way. Fred Wyshak was trouble.

That made two of us.

Fiumara was never indicted.

———

By that summer of 1993, we'd accomplished a lot, despite the efforts of the FBI and the USAO to stymie us, but we were starting to drag. It had been such a long hard slog that I could tell that the burnout factor was pretty high. There was grumbling in our little unit about the long hours, and complaints about some of my decisions, and worry about when the investigation would finally yield the indictments we'd been seeking. Tutungian and Scanlan were still the backbone of the group. Real power houses. If those guys had been marines, they would have taken hill after hill and then set their sights on a mountain. The big lug Pat Greaney had been a great addition to the team, and a loyal friend for me when I needed one.

It was still the original six, but they got a lift when I brought in Tom Duffy. For almost two decades, he'd been doing investigations with the DA's office in Worcester, and he brought the group some fresh energy and enthusiasm. A little later, I picked up another investigator from the same Worcester DA's office, Steve Johnson, who'd done a ton of undercover work and knew his way around in the dark. And finally, we lured in Dan

Doherty, a real godsend. He was one tough guy—shrewd, street smart, resourceful, the kind of guy you'd always want on your team. He knew all about Bulger from the DEA, and he was in with all the players from the State Police, the USAO, and even the feds. As soon as he started, it was like he'd been in with us from the beginning. With these guys, I figured we had the manpower we'd need for the next push.

———

Even if the USAO didn't move on Fiumara, we managed to grab enough of the other middlemen in the organization to more than make up for it. In December 1993, we targeted Mike Dezotell, a flunky for Yerardi, and bugged his car while he drank himself silly at the Marriott Hotel in Newton. The guy could not shut up. Who paid, who didn't, who had to be eliminated for not paying. It was a pretty good index to the Boston underworld. We also grabbed a veteran bookie named Jimmy Katz, who knew a lot about Whitey's bookmaking network. But Chico remained our ace in the hole, the one man whose testimony could bring down Whitey's empire.

Confident that we had the makings of a major case, in the spring and summer of 1994 we started bringing a stream of bookies and loan sharks before a grand jury that was convened to consider Bulger and the other conspirators, like Flemmi and Salemme. Fred Wyshak made the presentations, and what a workhorse he was. He enlisted a sidekick, Brian Kelly, a brilliant lawyer who also brought some much-needed humor to the duo. People started calling them Batman and Robin.

In the federal system, a grand jury is only impaneled for eighteen months before it expires, and when it does expire, the prosecutors have to start all over again with another grand jury, if that is even possible. This one would close down on September 12, and it was now early summer. That didn't leave us much time. Our case was cumbersome anyway, with all the witnesses and evidence we'd assembled, but it had gotten badly bogged down with some subpoenas we needed to get out on a number of bookies around town. The subpoenas had come from the USAO in May, and my instruction from the USAO was to let the FBI participate in serving the subpoenas. We had a big urgent meeting with Quinn, Farmer, his protégé Jamie Herbert, and Wyshak. We decided that the FBI would do half the list, and we'd do the other half. Remembering Fiumara, I let the feds pick the people they'd serve, in case there were any informants in there that they wanted to handle in their own way. I thought everything was all set.

We got ours done in a matter of days. If anything, the bookies we were serving were eager to go to court; they were tired of being shaken down by Bulger and Flemmi. Their information was from the bottom of the organization, but it would add important details to the picture drawn by Krantz, Roberto, Katz, and the rest about the top.

On the FBI side, though, there still was no action at all. This was toward the end of July, and Wyshak was getting frantic. He pleaded with the FBI to get cracking. When the feds continued to do nothing, Wyshak told us to go ahead and take over the FBI's list. It was either that or screw up our case. But when word got back to the FBI that we'd gone out with the subpoenas and started pounding on doors, Quinn lost it. An agent in the office told me he started raging at me, wondering what the fuck I was trying to do.

Quinn never told anyone what his problem was. I assumed it was just that there were informants on his list, and he couldn't deal with it. But an agent in his office passed on to me a better explanation. "We don't do South Boston." He said it in a tone like it was obvious. And it was.

South Boston, of course, wasn't just any part of the city. It was Southie, Whitey Bulger's base of operations. It was the feds' way of saying, "Don't do Bulger." It was one thing to be careful with informants but another to be careful with Whitey himself. What were they afraid of, exactly? Was Whitey so powerful that he posed some threat to the FBI? Or was it something else, like they owed him special treatment? The informants could help the feds out, make their lives easier, save them some trouble. But Whitey? What could he do for them?

———

We felt resistance on many fronts. We were trying to pull everything together for the grand jury to get indictments on Bulger, Flemmi, and Salemme before time ran out. We still wanted to strengthen the financial case against Bulger and Flemmi. Knowing our needs, another assistant U.S. attorney thought we might be interested in the Tim Connolly incident. A former tavern owner in Southie, Tim Connolly wanted to make something of himself as a mortgage broker, until he ran into Bulger and Flemmi. This is another aspect of the FBI's staying out of South Boston. The feds wouldn't have to confront Bulger and Flemmi's activities there, and the fact was, despite their reputations as Southie loyalists, Bulger and Flemmi would stick it to a Southie resident just like anyone else.

Tim Connolly was out walking his dog on a hot summer day when, with a screech of tires, a car pulled over. Bulger and Flemmi were inside, and they shouted at Connolly to get his ass over to Bulger's Rotary Variety Store. Connolly had no choice but to leave the dog at home and go straight there. Ushered into a storeroom, he found Bulger and Flemmi. Bulger held a hunting knife, a long one with serrated edges. He sat Connolly down and explained that he was outraged that Connolly had been slow handling a refinance for someone who owed him money.

"You fucker!" he suddenly screamed and, spotting some empty cardboard boxes along the wall, lunged at them with his knife and plunged the blade in to the handle, again and again, with a sickening ripping sound. Then he extracted the blade and brought it close to Connolly's face, then down his chin, and pressed it tight against his throat.

"I'm going to let you buy your life," he told Connolly.

The price was fifty grand, payable immediately. Connolly didn't have it, but he vowed to produce it, and Whitey and Stevie let him go. He ran out and got a bank loan for half, then for ten grand more. When Whitey demanded the balance, Connolly was tapped out. Desperate, he turned to Tom Reilly, the former assistant DA, who'd returned to private practice by then, and told him what had happened. Because racketeering is federal, Reilly told Connolly to speak to the FBI.

Tim Connolly had no reason not to. He called the Boston office of the FBI, and it sent out an agent, John Gamel, to have a talk with him. Gamel came from Worcester, where he had been a newscaster on a little-watched UHF station, and I'd never forgotten his heavy mustache and serious eyebrows; but most of all I remembered his immense height, somewhere north of six foot six. He was one of the few agents who had come to the FBI as a second career, but he retained the quality of a rookie through all the years I knew him. He never seemed to learn from experience.

Gamel interviewed Connolly at length, took down all the information, and then went back to the office. Nothing came of it. Happily, though, Whitey thought better of killing Tim Connolly for the balance, and he soon forgot about the whole thing.

That was way back in 1989. Now it was 1994. The Connolly incident sounded like a perfect example of Bulger-style extortion. Wyshak asked Farmer if we could use Tim Connolly in our case. Farmer stalled us, but finally provided the information we needed about Connolly. The problem was that he waited to deliver this piece of generosity until *after* the five-year statute of limitations on the Connolly matter had expired. It was over. It could not be a part of Whitey's indictment.

By now, John Gamel started paying closer attention to us. Before, he'd just been there, but now he was taking an active interest, curious about why we cared so much about the Connolly case, and where were we in our investigation. Then again, that was not exactly a secret. Any number of people in the USAO knew how things stood.

The truth was that we were going like crazy to meet the shutdown date of September 12 for the grand jury, and we wouldn't get indictments until then, if we got any indictments at all. Tutungian, Scanlan, Doherty, Johnson, and I were shuttling into and out of the courthouse every day, testifying, monitoring, and conferring with Wyshak and Kelly, who were even more crazed than we were trying to usher it all through. The others on the team were staying as close as possible to Bulger, Flemmi, and Salemme, the three we really wanted, if we could get the arrest warrants in time. Bulger they never got. The guy was impossible. You could make a guess where he was, but you'd never know. Along with several others, Patty and Gale were out following Salemme and Flemmi around. They weren't nearly as much of a problem. Especially Salemme. Big guy in a big car—you couldn't miss him.

And then, a few days before the end date, Flemmi and Salemme were gone. Vanished. Didn't show up anywhere. And we had to figure that Bulger had split, too. Days away from the indictments, they all scrammed. We couldn't believe it.

———

Despite our frantic efforts, we didn't get done anyway. We missed the dead- line, and the grand jury expired. Eighteen months and—nothing. With the main targets gone, we would have had trouble arresting them anyway. Still, it took a little of the wind out of all of us, no question. But we rallied.

Wyshak, as determined as ever, said he would convene an entirely new grand jury. All the evidence and testimony we previously brought to the prior grand jury would need to be read into the record to the new grand jury. A lot of it was a matter of reading the original testimony back into the record, page by page. The job fell to several of us in the unit—particularly Johnson, Tutungian, and Doherty—and we all got sick of it quickly, but we carried on.

Maybe two or three weeks later, Salemme and Flemmi slunk back into town. Patty and Gale spotted them. Somehow, they'd figured out the coast was clear.

We kept at it, though, week by week. The new grand jury was finishing up its work in late November when Wyshak ushered me into his office at the courthouse and shut the door behind us.

"We've got a problem, Tommy," he said. "Stern's not going to indict Bulger. He might not do Flemmi either."

"What?" I exploded. "You're kidding. What does the guy need?"

"He says the FBI's told him they've got something going that would make a much stronger case against them, but they won't have it together until spring."

"Spring? You're kidding me. This can't hold until spring. By then they'll be in Madrid or some goddamn place. They've already blown town once."

"I hear you, and I agree. I'm just telling you what Stern says."

"Doesn't he get it? We don't need the perfect case. We just need a case that will get those guys off the street."

At Wyshak's recommendation, I met Stern's top guy, Jonathan Shiels, and laid it out for him. Besides Wyshak and Kelly, Shiels was one of the few I liked in OC over there. I trusted him, and that is saying a lot there. He reiterated Stern's line that they were more likely to send Bulger and Flemmi away, and for longer, if we waited until spring. Apparently a concerted effort by the FBI to target the Rotary Variety Store was being planned.

Shiels was the messenger but I couldn't believe in the message. He knew how far we'd come. He also knew—not that he said anything—that the FBI had a problem with Bulger. Once again the USAO was the FBI's puppet.

"Jonathan, if we indict Bulger things will open up. You'll see, people will start coming out of the woodwork on this guy. The more people cooperate, the stronger case we'll have. I don't buy this spring offensive. It's just a delaying tactic."

"It's Don's decision, Tommy. I'm just passing it along."

"Well, Jonathan, listen to me. Tell them this. If Bulger and Flemmi are not indicted it will be the official public stand of the State Police that the United States Attorney's Office had the opportunity to do so but refused. You clear about what I'm saying? The official public stand—you tell them that."

He said he would definitely pass that along.

————

The FBI was feeling the heat, too. Aware over the years that we were working on Bulger, Dennis O'Callaghan, assistant agent in charge of FBI Boston, starting meeting with his equivalent in the State Police, Lieutenant Colonel Bud Riley, the head of the Division of Investigative Services.

A big, rumpled guy, O'Callaghan had always styled himself as one of the clean ones, and he always talked like the last thing he wanted was to damage the Bulger and Flemmi investigation. But he often complained to Riley about how I wasn't working with the FBI. "You've gotta work with the FBI, Tommy," Riley would tell me after meeting with O'Callaghan.

"You've got to get along." Riley knew that Greaney and I were close to Colonel Henderson and would often half-jokingly call us "the kitchen cabinet."

O'Callaghan and Riley went back a long way together, and they had any number of friends in common. O'Callaghan knew the landscape well enough to know that if he wanted to gum up our investigation, Riley was the man to see. Buddy Riley was also looking to advance and knew it wasn't in his best interests to go against the FBI.

— CHAPTER 15 —

It was around this same time that I started to I have trouble breathing. It developed over time, but then it got serious and eventually there were moments when I was gasping for air. I'd run pretty regularly in my college years, and I kept it up as I got older, running four, five, six miles a day, and maybe lifting some weights as well. It was important for me to burn off some of the stress of the investigation. But as weeks passed I'd noticed that I couldn't keep it up the way I'd always been able to before. I'd get not just winded, but wasted, like I had nothing left. I figured it had to be the stress. It was hard out there, getting it from everybody. I kept going, and it just got worse and worse, to the point where, when the weather warmed up, I couldn't keep up with my little kids when we were playing whiffle ball on the beach on a rare day off. At night, I kept waking up with cold sweats. I'd be drenched and shaking. And after a few months of this, I woke up one morning and my ankles were all swollen up. I thought—that can't be stress, can it?

Marguerite made me go to the doctor.

So I went to my doctor, Jack Kelly, and told him what was going on. I don't know what he was thinking, but he had an X-ray taken of my chest. After it was developed, Dr. Kelly looked it over with me, but he didn't say anything. He said he'd like the pulmonologist to see it. But rather than have me take it to him—he was just upstairs—he took it up himself. I waited there for a while, getting a little nervous. When Dr. Kelly returned, he asked me into his office, sat me down, and said I had lung cancer.

That was pretty terrifying. That was a Thursday. I took Friday off, and I stayed home with my family that weekend. On Monday, Dr. Kelly had arranged for me to be seen at Dana Farber, and I went over there for some more tests, and other pulmonologists reviewed my X-ray and determined that I didn't have lung cancer at all, but a rare disease that can look a lot like lung cancer. It's called sarcoidosis. It's caused by an antigen—a tiny pathogen that causes the immune system to overreact. It gets into the lungs and stays there, wreaking havoc in your body.

"So it's not stress?" I asked.

"It can be stressful, and it may be compounded by stress, but it is not caused by stress," the pulmonologist told me. "Why, are you under stress now?"

"A little," I said.

"A difficult investigation?" he asked. He'd seen on my chart that I was with the State Police.

"You could say that." I looked up at him. As the pulmonologist explained it, no one knew what caused the disease, but there were certain things to look for, chiefly some form of pollution, usually in the air. He asked me if I had been in any really dingy, stinking places in the last few months. And I told him I had—in Springfield on a matter entirely separate from the Bulger case. A gang had created a kind of headquarters in the gym of a high school that had been abandoned after a sewer pipe had broken and flooded the gym with raw sewage. On the walls, the stains went twenty feet up. It was the beginning of December, just as we were gearing up for the arrests. Our job was to wire the place for sight and sound, since it wasn't visible from the outside, and we hadn't been able to develop any informants. It wasn't easy drilling holes into the concrete walls for the surveillance equipment. I must have been in there three or four days. And the place really stank. Everything stank—the walls, the air. It was like the Whitey case. There wasn't a clean thing in it.

The doctor figured that was probably it, but we would never know for sure. He gave me some medication to help with the breathing. He told me the swelling would probably go down on its own. In the meantime, he told me I should do my best to ease off.

"That a possibility?" he asked.

"Not really."

"Well, go as slow as you can," he said.

Right. My breathing problem got a little better, perhaps from relief that it wasn't due to anything worse. But one other concern rose up to take its place—that I had to keep quiet about my condition. If people wanted to get me off the case, all they had to do was say I had a health condition and I'd be gone in the morning. So the word was that I was absolutely fine.

— CHAPTER 16 —

Then in mid-December, Stern caved in. He decided to indict Bulger and Flemmi along with Salemme and the others as soon as the grand jury had finished its work; it was now slated to do that in mid-January. Since this was our case, we'd do the arrests, but Stern wanted the FBI in on them, too.

When word came down from Stern, I started in. Bulger, Flemmi, Salemme. There were others like Bobby DeLuca—who'd be targeted, but these three were the essential ones, the ones we'd been gunning for since 1990. I thought a lot about the smartest sequence of arrests. Bulger first, then Salemme and Flemmi, because of their relative power? Or work our way up, as we'd done in the case? Whitey and Flemmi ran the Irish mob and virtually *were* the Irish mob, far and away the most powerful and terrifying mobsters in the city. Salemme was solidifying his hold as Mafia boss, not just in Boston but in all of New England. Between the three of them, they controlled all there was of mob activity in Boston and some way beyond.

Flemmi was the bridge between them. Or more exactly he was two bridges, linking to Whitey on one side and to Salemme on the other. So he joined the two of them together. It was enough to make us wonder once again if the line between the Irish and the Italian mobs was really as bright and clear as we'd thought. By getting Flemmi, we were getting a major Whitey connection and a major Salemme connection, too. Reaching to each, he'd help us get all three.

So we claimed Flemmi for ourselves. We'd go in with the FBI on capturing Salemme, since we had good information on Salemme's where-abouts. The FBI wanted Whitey. I had a talk with Quinn, and he assured me that his agents knew Whitey's location—not that he would reveal it to me—and they were on him. That was the extent of it. I didn't tell Quinn my plans for the arrests, or even say if I wanted the feds in. At that point, I didn't trust Quinn as far as I could throw him. I figured that, with Whitey's celebrity, once I told the feds their role, they would finally be under some pressure not to screw it up. The bottom line was that we had no choice. The U.S. attorney told us they had to be involved. Besides, I was going to set it up so that they wouldn't move on either Salemme or Bulger until we had Flemmi in custody. After that, we'd join in on getting Whitey, too.

I kept all this dead quiet, not saying a word to anyone. I didn't want any leaks. The less time the FBI had to interfere, the better.

Just after the New Year, we learned that the grand jury would finish earlier than expected—in another week, on January 10. I still wasn't going to spill the plan. Finally, Dick Swenson, the agent in charge of the Boston office, called Colonel Henderson and summoned us from the State Police, starting with Colonel Henderson, to the FBI conference room, to break some important news.

"We've received information that Frank Salemme is preparing to flee," he declared solemnly. "We'll need to move on him right away."

I was really starting to hate that voice. "What information is this?"

"That he's preparing to flee," Quinn replied.

"And the source?"

"Also confidential."

"A good source, Ed?"

"Highly reliable."

Confidential had come to mean nonexistent, but I knew I wasn't going anywhere with that. Trying to keep the arrests as quiet as possible, I didn't advise even my own people of the arrest teams and assignments. I wanted to wait to make sure that the indictments would be handed down. I believe, though, that the FBI felt we would leave them out of it. By claiming inside information, Quinn was sure to stay in on at least one of the arrests.

Although the grand jury wasn't quite finished, Quinn forced our hand. As usual, there was no saying no. Wyshak dutifully went to the court and, pleading emergency circumstances based on the information about Salemme, asked the court to issue arrest warrants in advance of the official indictments. Granted.

So much had gone into this—the layers of investigation since we started on Whitey in 1990. This would be the culmination of our hard work. Everybody on the team had sacrificed. We'd all given everything we had.

And now I was praying that we could pull this thing out. Things had gone wrong so many times that I'd gotten spooked. I didn't have time to think about whether the cause was an accident or deliberate sabotage. But I couldn't let myself be distracted. Now more than ever, I had to focus on what I needed to do, and let everything else go.

Just as I had back in September, I had the people in my unit out on the street keeping tabs on Flemmi and Salemme. As usual, nobody got a look at Whitey, but we'd have to take the feds' word that they had him. Patty and Gale had been tailing Flemmi for several days now, and for weeks before that, and they had him down cold. I'd bring in Tutungian to help out there, too. Johnson had Salemme along with a couple of troopers: Darlene Decaire, who was great at surveillance; and Mark Caponette, who was more of a tech specialist. Even with my best people on them, both mobsters moved into and out of view. It was midwinter now, the season of heavy coats and warm hats, of staying inside, and it wasn't so easy to stay with people.

At the end of December, just as we were gearing up to make our arrests, we had gotten some information that the notorious hit man John Martorano was living near Boca Raton, Florida. This was huge. A one-time member of the Winter Hill gang with Bulger and Flemmi, Martorano had fled race-fixing charges over fifteen years ago, and he'd been a fugitive ever since. He'd been as tight with Whitey then as Flemmi was now, and had as fearsome a reputation. Not only was Martorano a federal fugitive, but we had evidence that he was still involved with Bulger and Flemmi.

It killed me, but Martorano was too important to ignore. I had to take off two of my best, Sly Scanlan and Stevie Johnson, to fly down to Florida and take a shot at grabbing Martorano. At least we knew Flemmi and Salemme were around. The line from the FBI about Salemme's splitting was just that. He and Flemmi were there for the taking, and Bulger, too, for all I knew.

— CHAPTER 17 —

Early on Wednesday, January 4, 1995, Fred Wyshak gave me the call. "We've got the warrants," he said. It was go. Get Whitey, Flemmi, and Salemme. I was in Framingham at the time. "Hey, Pat, let's go!" I shouted up the hall to Greaney. Then I called Gale and Patty. They were out on the street, doing Flemmi. "It's now. We've got warrants. You got him?"

"He's slipped us," Gale told me. She was with Patty in the North End. "We'll get him, Tommy," they radioed back. "Don't worry. He's here some-place."

By now Scanlan and Johnson were headed to Florida, and I'd had to put a couple of young troopers on Salemme instead. Best I could do. The rest of the unit—Tutungian, Duffy, and the rest—were already out on the street. Then we went out to the parking lot, our breath like smoke in the icy January air. We brought along Lieutenant Kevin Horton, for an extra pair of eyes—in charge of catching violent fugitives, he had the desk next to me at SSS—and the three of us jumped into Pat's Crown Victoria. With Pat at the wheel, I rode shotgun so I could work the radio and try to coordinate everybody. It was like a military operation, a convoy in strange territory. We roared down the turnpike into Boston, and then, with Patty and Gale hovering in the North End, we fanned out to the other places we knew Flemmi liked to go.

A guy like Flemmi doesn't jump out at you. Mid-fifties, medium height, stocky, dark hair, severe looking. There must have been thousands of middle-aged men in Boston just like him. Lately, though, Flemmi had been going with a pretty Asian girl who'd help us make him if it came to that. Flemmi'd been living in Milton in a big house with a tennis court in the back. He'd shared it for years with a harsh-looking brunette named Marion Hussey, but he'd always had a girl on the side, starting with that teenager Debbie Davis, the one who disappeared later at twenty-six. Like her, Flemmi's girls since had always been slim and pretty, and much younger than he was. Patty and Gale had been shadowing Flemmi for a while, and they had the Asian pegged at about twenty-five. "She doesn't usually show until evening," Patty had reminded me on the radio. "And he doesn't sleep in."

We knew their hangouts, but we didn't know which one they'd hit today. Tutungian and Doherty hunted for Flemmi at some of Whitey's places in Southie, and we'd try Milton, a nice suburb south on 93, about the last place you'd expect to find a mobster. People are creatures of habit, and mobsters are no different. They go someplace once, they'll be likely to go there again. But now we tried the usual places and got nothing. No action at Flemmi's house in Milton. No sign of his car there either.

We toured through the North End, working our way down Hanover—colorfully lit for the season—and some of the side streets, then around again. Then it was back to Milton again, and around once more.

Nothing.

That first day came and went. I returned late to Worcester that night. Dead tired, I crawled into bed beside my wife, but I scarcely slept. I tried to keep my breathing smooth. My mind was still in Boston, trying to pull Flemmi's face out of the dark.

Quinn assured me he had Whitey. His man, Gamel, was clamped down on him. I worried about that, of course. By now, I'd realized that the truth and what the FBI told me didn't have much to do with each other. I concentrated on our own search. The longer it took to grab Flemmi, the less likely it was that the secret would hold. Where was he? Was he still around? We all felt increasingly edgy when we went out to search the same places, only to get the same results. Had he gotten word, and left?

If you're trying to find someone in a city like Boston, you have to make choices. We concentrated on the most promising spots, and we were thorough. We positioned our search cars so we could see *everyone* coming and going—without anyone seeing us. Sometimes you can feel when you're getting close, before you know just why. I had a good feeling that afternoon that we were finally on the scent.

Just then we got a call from the FBI. "We've lost Salemme. We had him, and now we don't. Can you help us out here?"

"Jesus," I said. "OK." We depended on the feds to take the lead. They'd acted like they were all over him, and they'd made a big deal of deploying a surveillance plane for this, plus an elite surveillance team.

When the feds told me where they'd last seen him, near the waterfront in South Boston, I knew where he was going. To Eastern Pier Seafoods, a restaurant he liked by the waterfront. It was a big place in the middle of a parking lot. I swung in there, and sure enough. Right in front of the restaurant, a big, obvious guy talking to a younger man who looked dangerously thin, almost gaunt. I knew who that was, too: his son, Frank Jr. We knew from intercepts that Junior had contracted AIDS—he claimed from a prostitute, but who knows? He didn't have long to live. If Frank Sr. had any idea that the arrest warrants were coming, this would make for a pretty heavy good-bye.

I called in the location to my guys, who passed it on to the FBI surveillance team, and then returned to the hunt for Flemmi. We were at it the rest of the afternoon until it started to get dark around five, five-thirty. Time was running out. I couldn't let this go another day. I checked in with everyone, and we decided to concentrate on a restaurant called Schooner's, down by Faneuil Hall, the tourist hangout. It was a hunch, but I've learned to trust hunches. I had reasons: it was owned by Stephen Hussey, the son of that longtime live-in of Flemmi's, Marion Hussey. Stephen was Debbie's brother. Debbie was virtually Flemmi's stepdaughter; he had known her nearly since infancy and he'd assaulted her when she was a child, then started in on an affair with her when she was in her teens. She'd started to do drugs, then danced in the Combat Zone, and then, at twenty six, she was gone. Still, Flemmi remained tight with her brother, and Schooner's was about his favorite hangout. Stephen had been rehabbing the place, trying to turn it into something, and the work was finally done. I guessed that, if Flemmi was planning to run, he'd stop by to see Stephen there first.

Patty and Gale were watching from the sidewalk, trying to stay warm, and Doherty and Tutungian watched the place from the other side in their car. Greaney, Horton, and I hovered in the North End, maybe a quarter of a mile away, checking around there, just in case.

"Anything?" I asked Patty.

"Not yet. Lotta people around, though. Looks like things are heating up."

"John?"

"Nothing here. We've got the side door, though, and an angle on the front."

"Well, hold, guys. Let's give it some time."

So much of surveillance is just waiting, but we were all getting frustrated.

A little after six, Duffy radioed that he wanted to pack it in. "Nothing happening here. We're wrapping up."

"Negative, Duff. This is our best shot. Hang in."

A little before seven, Patty called me by radio. "We think we see him." Excitement in her voice, but she was trying to tamp it down. "Front door, Schooner's. Baseball cap, Asian with him. Anyone confirm?"

"Out front?" Doherty asked.

"Affirmative."

"Oh, yeah. That's him." It was Patty Gillen.

Doherty and Tutungian followed Flemmi and the girl back to a side street where they'd parked Flemmi's white Honda. He unlocked the car, opened the side door for the girl, then swung around to climb into the driver's side. That's when Doherty and Tutungian roared up, pinned the Honda in place, and then jumped out with their guns drawn, pointing them two-handed at Flemmi. Doherty screamed, "DEA! Steve Flemmi, do not move! Stay right where you are!" And the two of them closed in on the car. Flemmi dived under the dashboard, but the girl stayed frozen in her seat. Danny rushed the car, ripped open the door, and thrust his gun inside.

"Steve Flemmi, you are under arrest. Put your hands up on the dashboard. Now. Put them where I can see them."

Doherty pressed the point of the gun up hard against Flemmi's temple. "Hands on the dashboard," he repeated. "Or I'll blow your fucking head off. Now! OK, out of the car, Stevie. Real slow and easy. Any quick move and you're dead." He kept his gun pressed tight against Flemmi's head to let him know he meant it.

On the other side of the car, the Asian girl could barely breathe. Tutungian was there, and, his gun on her, he got her out and patted her down.

"Hey, guys, c'mon," Flemmi said when he was against the car, like he could talk his way out of it. "C'mon now. What's going on here? Hey!" Danny paid no attention, snapping the cuffs shut tight.

Flemmi spread his legs and Doherty patted him down. He pulled out a hunting knife Flemmi had tucked under his belt and a can of Mace.

As soon as Doherty had stuffed Flemmi into the backseat of his car, he called me.

"We got him," Doherty said.

"Great work."

———

The FBI had given Salemme to its Special Operations Group. Sometime after I'd provided Salemme's location, the feds lost him again. They assured me their surveillance plane would pick him up, but that's not so easy in the dark, and their cars didn't do any better, and Frank Salemme disappeared into the last of the rush hour traffic.

———

Then there was Whitey. Although the FBI was supposed to move on Whitey the moment we had Flemmi, when I arrived at the South Boston address they gave me for the arrest team, I found no action at all. John Gamel was sitting in his car with a couple of other agents on Silver Street, a row of vinyl-sided houses, many of them still strung with Christmas lights, not far from the center of the neighborhood. If Gamel was trying to look inconspicuous, he wasn't doing a very good job. At six-six, he was way too big for his FBI-issue sedan, and he had that unforgettable mustache, and it looked like the three of them had been sitting there for hours.

I tapped on his window, and he rolled it down.

"What are you doing?"

"Watching that house up there." He nodded toward a two-story house a few numbers up the narrow street. It still had a wreath and some reindeer out front.

"Why?"

"It's his girlfriend's, Theresa Stanley."

"You sure? Doesn't look like it. I thought her house was farther down."

"That's our information. We've had it under surveillance."

"So why are you waiting? We've got Flemmi. Let's go."

He stepped out of the car, and together we approached the house. Most of my team had gathered by now, but I had the rest of them stay back on the sidewalk with a couple of the FBI agents, to make sure Whitey didn't slip out the side while we went in the front. Gamel and I went up the steps together. For something like this, you need to be prepared, but you don't want to overdo it by sticking a gun in someone's face. I pressed the bell.

Nothing happened—and then a hallway light switched on. Not what Whitey would do, surely. Finally, the door swung open and an elderly woman stood before me. Not Theresa Stanley. And the taller man beside her wasn't Whitey either. I introduced Gamel and me.

"We have a warrant to search the house for Whitey Bulger," I told her.

"This house?" The woman looked startled.

"Isn't this the home of Theresa Stanley?"

"Oh, no, officers. Hers is down the street." She stepped out onto the landing, and pointed. "There. That's hers. Four doors down."

We still glanced around inside for a moment and saw that the woman was obviously telling us the truth. As we left the house, I shot Gamel a look.

At Stanley's house, there were no Christmas lights, and all the windows were dark. By now, seeing all the law enforcement officials about, some neighbors had crowded onto the street. This time, Gamel and I positioned ourselves on either side of the door to have some protection in case Whitey burst out, guns blazing. I pressed the buzzer. I could hear it chime inside, but no lights came on. I tried again but got nothing.

We stepped around to the rear of the house and found a back door. Tutungian went back to his car to get out a battering ram from the trunk. Tutungian drove it into the door, and smashed the door in. I stepped inside, my gun out. "State Police!" I shouted. "We're here to exercise a warrant on Whitey Bulger. Whitey, if you are in here, come out now." I added that anyone who assisted him would be subject to arrest as well. The house remained silent, except for the ticking of a clock on the wall. No one emerged from the shadows.

Inside, I snapped on the lights and found a spare kitchen, which gave way to a bleak hall. There were four or five of us, and, guns out, we went slowly through the house, room by room, flipping on lights, checking behind couches, under beds, and in closets. We saw no sign of anyone, and, stopping periodically to listen, we heard nothing.

There was a crawl space by the stairs. We peered deep inside with a flashlight, but found nothing except boxes and old clothes. I ventured downstairs into the dark basement, looked into corners, looked behind the furnace. Nothing.

The only hint of Whitey was a picture of him on the mantelpiece. He is standing with Stanley by the sea someplace. He is glowering at the camera. She is smiling.

And this was where the feds were convinced they'd find Whitey? If Gamel felt any embarrassment, he didn't show it.

When I came out of the house, lights were on and up and down the street, and along the sidewalk, people were gathering, talking eagerly among themselves. A TV reporter, Ron Golobin, had gotten word of the Flemmi arrest and was set to run with it on the eleven o'clock news. That was still fifteen minutes away, but the station had run a teaser at ten-thirty, and it seemed that everyone in Southie had gotten word. When I got back into my car, it was like someone had thrown on the master switch for all of South Boston. Lights came on, traffic picked up, the bars filled up, and the sidewalks were jammed with people going in all directions.

Desperate to make the most of our last chance, we rushed over to a town house in Quincy, the home of Whitey's other girlfriend, Catherine Greig. She didn't show much delicacy. As we pulled into her driveway, she emerged from her front door in a heavy coat to meet us on the front steps. A sturdy blonde, she crossed her arms across her chest and spread her legs slightly to let us know she was in charge. Just as Whitey would have. Then she demanded to know if we had a warrant to search her house. When we said we didn't, she threw us off her property. "Go fuck yourselves," she said.

That was where our last best chance to arrest Whitey Bulger ended.

———

Duffy called me on the radio as soon as I got back into the car. "You won't believe it," he said.

"What?"

"The Feds. Jesus Christ. What they do."

"What?"

When the feds heard about the arrest of Flemmi, they'd rushed to the scene, and they planned to take Flemmi to the FBI office downtown for booking. Duffy and Decaire had hurried to provide backup, and Duffy checked with me while I was racing to South Boston to grab Whitey, and I thought screw it. I told Duffy, "Go ahead." So long as Flemmi was in custody, I didn't care who held him. We needed to concentrate on Bulger.

Now Duffy was calling me to say that Quinn wanted to keep Flemmi, not just book him.

"That's ridiculous," I told Duff. "They don't even have a facility."

"That's what I told him, but they worked out some deal with Braintree PD."

So I called Quinn and asked him what the hell was going on.

"We're taking Flemmi into custody in Braintree," he repeated, as if this were fact.

"Ed, no. Sorry, but we arrested him, we have a facility of our own in Framingham, we'll be taking him there, and that is all there is to it."

For once, Quinn had nothing to say back, so that's how we left it.

I called Duffy back, and told him to take Flemmi to Framingham.

"Will do," he said. I could hear the relief in his voice.

A little later he called back. "There's something else, Tommy."

"And what's that?" Duffy didn't usually require any encouragement, so I knew this was troubling him. It turned out that while the FBI had Flemmi, Duffy saw an agent, Charlie Gianturco, take him aside and speak quietly to him. Now, Charlie was the brother of Nick Gianturco, my FBI buddy who worked with me on the Oreto and Naimovich cases. I'd seen Charlie around, but I'd never warmed to him. Nick had been fun for a while, but Charlie struck me as too slick.

"You'll never guess what I heard Charlie say," Duff told me.

"What?"

"He was there with Flemmi in the holding area they have. Just the two of them, off to one side. Charlie was quietly speaking to him, and this is an exact quote. 'This thing of ours, Stevie, it is no more.' " He let me think about that for a second. "This thing of ours, Tommy. That's La Cosa Nostra. That's like what it means."

"Yeah, I know."

"So what do you make of it?"

"I have no idea." But of course I did. It was too much to say. Gianturco and Flemmi, they had a bond of some kind. It wasn't just the words but the way he spoke them. If Gianturco was in that tight with Flemmi, he'd have to be in with Whitey, too. Tighter than he would ever be with us, in any case. Now I had to wonder: Just how deep was the FBI in with the mob?

PART THREE

The Big Reveal

— CHAPTER 18 —

For the next forty-eight hours we raced around Boston investigating reports of sightings of Bulger and Salemme, but we didn't find a trace of either of them. By Monday, it was clear they were gone. If it had been hard to find them in Boston, it would be nearly impossible to find them anywhere else. Whitey had plenty of money, even more ingenuity, and a powerful reason to disappear. He could have gone to New York, or farther down the coast, or to the other side of the globe. Nothing was beyond the realm of possibility.

It was beyond frustrating. For years, we'd busted our asses to get Whitey and now we'd reached out and grabbed only air. The most vicious criminal in Boston's history, and the FBI had let him go free. It was insanity. If I hadn't known better, I would have taken the elevator to the eleventh floor of the McCormack Building, charged into Quinn's office, and had it out with him.

But I knew that wasn't the way. In this business, like most businesses, you have to stay cool. I carried the fury with me for a few days, but inside. If I let it out, I'd be the problem. That was what the feds wanted: to infuriate you, and then, if you should actually get mad, wheel on you for being unprofessional, claim you are impossible to work with, and push you off a cliff. I might be burning inside, but I was going to make like I understood entirely why the FBI had let a psychopathic killer go. Anybody would.

Even though I did my best to act the same, everything changed for me with the FBI. No longer would I give the feds the benefit of the doubt on anything. Whatever they said, I'd believe the truth was anything *but* that, unless I had solid proof otherwise. No more "innocent mistakes." To hell with that. There had been way too many examples. The mistakes were on purpose, and the purpose was to kill off our investigation.

Now, why? How could the FBI possibly benefit from that? It obviously didn't help the Bureau's image to obstruct the efforts of another law enforcement agency, especially not one that it had joined up with, and certainly not in an effort to put away the most terrifying mobster in Boston's history. And for what?

Well, the answer was inescapable. The FBI was trying to protect Whitey Bulger. That was more important than anything else, and it influenced everything the feds did, whether it meant exposing our stakeouts or revealing our wiretaps or lying to us about all of it. But why? Why protect *Bulger*, of all people? Again, the answer was staring me in the face. It had hung over the FBI for years; it had even been hinted at in a *Boston Globe* article a few years back claiming that Bulger had a "special relationship" with the FBI. And that was code for only one thing.

Whitey Bulger was an FBI informant, and Flemmi was, too. Had to be. It was the only thing that made sense. The FBI had informants everywhere; the mob landscape was thick with them. Why not Whitey and Flemmi? They were feeding the FBI information, probably in exchange for protection from prosecution for their crimes. Hence Charlie Gianturco's remark about "This thing of ours." It was a joint venture. The FBI and Bulger and Flemmi. One hand washed the other. Partners in crime. Call it whatever you liked. It was lunacy, but it was there, as obvious as it was astounding.

It didn't really make sense on any level. Everyone in law enforcement knows that when you enlist an informant, you never take the top guy. Ever. Make the top guy an informant and you've given him superpowers—you've made him invulnerable to prosecution, and, to the extent you share inside information with him, you've made him almost omniscient besides. So you have taken the most dangerous criminal you know, and made him a whole lot more dangerous. If the idea is to reduce crime, this is a ridiculous way to go about it. No, you want to inform up, not down, since down isn't worth it, and there are plenty of better ways to get down. And, for that matter, you'll never get good information sideways either about the Mafia, for example. High-level informants keep that information for themselves, and use it for leverage. Aren't the kingpins likely to know more about crime? Yes. But they won't tell you. They are likely to receive far more information from you than they give you back, and they'll enjoy the protection to boot. Worse for the FBI, once an informant like Whitey starts committing serious, unforgivable crimes like murder, and the FBI has helped hide them, then Whitey has the FBI as a buddy for life, for the feds can't walk away from a relationship they have to conceal. The FBI might as well be a coconspirator, as guilty as the triggerman. And each new crime gives it one more reason to protect Whitey from prosecution.

In its mounting desperation, the FBI had come through for Whitey big-time, by tipping him off to our arrest. But that was just the latest favor. The informant status was why neither he nor Flemmi had *ever* been arrested for anything since 1965, why all investigations against them came to nothing, and why the feds were determined that ours wouldn't come to anything either. The FBI had placed Whitey and Flemmi inside a zone of safety. They could touch you, but you could never touch them.

For the feds, Whitey had changed everything—and he changed everything for us, too. It was like he had tipped over the McCormack Building where the FBI had its offices, so that nobody there knew anymore which way was up. I can't imagine that Quinn wanted to lie to me, over and over, but he had to. I doubt he and his colleagues wanted to knock out our wiretaps, foil our surveillance, and all the rest. Truth didn't matter anymore; it was all about self-protection. The FBI was in too deep to do it any other way. If the facts got out, the Bureau would never be the same.

Deep as the FBI was in, it had just gone deeper still. I knew what had happened. Someone deep in the Bureau had tipped Bulger off to the coming arrests. Just like back in September. All three had fled then, but this time only Whitey had gotten out scot-free. Salemme had wriggled free, but Flemmi waited too long.

Still, it was astounding to think of Bulger as a snitch. That was yet another consequence of his reputation as a vicious, bloodthirsty killer: everyone agreed with whatever he said. Who'd ever argue? Loyalty may not be pervasive in the mob, but everyone hates rats, and no one more than Bulger. He *feasted* on them. Whether this was because Bulger didn't really think of himself as one, or because he wanted to show he couldn't be one, he was infuriated by anyone who ratted on him.

And he wanted to get that word out. Everyone seemed to know the story of the mob-connected deckhand, John McIntyre, who Whitey tortured beyond endurance for telling the DEA, Customs, and the Quincy police about a cache of weapons that Whitey'd sent the rebels in Northern Ireland. (Whitey had a soft spot for Irish militants.) Acting on a tip, Irish authorities intercepted the weapons off the Irish coast. The leak drove Whitey into a further frenzy when thirty-six tons of his marijuana were seized by Customs as the shipment entered Boston Harbor. Bulger, Flemmi, and Weeks were supposed to get $1 million each from the proceeds.

The DEA was one of the law-enforcement agencies that had flipped McIntyre to get the information about the shipment. No one knew how Whitey figured out it was McIntyre. Now it's obvious—DEA to FBI to Whitey. Then it was a complete mystery.

A few weeks later, McIntyre was invited to a house in Southie for a party. He arrived at the door with a case of beer under his arm, and pressed the buzzer. But there was no party. There was only Whitey Bulger, ready for him with some chains, a heavy rope, and a pair of handcuffs. He threw McIntyre down into a chair, chained him tight to the chair, and cuffed his wrists behind the chair back. Then he leaned in, close enough that McIntyre must have smelled Whitey's breath. "I know you're a snitch, you piece of shit," he told McIntyre. He teased McIntyre with the thought that maybe he'd let him off with a one-way ticket to South America. But then he reconsidered. He had a better idea, and brought out the rope. He looped it around McIntyre's neck and slowly pulled it tight. McIntyre kicked and bucked in his chair, straining for air. His face turned beet red as he struggled in agony. But he would not die. Hard as Whitey squeezed, McIntyre managed to draw in a little air and hang on. Finally Whitey relaxed his grip, pulled out a revolver, and cocked it in front of McIntyre's eyes. He bent down to whisper to him in his raspy voice, "Do you want me to shoot you in the head?"

"Yes, please," McIntyre mumbled, his eyelids fluttering in distress.

Whitey obliged. The bullet knocked McIntyre's chair back onto the floor, but somehow didn't kill him. So Whitey bent down and fired several more rounds point-blank into McIntrye's face.

Then he took a pair of pliers and a knife, reached deep into the back of McIntyre's mouth, grabbed his tongue tight, and ripped it out from the back of his throat.

That's what Whitey thought of informers.

Of course, the FBI must have known of this crime, too, but it never said a word.

———

I choked down my anger about the FBI on this truth: having Whitey off the streets was almost as good as having him in custody. He wouldn't be around to scare off anyone who wanted to come forth with information about him. Every day that the rumors spread, Whitey was less a criminal mastermind and more a snitch. And the rats would start lining up to return the favor. And I was sure the revelations would add up, way beyond the racketeering and bookmaking we had him for, and deep into drug dealing, extortion, and murder. If we could make those charges stick, Whitey was gone forever. And in the meantime, Boston had one less mobster roaming the streets.

That was my thought, but that wasn't how my guys saw it. They wanted me to go straight at the FBI for what it had done. Several of the guys came into my office to tell me so.

"I know, I know. I feel just like you do. But I keep telling you guys. Now is not the time. We don't have the manpower right now. We've got to stick to the plan. We've got to stay focused. Just wait, OK? More and more stuff will come out on Whitey and Stevie, and the FBI will have to come clean eventually."

They weren't buying it, and I couldn't say I blamed them. But it was the truth. We had to be patient, and we had to wait. We had no choice. But one thing was true. With Flemmi in a holding cell right now, pondering his choices, I didn't want to be the FBI. Still, my health wasn't so great, slowing me down to half speed some days. And my guys were struggling, too. Chuck Hanko had called it quits, burned out by the long hours, the stress, and the craziness with the FBI. Mark Caponette would be able to handle the tech stuff, so we wouldn't lose too much there. The versatile John Cahill soon followed suit. I could tell that some of the others were thinking there had to be an easier way to make a living. And if they weren't making good money, at least they should have the satisfaction of seeing Whitey in handcuffs, a state trooper on either side holding his arms. I tried to bring in more fresh blood, but this kind of work requires a certain personality, and often that was difficult to find.

— CHAPTER 19 —

Whitey might be gone, but Steve Flemmi was with us, and he was going to stay with us.

Late the night he was brought in, I went down to see him in the holding cell in Framingham. Not since the Busy Bee, when I took a booth next to him, had I seen him close up. And that was more out of the corner of my eye. This was straight on, on the other side of a set of iron bars. I'd been chasing the guy for nearly five years, and now here he was, caught. Prisoners don't usually look like much. Mobsters derive their strength from their circumstances—their minions, their machine guns, their piles of cash. Strip away all that, and you get just a guy. And that's what Flemmi was to me. They say he could be very up and down emotionally, and I got a feeling of that now, like he was forcing himself to be up, to be outgoing, as he tried to lay on some charm.

"Hey, Tommy, howya doin'?" he shouted out to me from inside his cell when I came down. It was like we were old friends, even though I was the guy who'd gotten him locked up. But we did have an odd connection: I'd followed him on surveillance, and he'd followed me through the FBI.

"C'mon, Tommy. What's going on here? Why'm I in here? I don't get it. I didn't do anything. What, you have something on me?" Like that—he was acting like he was just curious, like he had no idea. But hopped up— and obviously pumping me for information that might help him wriggle out of this.

"Stevie, you are charged with RICO offenses and will be brought to court in the morning."

He and I certainly weren't friends, or anything close. The feds might have been friends with him, or acted like friends. But where were they now? That was starting to eat at him, I could tell. They'd been the ones to book him, but they hadn't come back to check on him, see how he was.

I watched Flemmi pace around his cell, one not so different from the ones I watched at Walpole. He was caught, caged. We had him. Flemmi had been big, but now his world was down to a box about eight by eleven, with a cot and a toilet and a sink. Despite all his energy and false cheer, his eyes were dark, and his head sagged a little.

I spent a few more minutes with him; then I tapped on the bars of his cell and told him good night.

"Good night," he scoffed, as if it were a joke. "Yeah."

————

For Flemmi, this was a new one: in jail, facing a mound of indictments, and Whitey off God knows where. I knew what he was thinking. Not that he ever said it—I could just tell by the way he'd slowed down that he'd been working the idea through. Clearly, to him, the FBI wasn't planning to swoop down and save him from prosecution. But he still had leverage. Blackmail. The FBI didn't want a Steven Flemmi tell-all, and he was sure that it would do anything to keep him quiet.

But Flemmi didn't want to talk either. It would go far better for him if he *threatened* to squeal than if he actually did. A threat might move them. Actually doing what he threatened would end everything between them. There was another angle, too. Calling himself out as an FBI snitch was likely to infuriate his fellow gangsters, especially the ones he'd ratted out. They'd want to strangle him and rip his tongue out, too, and there are plenty of opportunities for that if you're in a general prison lockup.

It was far better to threaten, but if the FBI wasn't going to come through for him, then he had no choice but to treat the feds like the enemy they'd become and shout from the mountaintop that he'd been in bed with the FBI all these years, and shame them for harboring a monster. It might not work, but it would show those bastards who they were working with. Flemmi didn't want to do that, but what was he supposed to do? He waited and waited for the feds to come to his aid, and they never came. There it was. They wanted a rat? Well, now they had one.

————

And then Flemmi made his choice. Because it involved the federal RICO statutes, Flemmi's case was heard by a federal judge, chosen at random. When the judge turned out to be Mark Wolf, we were apprehensive. Judge Wolf had a reputation for being surly and difficult. If you bade him good morning, you were likely to get a scowl back. One time, when I was testifying on the stand, he actually rolled his eyes and moaned in response to what I was saying. He was so afraid of being second-guessed that he demanded mountains of legal paperwork from us to make sure he covered everything and none of his judgments would be overturned.

For all that, I ended up admiring Judge Wolf enormously. Unlike everybody else on the case, he was not cowed by the FBI or the USAO or even his former bosses at the Department of Justice, although I'm sure a lot of the people there would have liked to tie cinder blocks to his ankles and drop him into Boston Harbor. Judge Wolf didn't particularly care what people thought. He kept his own counsel, and he went wherever the evidence took him.

Judge Wolf undertook the case in January 1995, but it didn't get going until much later. When it finally did, the first order of business was to weigh in on the usual defense motions to dismiss the case. These claims are usually nonstarters, but Steve Flemmi's attorney was a heavyweight, Ken Fishman. He'd handled plenty of mob cases, and, given the evidence we had against his client, he knew that the only way he had a chance of winning was to change the game.

By now, the FBI had made no overtures to Flemmi. It would obviously not be a party to any rescue, or to any plea for a complete exoneration on the basis of services he might have made to the bureau. Flemmi was on his own.

It was time for revenge.

With Flemmi's copious input, Fishman put together an extraordinary exculpatory affidavit from Flemmi that, when it was released to the USAO and made its way to the papers, sucked much of the oxygen out of the city. In it, Flemmi argued that these charges against him should never have been brought, for the reason we had long suspected. He had been an informant for the FBI off and on for almost thirty years, and as such he had been granted immunity from prosecution for any crimes he might have committed during this period.

And there it was. Steve Flemmi was an informant of the FBI, and Whitey Bulger was, too.

At that point I can't say it was a surprise, but it stunned me nonetheless. To me and my fellow investigators it felt like this truth was going to remain unspoken forever. The mobsters, the FBI, and the USAO didn't traffic in truth; it was not their language; they said everything but. It was all lies or half-truths or deceptions. So to hear the truth now—especially a profound, central, dangerous truth like this, revealed in a federal courtroom—it was like seeing snow for the first time. You'd heard all about it, but it still seemed impossible. Now, there was Flemmi saying it open court: the FBI had been in bed with two of the most despicable mobsters in the history of Boston.

For the rest of the affidavit, Flemmi did his best to blow up the FBI. It was all the FBI's fault. Anything illegal that Flemmi did—the FBI said it was fine. He never claimed the FBI *made* him do it, of course. But it was damn close: the FBI *let* him do it. And there was a certain logic to it. If he was to fit in with the gangsters he was spying on, he had a reputation to protect.

Flemmi had been with the FBI since the mid-1960s, having been introduced to the organization by his brother—another unhinged mobster, Jimmy "The Bear" Flemmi, who'd been recruited the year before. Steve Flemmi, in turn, had eased in Whitey Bulger, whom he'd met through Winter Hill. For much of that time, he and Bulger had been handled primarily by John Connolly. This was no surprise, given that we knew Connolly handled all the top informants. When some FBI superiors were starting to worry that Connolly might be getting too close to the two mobsters, they brought in John Morris, a midwesterner known for his strict principles, to ride herd on him. But it went the other way. Connolly's rogue charm outdid Morris's principles, and soon Morris was fawning over the two mobsters even more than Connolly was. Flemmi claimed that John Morris had told him straight out that he needn't worry too much about the law. Do what you want. Just don't kill anyone, and the FBI will protect you. That, he said, was the message.

Flemmi said Morris laid out the rules to him at Morris's house in suburban Lexington, where he and Whitey—"Mr. Bulger" in the affidavit—had gotten together with Morris and Connolly to talk things over. The implication was that this was a meeting of four serious professionals, but the cozy setting suggests otherwise. These are Flemmi's words:

> *I specifically recall meeting on one occasion at Mr. Morris's home in Lexington, Massachusetts, and during a conversation in which I was asking the agents present about whether certain individuals were informants and who should Mr. Bulger and I stay away from, the issue of our criminal activities came up. Mr. Morris told Mr. Bulger and I that we could do anything we wanted so long as we didn't "clip anyone." On several occasions, in the course of similar conversations, Mr. Bulger and I were assured that we could be involved in any criminal activities short of committing murder and we would be "protected." I operated and relied upon this express agreement with the FBI.*

While Flemmi was trying to paint his deal with the FBI as a straight business deal, a matter of neckties and briefcases, the truth of it was, as Morris testified later, a little different. By then, Morris had received immunity, and he was freer to say what really went down. As he laid it out, this wasn't really business. This was a bunch of pals swapping favors. It was like the mob: friends never *paid* friends for a hit. The whole arrangement was set up out of friendship, and much appreciated. And within the FBI, you helped out other agents just to help them out; no one expected anything like money.

So here, in Morris's telling, the deal actually was pretty loose—you do things for us, we do things for you, no problem. It wasn't a contract; it was more a friendship. This is what friends do. We're all in it together.

But, with Whitey and Stevie, this was a deal with the devil. If the FBI agents ever imagined they'd get anything close to full value from their friends—well, they didn't know their friends. Mobsters know more about exploitation than feds do.

While this setup was surely extreme, it wasn't too far from the arrangement that the FBI has with all its informants, which is rarely formalized and is never subject to oversight or review. While there is an informant policy, nobody ever pays any attention to it. Handlers make up policy with informants as they go along.

That's not how we do it in the State Police—or at least not how we did it while I was there. We'd learned that whenever our officers get into trouble, an informant is usually the reason why. So we paid attention. We examined the informants closely, watched what they did for us, and documented the results. The informants were constantly being evaluated to see if they were worth it, and we tossed the ones who weren't. This was the system that we'd had in place since the Naimovich case, and it had worked well. We had a policy and we followed it. It was ridiculous to do it the FBI way: the feds simply ignore whatever policy they have.

According to Morris's testimony, the get-together at his house in Lexington was no business meeting. It was more a jolly foursome getting ripped over dinner—drinking, talking, swapping stories. There were plenty of these gatherings. Whitey would usually come with a nice bottle of wine and everything would have been grand except that Morris would sometimes get a little tipsy, and his wife was so horrified that her husband was entertaining a couple of murderous gangsters in her house that she went upstairs and hid in the bedroom. Morris later divorced her and took up with his secretary at the FBI office, and, according to court testimony, he used money from Bulger and Flemmi to fly her places to meet him.

But that wasn't the half of it. As Morris acknowledged, Connolly once brought along a special guest: Joe Pistone, the former undercover FBI agent who, under the name Donnie Brasco, penetrated the Bonanno family in New York. As Brasco, Pistone almost became a made man. Alarmed that he was getting in way too deep, the feds yanked Pistone back into the fold. His testimony and evidence led to two hundred indictments, as well as the brutal murders of some of the mafiosi who'd vouched for him, allowing him entrée. One of them got his hands chopped off.

Still, even after he ended his undercover work, Pistone had a lot of mobster in him. He must have been interested to meet the notorious Whitey Bulger, and Bulger might have been curious about the shadowy Pistone. So there it was—a dinner for five with two FBI agents, two gangsters, and a former undercover FBI agent who'd been both.

———

In producing his affidavit, Flemmi was pure mobster, hungry for revenge. Despite what the feds had done for him, he was going to blow them sky-high. He produced an exhaustive list of dates, times, and locations for his many meetings with Connolly and Morris through the years, when they supposedly sanctioned the growing list of crimes committed by him and Whitey. In his telling, since he and Whitey were in so tight with the FBI, how could they be prosecuted under the antiracketeering laws? It didn't make sense. They weren't with the mob. *They were with the FBI!* Flemmi was like Donnie Brasco, but in reverse, coming from the mob to the feds. As Whitey had once put it, Flemmi wasn't a straight-out bad guy. He was a *good* bad guy. That shouldn't merit incarceration but commendation. It was like being back in the military, where they gave medals for bravery.

— CHAPTER 20 —

Whitey and Salemme may have slipped away, but we still had that intel on Johnny Martorano, living under a false identity in Florida. I'd sent Johnson and Scanlan to bring him in. I'd had to take them off Salemme to do it, but Martorano was that important. Back in the day, he'd been second only to Whitey as the biggest mobster in Boston. I knew about him from my earliest days in OC. His was one of the fat files. He was a hit man for Winter Hill back when he and Whitey and Flemmi were all vying for the top spot occupied by Howie Winter. As a killer, he was up with Whitey as one of the most proficient ever. By now, we had him for twenty murders, officially, to Whitey's nineteen. Newspaper accounts tried to put Martorano at fifty.

Unlike Whitey, Martorano didn't kill to send a message; he killed to get someone dead. If Whitey sprayed his victim's face with machine-gun fire, Martorano used a single bullet, fired from a snub-nosed thirty-eight into the back of the head while his victim sipped coffee in a coffee shop or idled at a red light. No one ever saw it coming. Nothing flashy or traceable. Just done. After hours, Johnny himself always stood out. He had all the charm of gunmetal, but he could dress. He loved the glittery nightclubs, where he played the old-school hood in the Italian double-breasted suit and alligator shoes, his fingers bright with jeweled rings, chasing some pretty girl half his age.

Martorano was as street-savvy as they come, but he had some blind spots. When Howie Winter came up with a cockamamie racing scheme to make some quick money when he was in a pinch, Martorano went in with him. And when Winter slipped up and got arrested for it, Martorano did, too.

At the time, Martorano had no idea, but as things turned out, this was not just bad luck. Rather, it was some bad luck that was visited on him by Whitey and Stevie as top-echelon informants. Martorano considered them his two best friends in the world; each was a godfather to one of Martorano's two sons. Martorano had risked his life to save those guys, and thought nothing of it. But they sold him down the river. They'd used the FBI to take Martorano and Winter down, in order to clear the way for themselves to take over as the undisputed rulers of the Irish mob. Winter Hill had been Howie's; now it was Whitey's. For Whitey, it was a move out of a military manual. Surprise strike, high-value target, minimum risk. So the big boys went down: one to prison, the other to a life on the lam.

Or maybe they thought they were nice to Martorano. After they sicced the feds on the two, Whitey and Stevie did Martorano the favor of warning him that the feds were coming. "Maybe you should go away for six months or so, treat it like a vacation," Bulger had told him. But there never seemed to be a good time to come back. Bulger and Flemmi started sending him money through George Kaufman, but never very much. Martorano had had a nice bookmaking business going, but it fell apart when he left. Meanwhile Bulger and Flemmi's expanded. Still, Martorano had been grateful that his friends had looked out for him, and that gratitude didn't wear out even as his fugitive years reached fifteen. If it weren't for Whitey's flight, people would be asking, "Where's Johnny?" Then again, the two fugitives had something else in common: a suspicion that the FBI might think it was better off leaving them wherever they were.

To us, Martorano was key, since he was a serious player, a contract killer, who knew about Whitey from way back and had been a fugitive for fifteen years.

And so we sat up when we first heard, back in the fall, that Martorano was in Florida, and that he was back in the loan-sharking business with Steve Flemmi. Our source was Jack Kelly, a sometime mobster, full-time deadbeat, and occasional informant. He was the son of John "Snooks" Kelly, the famous coach of the Boston College hockey team who led the Eagles to their first national championship in 1949. Jack was a lifetime junkie who'd do anything to support his habit. Robbery won him serious jail time, and then he fell in with Flemmi to do some loan-sharking and leg breaking and other rough stuff. He never cleaned himself up, though, and by the time we got to him he was wasting away from the liver disease that would eventually kill him.

The mob provides no health benefits, needless to say, so we won him over with an offer to help pay for his health care if he helped us. Sensing that he was on the way out, Kelly claimed that, after a life of crime and deception, he wanted a chance to make things right, but this didn't make him any easier to work with. No informant is a picnic, but Kelly was a real rattlesnake.

I put Tom Duffy on him. Duff had taken some serious nut jobs before. Eventually Kelly's snappishness and mood swings wore him out. But not before he'd given us the word about Martorano—not as a killer, but as a loan shark. Kelly didn't know where Martorano was based, or how he got the funds, but he was putting serious dough out on the street through Flemmi's bookie manager, Joey Yerardi. That was Kelly's line, anyway. We'd been keeping tabs on Yerardi but had gotten no hint of Martorano's operation. At first we didn't believe it. We couldn't imagine that Martorano would reconnect with Flemmi after all these years, or that a loser like Kelly would know about it. When informants need something from you the way Kelly did, they'll tell you anything you want to hear.

"He talks to Yerardi," Kelly insisted. "He does, goddamit."

"You're shitting us," Duffy told him.

Kelly got squirmy. "They talk, man. Yerardi and Martorano talk on the phone. They do. I know they do."

"Prove it," Duff said. "Call him. Or get him to call you. Go on, get him on the phone." Somehow Kelly worked it out with Yerardi. Martorano did get on the phone with Kelly.

When we listened to the tape of the call, it seemed to us like it might be Martorano, although none of us had actually ever heard his voice. He had a tough-guy Boston accent. He was definitely talking about street money. But even if it was Martorano, the call didn't bring us any closer to locating him, since he was using a cell phone of Yerardi's.

This was back in December, when things were heating up on Whitey and the others, and we were in front of the grand jury every day, first re-cording evidence and then reading it into the record. Everyone was going full out. But then, I'd had Steve Johnson with me for a couple of years. He'd been an undercover cop working on drug investigations in Worces-ter. One tough guy—you could not wear him out. Summer could not get too hot for him, or winter too cold.

So I turned to him to find out Martorano's whereabouts from all the Whitey tapes. These were the ones of all the bookies, loan sharks, extor-tionists, and other high-level mobsters—hundreds of hours, easily. I had a good idea that the information was in there, but it was worse than try-ing to find a needle in a haystack, because at least you know what a needle looks like. We couldn't tell what a clue might be, or what it might be a clue to. For something like this, people were not going to come out and use Martorano's name, or their own; they'd use code words for him, like Ice Man or Fingers, and just be cryptic about the whole thing. Just about ev-erybody assumes their phone is being tapped. "That place," "The guy we know"—these were the expressions they used. So which one was the clue?

There were hundreds of hours of tapes, and practically all the calls were scratchy, hard to hear, and herky-jerky because of those minimi-zation rules, so the conversations were almost impossible to follow. But somewhere in there I was pretty sure there were clues to what Martorano was up to, and where.

Most people would have said: Forget it. Or put in a half-assed effort. Not Stevie. He went through all the tapes, listening and listening for some reference to a place where Martorano might be holed up. A head-splitting effort, and it took weeks, but God love him, somehow he pulled out that Martorano was down in Broward County, Florida, living under the name Vincent Rancourt. Incredible.

When I heard the alias, I knew it was right. Rancourt. Ran from court. That was Martorano. Clever, and in your face. Or so we thought.

This was the very beginning of January, and we were closing in on the arrests. I'd decided to pull Johnson and Sly Scanlan off the Salemme tail and fly them down to Florida on Martorano instead. They arrived Wednesday, January 4, the day we finally got the arrest warrants up here and started scouring the city for Flemmi. Looking back, I'm convinced that if I'd had those two on Salemme, he never would have gotten away. But life isn't lived looking back.

Once they had the name Rancourt, Johnson and Scanlan went to the Registry of Motor Vehicles down there and got an address. No problem. It was in Deerfield Beach, just south of Boca Raton. The registry also kicked out the photograph shown on his license. A lot of state registries didn't do that then. This one showed Martorano, no question. The face of a killer—blank and mean. They watched the house for a couple of days before they saw someone they thought was Martorano.

In the meantime I had approached Ed Quinn at the FBI and told him. "I think we've located Martorano. He's in Florida."

Quinn snickered at that and said that we were wasting our time on this one. "If he's there, he looks nothing like he used to. I doubt your people will recognize him."

A few years back, I might have listened. Not now.

"Well, we're going ahead with it," I told him. "I've got a couple of my guys down there already. We'll need the warrant from the race-fixing case." I gave him the details, even though he said he had them already. It was a federal case and a federal warrant, so I had to go to Quinn to get the warrant.

"No problem, Tommy," he said. "If you need it, you'll have it." He didn't sound too enthusiastic.

By then, Johnson and Scanlan had made contact with the police in Broward County. Local police usually help out on a collar like this, and they agreed to send out a couple of deputies. Along with the Broward deputies, my guys staked out the Rancourt address. It was a ranch-style house on a quiet street of a bedroom community, like Martorano was just another commuter.

That afternoon Stevie Johnson called me from his car. It was Thursday, January 5, the day I was racing around trying to find Flemmi. "We've got the house. I'll let you know what we find."

"Do that."

I didn't hear back from him until the next day. I'd had Flemmi to deal with, plus a ton of media.

"He's here, Tommy," Stevie told me, a little breathless. "Or at least somebody who looks a helluva lot like him. A real bear. We're at his house. We can see him moving around inside. We should grab him."

"Well, you can't move yet," I told him. "I'm still waiting on the warrant from the FBI."

It was a frustrating situation, no question, and I felt for the guys out there, waiting. "Just hang on."

I called Quinn again and asked what was happening with the warrant. "We need it now," I told him, an edge in my voice.

Quinn was all oil. "Let me get back to you." It was like he'd forgotten all about it.

"Ed, come on! We're ready to make an arrest. Let's go. We need that warrant."

"I'll call you back."

He rang me maybe an hour later.

"Sorry, there's no warrant."

"What do you mean, no warrant?"

"We can't find it."

"Of course you can. It's in your computer. For chrissake, dig it out for us, all right? Now. We need it right away. We're all set to grab him, and we need to move now."

It was getting to me, this pseudo calm of Quinn's, like I was going wild asking for a warrant for Martorano's arrest when my investigators were outside his house right then.

I called Wyshak and asked him to help us out. He got in touch with the assistant U.S. attorney who was on the race-fixing case. He was no friend of the Bulger investigation, but he was able to produce the warrant for us. Shortly after Wyshak called to let me know, Quinn called back. "Oh, by the way, there's something else." With the FBI, that's never good. He said an agent, Mike Buckley, was going to be down in Florida for a conference and would be arriving Sunday noon. "Could you hold off on the Martorano arrest until Monday anyway so Mike can get in on it? He can bring the warrant down with him."

That time, I said nothing, afraid of what I might say if I said something. I knew what was up. This whole thing with the warrant was Quinn's way of making sure the FBI would be in on the arrest.

"That work for you, Tommy?" Quinn asked.

Every part of me screamed No! But he had us. "I guess it'll have to," I said.

I called Johnson to let him and Scanlan know. They sure weren't happy about it, but there wasn't much anyone could do. It was a frantic weekend for me anyway, since I was dashing around trying to pick up Whitey's and Salemme's trail. But the wait nearly killed all of us. I didn't sleep too well, either night, thinking that Martorano might slip away just like Bulger. How much of this were we going to have to take?

The warrant came down with Buckley, and it was the original federal one that was supposedly lost. Having Buckley there would make it look like an FBI arrest, not one of ours, but what the hell. We work with the FBI; they don't work with us. What else is new? I just wanted Martorano taken into custody. I didn't care how.

Johnson and Scanlan, along with the two deputies, had kept tabs on the house over the weekend, checking for any signs of unusual activity. Worried that Martorano—if Rancourt was Martorano—might notice the same car going by the house, Johnson asked Buckley to rent another car when he came to help with the surveillance, and give Martorano a different look. "Sorry, I'm not authorized to do that," he told my guys.

"You can't rent a car to pick up a fugitive, a guy with like a million murders?" Johnson asked.

Buckley had no answer to that one.

So on Monday morning, Buckley was picked up at his hotel, and he jumped into the backseat. Johnson and Scanlan were up front. They returned to the house for the grab. They parked a short way down the street and watched the house through their rearviews.

Before long, they saw a severe-looking man emerge from the house with a teenage boy.

The driver and the boy climbed into a tan minivan and pulled out of the drive. The arrest team revved up and, starting from their spot up the road, followed the van at a safe distance. The van went only a short way down the highway and then turned in at a strip mall. The minivan pulled into a parking space. In a moment, the driver stepped down from the van, and our guys were on him.

"John?" Stevie shouted out. "John Martorano?" He needed to be sure.

Martorano glanced toward him. "I think you have the wrong man," he said casually.

Johnson and Scanlan pushed closer. "Up against the van, John."

"You have the wrong man," the driver insisted.

"Well, let me check your arms then." The man was wearing a polo shirt in the Florida heat, and he brought his arms in tight to his body.

We knew all about his tattoos, and when he turned the inside of his right arm toward us, we could see the name plain as day. NANCY, in big block letters, for the wife he'd left behind back in Boston.

Scanlan showed Martorano his Massachusetts State Police badge. "Recognize that John?" the Broward County deputy asked him. "John Martorano, you're under arrest," Stevie told him, and cuffed his wrists behind his back.

Martorano didn't resist. It was hopeless. He had his son there, staring, and he'd probably reached the screw-it point that all fugitives get to eventually, where they're more relieved than anything else when their number finally comes up. Our guys took him to federal court down there with Buckley, and a couple of days later the U.S. Marshals flew him up to Boston to be arraigned.

We had him.

———

It couldn't have done good things to Flemmi's peace of mind to learn that John Martorano was coming to Plymouth, too. Just for him to be in the same city, knowing what he knew, and what he was bound to find out, was frightening. But to be in the same lockup?

— CHAPTER 21 —

The FBI always was shameless about PR. In announcing the arrest of Martorano, the feds somehow failed to mention that we were the ones actually to do it. And then they followed that up by announcing that the FBI was creating a high-level fugitive task force to capture the mobster it had let escape. This was in January, a few weeks after Bulger had fled. Wherever in the universe Whitey Bulger was, he would be hunted down—that was the message. The G-men would make this right. And who'd be running the show? Agent Charlie Gianturco, Mr. This Thing of Ours himself. And he would be assisted by John Gamel, who couldn't even find Theresa Stanley's house the night that Whitey disappeared.

It was a joke, but it didn't matter to us if Stern had put General Patton in charge. We weren't waiting around. We were going to do everything we could to get Whitey ourselves.

The FBI's big idea was to get Whitey Bulger on *America's Most Wanted*, and then wait for the phone to ring. The louder the feds yelled that they were in charge of the investigation, the more likely they would be to receive any tips.

Well, fine. But that didn't mean we were going to just let Whitey go. Early on, we'd picked up intelligence that Bulger might have slipped across the border to lie low in Montreal or Toronto. To develop the lead, we needed some phone records from the Royal Canadian Mounted Police. But somehow Gianturco found out about our request, called the RCMP himself, and persuaded the Mounties to send the phone records directly to him.

Once he had the records in his hands, Gianturco called me. He spoke as though he were leaving an answering machine message, even though I was there on the other end of the phone. "Tommy? Just wanted you to know I've got those RCMP records you wanted." Meaning he was in tighter with the Mounties than we would ever be, and that we would have to come to him if we expected to get any of the documents.

The fact was, of course, that even though we were a state police agency, we had full federal powers to subpoena evidence. It would have been nearly impossible to work on a fugitive case like Whitey's otherwise. When I first started doing OC in 1984, I was deputized by the U.S. Marshals, gaining for myself the federal power to serve process and make arrests related to their cases. That was standard practice for investigators like me in the State Police, and it was pretty much essential for OC. When the investigation into Whitey and Flemmi heated up, all of my people were deputized by the Marshals as well.

Then Gianturco heard about this. He professed outrage that we had such powers. Not that he ever said why, but it was clear: he was afraid we'd use them to track Whitey—and never mind how Whitey became a fugitive in the first place. Gianturco didn't care about reasons. He just wanted to keep us from showing up the FBI.

He took his complaint to Jim Farmer in the USAO, and Farmer called me. "Just wanted you to know that DOJ has worked out a new policy in Washington."

"Oh? And what's that?"

"Starting now, the deputies will all have to be approved by the FBI. So you'll be going through them on those."

"This national, Jim? Or is this just us?"

"Not just you. Everyone. Whole country."

"Could I see a copy of the order?"

"Of course. I'll get it right out to you."

I was curious to see the rationale behind the new requirements, and I had the feeling that none existed because, in fact, there was no such order at all. Sure enough, Farmer never sent anything. I asked several state police colleagues working on OC cases in other states if they had ever heard of such a policy, and none of them had. None of them were subject to any such FBI or DOJ review. It looked as though this new national policy was for us alone.

What Gianturco and Farmer didn't think of was that our investigation was a joint project with the DEA—this was why we could have Danny Doherty with us—and DEA was a federal agency capable of providing deputizations. Doherty went to his boss, who shook his head over the FBI's behavior and told Doherty he'd be happy to help us out. How many deputizations did we need?

———

Meanwhile, the feds were squeezing us on money. Back in 1991, Whitey did one of the more sensational things he had ever done: he announced that he held a portion of the winning $14.3 million state lottery ticket, which would kick out almost $90,000 a year. It was headline news across the country. Notorious mobster strikes it rich. Everyone wondered—was Whitey really that lucky? It didn't seem possible. Suspicion immediately turned to Billy Bulger. With his power over state government, it seemed he could easily get a winning ticket into his brother's hands. More likely, Whitey simply muscled in on the winning ticket after it had been pulled, claimed that he was in on it all along, and dared the true owner to say otherwise.

One problem for Whitey was that he had to go to the lottery office in person to collect, and show himself to the video cameras there. This provided one of the very few Whitey sightings on the case, and the only one that wasn't still pictures but video. Shot from above in blurry black-and-white, it showed a middle-aged man in a baseball cap moving stiffly to the counter for a brief exchange with a clerk and then making a hasty exit, head tipped down.

For Whitey the ticket's yield would provide cover for living expenses that were otherwise unaccounted for by someone who had no legitimate occupation. Now that Whitey had fled a federal arrest warrant, though, we could seize the lottery proceeds along with any other assets he had left behind. Normally, money like that goes to the lead agency investigating the case. That would be us, and we immediately put in a claim for it to the USAO, which decides these things. Of course, the FBI claimed it, too. Rather than adjudicate, the USAO ducked it, leaving the two of us to work it out between us. The FBI never engaged in any negotiations. It simply seized the money.

And the worse the FBI agents did, the more accolades they got. Within a year after letting Whitey slip through his fingers, and then being named to the task force that tried (without success) to find him, Gamel was named the Boston FBI office's Agent of the Year. Two months after that, he took over from Quinn as commander of all the FBI's OC efforts in New England, including the ones with us.

That was too much, and I called another assistant U.S. attorney, Jamie Herbert.

"Gamel's the Agent of the Year? And now he's overseeing Bulger?"

Herbert was usually an FBI apologist, and he didn't let me down. "This has nothing to do with Bulger. It's a career achievement award, honoring the guy for everything he's done."

More exactly, it was the annual award for the agent whose job it was to keep tabs on us that year. Later, when Gamel moved up, Stan Moody took over. His job was to watch what we were doing on Bulger, and to try to make it nothing. He was named Agent of the Year, too.

And there was Barry Mawn, who took over the FBI's Boston office later. He called our efforts to find Bulger "FBI-bashing" and told us that if we couldn't get along with the FBI, we should quit. New to the case, he declared that if we complained about anything the FBI did before he arrived, we were just whining about "ancient history." Mawn eventually rose to become an assistant director of the entire FBI.

Meanwhile, the FBI continued to work the press, and the feds managed to turn black into white in some of the most prominent newspaper accounts of their work with Bulger. This is from a *Boston Globe* report in March 1995: "In 1991, federal prosecutors, working mostly with State Police leads, began corralling middle-aged bookies accustomed to paying small fines and hammered them with money-laundering charges carrying stiff sentences. The goal was to force the bookies to testify about extortion payments. It began to work, and the FBI jumped on board."

This may sound right, or nearly right, but it is completely backward. If the *Globe* was talking about the USAO, it was not the entire USAO but just a couple of assistant U.S. attorneys who were willing to buck the system to do what was right. And the FBI did not "jump on board." That's crazy. The truth was just the opposite. As soon as the investigation started to work, the FBI tried to close us down. In the same article, the *Globe* hailed Ed Quinn, saying his "reputation for integrity" had "bridged the historical animosities and suspicions held by State Police" toward the FBI. Hardly. In fact, Quinn had fueled those animosities and suspicions, and he continued to do so. Toward the end of the story, the article landed on the truth of the matter: "Two years ago, a high level law enforcement official told the Globe that there would be as much trouble as glory for the FBI in building a case against Bulger. He saw a public relations debacle down the road if Bulger went to trial and used his role as a bureau informant as a defense—that he was only doing what the FBI told him to do." Dead right. And that fact explained everything else. Such conflicting media accounts—within the same article, no less—revealed that, along with all the battles we were fighting, we were in a war with the FBI over public opinion.

— CHAPTER 22 —

The FBI didn't do everything wrong. It had some successes, but the thing with the feds was that you never knew what to make of them. By this time, I simply did not believe them unless their claims were corroborated by an independent source, and even then I couldn't be sure. Whenever I talked to people from the FBI, I had to listen on two tracks—the track of what they were saying, and the track of what I could believe.

In August 1995, the summer after Whitey fled, Colonel Henderson received a call at home from Dick Swensen of the Boston office saying that the FBI had just captured Frank Salemme Sr. in the Palm Beach home of one of his girlfriends. It was a rare success for the Bureau, and the feds were crowing. They didn't alert us to the arrest ahead of time as I'd done with Martorano, but I knew not to expect them to share. They said they'd gotten a tip-off from a broadcast of *America's Most Wanted*. I had to roll my eyes. That was like saying a little bird told them.

Still, Salemme was in custody, and we were good with that.

———

That left Whitey.

We continued to chase leads, and in mid-1996 we obtained information about a counterfeiter who had supposedly been creating false IDs for him. The counterfeiter specialized in driver's licenses, and he'd helped any number of criminals in the past. That was big. If we had the alias under which Bulger was operating, we'd have a good shot at him. First, we'd need to get to the counterfeiter. Johnson, Tutungian, and Doherty went to have the conversation with the guy, and put him to use. Unfortunately, the

FBI had found out about the counterfeiter, too, and insisted on pushing into any interview. Once again the USAO wanted the feds to participate.

We weren't entirely convinced that the counterfeiter—whose name I still cannot divulge—was telling us the full truth, but we felt there was something there. Gamel, who was in charge by now, was sure our man was a compulsive liar who couldn't be trusted. But could the FBI?

After the Mounties incident, we'd decided that the rule of thumb with the FBI was: the feds hold back any information that might help us find Whitey, but they broadcast anything that makes us look bad. Like when we learned later that the FBI had developed some information from another South Boston source that Bulger was using the name Thomas Baxter and driving a black Mercury Marquis. Both pieces of information proved true, and both would have been immensely helpful in any effort to dig out Bulger. The FBI never used the information and never let us know about it either.

The counterfeiter, however, was meeting Kevin Weeks on a fairly regular basis. Young and surly, Weeks was a close associate of Bulger's and was often described as his surrogate son. Weeks was a bouncer at the Triple O's, which was the successor to the old Killeen hangout, the Transit, and was owned by Whitey. I'd seen Weeks racing down the sidewalk, probably to alert Whitey to the arrest warrants, that big night in Southie when the town lit up. Weeks's brother went to Harvard, and Weeks himself always made out that he could have gone Ivy League himself if he hadn't decided to hang with Whitey. He was canny, no question, and I bet Whitey taught him a few things.

Like Whitey, he was just about impossible to tap, and I don't think it was because he was getting tipped off. I think he was just smart that way. He was murder to tail. He knew all the tricks—running red lights; shooting across several lanes to make a sudden exit off a highway before we could react; or banging sudden illegal U-turns on one-way streets.

Concerned about his safety, the counterfeiter never came to us, and we never met anywhere we might be seen. Instead, we sat down with him well outside town.

Electronic surveillance of Weeks was difficult, but we did manage to get some information on his calls from the pay phones he used around the city, and, with a court order to the phone company, we were able to get a pen register on Weeks's phone. That doesn't record conversations—it records just the numbers dialed on a phone—so courts let us put one in fairly liberally. Our counterfeiter reported that Weeks didn't just need a phony license or two for his client; he'd also need "clean" names—ones without any criminal history—to go with the licenses. Johnson dug those up for us. He pulled them off lists of the recently deceased. It was just a name—Bulger would have to fill in the ID, with address, profession, and all the rest. But if Bulger ever tried to use the name, we'd have him. Weeks also provided the counterfeiter with a photo to use for the phony ID. To me, it didn't look like Whitey Bulger at all; it looked much more like his brother Jackie, and probably was. Obviously, Weeks was having trouble getting a good current picture of Whitey, just like we were. And Whitey couldn't have been too pleased with what Weeks sent either. Whitey provided a fresh photo and told our guy to try again. We pocketed a copy of that one. Whitey was a little worn, but that cold stare of his burned right through.

Weeks had an unusual hobby, one we figured we could make use of. Paintballing. He loved running around shooting other guys with blobs of paint. That pen register we slapped on his phone suddenly started kicking out a lot of calls to a paintball club outside Chicago. Why Chicago, all of a sudden? That wasn't exactly the paintball capital of the universe. It occurred to us that maybe he was going to meet Bulger to drop off some phony IDs. He'd make it appear like he was going on one of his paintball trips.

Still worried about the FBI, I told no one outside our unit about Weeks's movements, or about the names we'd generated. Any disclosure could get the counterfeiter killed. I sent Johnson, Doherty, and Tutungian to Chicago to try to follow Weeks, but told them to keep their distance. It was essential that Weeks have no idea they were on him. If Weeks sensed he was being followed, he'd tell Bulger, and Bulger wouldn't touch those IDs. Well, hard as it is to follow someone on unfamiliar city streets, it is doubly hard under those circumstances, and they lost him.

As we learned later, Weeks did indeed meet Whitey in Chicago on his paintball trip, and he talked over the IDs. He didn't dare bring them with him, though. That task fell to another Southie hood, Peter Lee, who delivered them to Whitey in New York. Whitey was leery of IDs that two other people knew about, besides himself. He knew a bad ID could be the end of him, just as we did. He used the IDs, but only briefly. Then he tossed them.

— CHAPTER 23 —

There was someone in Boston who knew where Whitey was. We never had any doubt about that. He chuckled about it sometimes, but he never had to sit for any official interviews on the subject until much later, when a congressional committee made inquiries, years after that fact. It was Whitey's brother Billy, of course, the cultured, apple-cheeked president of the state senate. He still lived in Southie, in a fine house that, as subsequent events revealed, was next door to Flemmi's mother's residence, where Whitey committed two of his most horrendous murders. Billy much preferred to present himself as a devoted father of nine who read the classics of Greece and Rome in the original Greek and Latin when not attending to the affairs of the Commonwealth.

In 1995, he was by far the most powerful figure in Massachusetts politics, easily surpassing the governor, and had been for over a decade, ever since he ascended to the senate presidency. People joked that he was a Bostonian Caesar, who ruled for life.

One of Billy's favorite quotations was from the Roman philosopher Seneca: that loyalty was the "holiest good in the human heart." And when it came to his brother, Billy was nothing if not loyal. He could be as cheerful as anyone, but if you asked him about his brother, his blue eyes would turn black. Like his brother, Billy arranged his life so that his reputation was such that he didn't have to reinforce it. People just knew. But on occasion he spelled it out—as with a State Police officer, Billy Johnson. In 1988, Whitey and his girlfriend Theresa Stanley were preparing to board a flight to Montreal when the female security guard attending the X-ray machine noticed some suspicious lumps in Bulger's duffel bag. She groped inside and found several blocks of $100 bills, adding up to a sum well in excess of the $10,000 you can legally take out of the country. She asked Bulger and Stanley to step to the side while she called the State Police. "Fuck you!" Whitey screamed. He grabbed the bag; tossed it to Kevin Weeks, who was there to see them off; and ran for the exit. Johnson, a plainclothesman for the State Police, caught up with him and demanded ID. The license was legitimate; Johnson didn't recognize the name James J. Bulger. The two barked at each other, but by then, Weeks had made off with the serious cash, leaving only a few thousand on Stanley, and Johnson had to let him go. Soon afterward, Billy's office called, asking for the official report on the encounter.

That was not the end of it, though. Although Johnson was a former marine and onetime Trooper of the Year, the incident was scrutinized by his superiors, and he was seen to be at sufficient fault that he was moved from undercover duty to the lesser job of cruising the airport parking lots. When he complained, he was court-martialed. He blamed Billy Bulger—not that he had proof. And Billy would never have provided proof. Years later, alone and miserable, Johnson ended up shooting himself in the New Hampshire woods.

And the State Police investigation into Whitey's operation that preceded ours? That was in 1983, and it was led by Lieutenant Bob Long and Lieutenant Colonel Jack O'Donovan, who was then chief of detectives for the State Police. It finally succeeded in planting a bug in the Lancaster Street garage where Whitey conducted business. The investigation, though, closed down after Whitey simply stopped talking anywhere near it. Afterward, Billy Bulger filed a bill that would require the retirement of a few State Police officers, most notably Lieutenant Colonel O'Donovan. There were all sorts of dire rumors, at the time, that this was payback, and Flemmi later told us they were true. He and Whitey were irrititated by all the attention they were getting from the State Police, and Whitey asked his brother to do something. And Billy did. Or he tried to. The State Police successfully fought it off. But that's what we were up against.

Old-line WASP and Harvard-educated Bill Weld was governor the year that Whitey disappeared. He'd come to office promising to clean up the corruption he associated with Billy Bulger. He didn't have to mention Whitey's name. And Weld knew all about Whitey, having been a U.S. attorney himself in the early 1980s (and later serving at the Department of Justice in Washington as head of the criminal division), at the time of the Lancaster Street investigation. He had to have known the rumors linking Whitey to the FBI.

So we'd hoped that once Weld took over as governor in 1992, he might go after Billy Bulger and loosen Billy's grip on the state. But no, practically as soon as Weld took office, he and Billy Bulger were cracking wise together at Billy's famous Saint Patrick's Day breakfast in South Boston. It was as if the senate president's having a killer for a brother was a big joke. That very first breakfast after Whitey fled, one held in March 1995, Governor Weld sang a ditty to the tune of a famous Boston song, "Charlie on the MTA," about a commuter lost in Boston's mass transit. Weld's song shared the refrain: "Will he ever return? No he'll never return. No, he'll never come back this way. I just got a call from the Kendall Square Station. He's with Charlie on the MTA!"

There were two U.S. senators there, and a host of other pols, and everyone found that hilarious.

Billy was involved in a scandal of his own, and this time it was Whitey who bailed him out. It was back in 1988, when Billy Bulger had received some questionable payments to facilitate the construction of an office building at 75 State Street downtown. It was a complicated deal, as it involved extensive permitting from the city's development agency and the biggest developer in the state, Harold Brown, a man who didn't have the best reputation. Billy was in the middle of it as a private lawyer with Tom Finnerty, a former DA who'd also grown up in Southie. For what seemed like scant effort, Bulger had received well over a quarter of a million dollars. The transaction made headlines—and a scandal that put Bulger on the defensive.

The FBI was called in to investigate, and this time Billy rode on Whitey's name and reputation, for the man overseeing the investigation was none other than Whitey's handler John Morris. And if that wasn't enough, Whitey sweetened the deal by handing Morris an envelope stuffed with $5,000 in cash. "Here," Whitey said, according to later testimony, "this is to help you out." Morris shut down the investigation soon afterward, and Billy was exonerated. No one at the FBI ever even interviewed him.

When the Massachusetts attorney general, Jim Shannon, heard about that, he demanded the FBI try again, with a little more heart this time. This time, the feds put John Connolly on it, and it was even more of a joke than the Morris version. Having grown up with the Bulgers, Connolly probably admired Billy even more than he did Whitey, and he thought of himself as one of Billy's closest friends. Connolly limited his investigation of Billy to a chatty two-hour interview in his legal office, during which Billy denied any impropriety. And Connolly saw to it that the FBI left it at that. When Connolly's FBI career ended a couple of years later, Bulger secured for him a no-show job at Boston Edison.

———

In early 1995, everybody figured that Billy had to know more about Whitey's whereabouts than he was letting on. Everybody also figured that he wouldn't say a word about it. Squeezed, the USAO turned to me and asked me if I'd interview Billy. This was just after the USAO had made a big show of having the FBI set up the fugitive task force to find Whitey. But it wouldn't ask Billy if he had any idea where his brother was?

As the unofficial stepchild of the FBI, the USAO gave the FBI line, and vice versa. So I had to think that the FBI lay behind this request, and the idea was to set me up. After all, Billy Bulger held the State Police budget in his hands. So I said no.

Later, the FBI interviewed Billy. The exchange was brief and, I'm told, quite civil. It yielded nothing. Billy insisted he didn't know anything about Whitey's whereabouts.

Many years later, however, it was revealed that Billy had taken a call from Whitey back in January, a few weeks after he fled. Billy arranged to receive it at a friend's house, where the phone would not be tapped. Although Whitey was a fugitive and a suspected multiple murderer, Billy said nothing to law enforcement about the call. He said later that he'd told his attorney, expecting his attorney to pass on the information, but no attorney ever did. Because of attorney-client privilege, it's impossible to say if the conversation ever took place. Much later, before a congressional committee, Billy was asked to divulge the contents of the call. He resisted fiercely, first invoking the Fifth Amendment, then demanding immunity. Finally, he said Whitey had told him only this: "Don't believe everything you hear about me." In return, on behalf of his own family, Billy said he expressed "concern" for his brother's welfare.

— CHAPTER 24 —

In the mob, you never know where the bullet is going to come from, and usually it's from the guy you least suspect. It's the same in law enforcement. I knew I had enemies at the FBI, but that went with the territory. I didn't think I had any serious enemies in the State Police.

They didn't emerge until Henderson stepped down in the spring of 1996. He'd been a big supporter of ours, and I missed him when he was gone. To replace him Governor Weld appointed Reed Hillman—a surprising choice, since Hillman was much more a political figure than a trooper. He'd raised a lot of money for the Republican Party and was close to Weld's lieutenant governor, Paul Cellucci. But he was only a captain, so he'd have to leap several ranks to become a colonel, the rank required for a superintendent. That was a first, and it meant there would be a lot of gaps in his experience. He came in knowing little about the full range of State Police operations, and almost nothing about investigations. As a trooper, he'd spent most of his time in central Massachusetts, well away from Boston, and most of that time he was a court officer. He had limited investigative and supervisory experience. That didn't sound good for us.

Around this time, Riley left to become head of Harvard's campus police. Major Nelson Ostiguy took over, and he kept the Division of Investigative Services on the course that Riley had set. He took the same line—Foley isn't a team player, can't work with the FBI, etc.—and he had a grudge against Colonel Henderson.

Pat and I were both considered Henderson's people, kitchen cabinet or no, and that made us perfect targets for Ostiguy, if he was trying to make his mark. He'd create the new by tearing down the old. Frighteningly for all of us, Pat had a heart attack that summer. The stress of the investigation, and all the cross fire, had to have played a role. I knew what that was like: I found myself fighting for air sometimes. But Pat wasn't able to return to the force, and this was sad for everybody. Great guy. And it also gave Ostiguy just the opportunity he was seeking.

Ostiguy went to Colonel Hillman and his second in command, Lieutenant Colonel Glenn Anderson, and declared that my SSS unit had a disproportionate number of sergeants, and some of them had to go—returned to patrol duties. It was absurd. Usually the commander of investigative services is fighting to *keep* his men, not lose them.

Hillman simply agreed. Sure, why not? Sounds good.

Once Ostiguy had Hillman's approval, he summoned me to his office, shut the door, sat me down, and let me know that some of my sergeants would have to go.

At SSS, I had seventy people altogether, and within it I was running a delicate and complex OC investigation with just a few of them. I couldn't manage without my sergeants. This he knew only too well.

"Sergeants Tutungian, Johnson, and Duffy will be transferred back to uniform duties," Ostiguy declared, reading off a list he had prepared.

If he had stabbed me in the chest I don't think I would have felt more betrayed than I did at that moment. These men weren't just my key investigators on the most important case the State Police had going; they were my friends, my brothers. They had my back, and I had theirs. Everything we'd gone through together on the case—the strategizing, wiretaps, surveillance, informants, arrests—we had gone through together. On the job, I couldn't imagine ever being as close to anyone else as I was to these three men. They were making this case, not me. If I lost them, I'd be lost, and the case would be as good as gone, too. And now Ostiguy was plucking them from the case, and sending them to Siberia.

"So that's what we have decided," he said, enjoying the moment. He would bring our investigation of Whitey Bulger to a halt. He didn't care how much it mattered, or how much had gone into it.

"Is this a done deal?" I asked.

"Yes."

"Then it doesn't really matter what I think, now does it?"

I left his office a dead man. If those three officers were sent packing, everything that I had been trying for in the last ten years since I arrived in Boston to work on OC had amounted to nothing. It was stunning. We'd killed ourselves doing our job. We'd brought SSS back from the dark days of Naimovich. It had become the best place to work in the State Police, and we were making the most important cases in the Commonwealth. And this was what we got.

It was a classic case of pointless revenge. Ostiguy wasn't really after me, much as it looked as though he was. He was carrying some water for Riley, who'd been convinced by O'Callaghan that I had it in for the FBI. Ostiguy bought into that, but he added a few cupfuls of hatred of his own. He wanted to get Henderson. He was upset because Henderson hadn't promoted him earlier. And now that Henderson was gone, he'd stick it to him by sticking it to me, since I was a Henderson man. And if he could knock out the Bulger investigation that was causing the FBI so much grief, so much the better. And Hillman felt the same: any trouble with the FBI was trouble for him.

I had to sit with that one a long time. I'd never felt so frustrated, so powerless, and so angry. Obviously, it wasn't about my sergeants. They were just a way of getting to me, just as I was a way of getting to Henderson. They were just a place to start. Without them, I'd be weakened. He could phony up some reason to take me out.

I can't recall now just how long I sat with this, but I never said anything to my sergeants. However long it was, by the time I was done I knew what I had to do.

I'd worked before with Hillman's second in command, Glenn Anderson, and I arranged to meet with him, just the two of us.

There was no need for preliminaries. He knew what it was about; it was the talk of the building.

"Sir, Lieutenant Colonel Ostiguy wants to take my sergeants," I began.

"Yes, that's right. We need them in the barracks. We have been studying the issue." It was somewhat halting. Anderson must have known this was BS.

"Let me ask you something," I replied. "How about lieutenants?" I asked. "Could you use a lieutenant?"

That surprised him. "You mean you?"

I nodded, once quickly. "If my sergeants can stay, I'll go."

"We do need lieutenants," he said.

He studied me. "OK then." He agreed to it so quickly it was clear to me this had been the ultimate objective all along. It was always about me.

"So where would you like to be assigned?"

I named a couple of areas in mid-state.

"How about station commander at Leominster?"

That was north-central Massachusetts, over fifty miles from Boston. Not exactly convenient.

"OK."

"Done."

He took me to see Hillman, to finalize the deal.

Standing on the other side of the desk, Hillman looked pale and almost bony. His eyes skipped around the room, landing everywhere but on me, and his hand was slippery when I shook it. Hillman didn't know much about our investigation except that it was getting him grief from the FBI and the USAO.

A moment or two later, Ostiguy came into the room. He stood directly behind me in a way that reminded me of Vinny Ferrara years back, and he didn't move until I turned around.

I told Hillman that I'd agreed to the transfer I'd just worked out with Anderson. "But it makes no sense at all," I told him. I ticked off the accomplishments of SSS, and the progress we'd made on the Whitey case. "We're at a key moment in the Bulger investigation, and I need these sergeants."

From the look on his face, that seemed like news to him. "You can work on Bulger when you need to, Tommy. It's fine with me."

Hillman said this so casually I didn't know how seriously he meant it, but I was going to take it and keep it. "Good," I told him. "I would like that. Thank you, sir." I had no idea how I could possibly keep the investigation going from Leominster. But I would find a way.

It wasn't a long walk back across the compound to my office, but it seemed to take forever, like something in a nightmare. I couldn't believe it. I was out. I'd taken myself out, removing myself from an active, daily role in an investigation that had been at the center of not just my career, but my life. I'd breathed this case. I ate it. I'd racked up so much time on it. Nights and weekends, yes, but also July Fourths and Christmases and birthdays.

I went upstairs to see my guys in the unit. They'd all heard the news. Tutungian, Johnson, Doherty, all my guys. They were all standing around with long faces, obviously stunned. "Tommy, are you really out?" Tutungian asked me.

"Out of here, anyway."

"Shit," Johnson said.

"Did you really offer to go?" they asked. "Was that your idea?"

"Guys, I didn't have any choice. The case can't be done without you guys.

"But listen," I told them finally. "I'm going to stay on the case, just not from here." I laid out for them how I'd stay involved from Leominster. That lifted spirits a little. We talked some about how it might work, but of course none of us knew yet how it would really work.

I wouldn't leave for a couple of weeks, and the guys kept coming into my office to see me and tell me how bad they felt about everything.

"So that's it?" Tutungian asked me one day toward the end. He had been there since 1990. He'd never given in to the hours, the pressure. He'd always been the beast of the group, just relentless, staying up all night to write an affidavit to get a wiretap, and then staying up all the next night to monitor it.

Now all we could do was look at each other.

"Yeah, it's back to the barracks for me."

"Leominster?" he asked, with some disgust.

"Hey, I'll be back," I told him. Then I smiled. "And I'm going to stay on your ass, don't worry."

———

I was home for a few days before I started in again at Leominster. All my guys in the unit called, even the ones I'd already spoken to, and told me how shocked they were, and all that.

One person from outside the force called, and that meant a lot to me. It was Tom Reilly, now the attorney general for the Commonwealth after a stint as our district attorney. He said he was calling to let me know how sorry he was about what had happened. "Senseless," he told me. "Just senseless."

I had to agree with that.

"I can call Hillman, you know. Put a stop to it."

"Thanks," I told him. "But it wouldn't work. If they don't get me out this way, they'll do it some other way."

"Well, the offer stands."

"I'm just glad to have the support of the attorney general."

Ostiguy had my replacement all teed up. I was hardly gone before he brought in Jack O'Malley. He was the head of something called the Criminal Information Section, which kept the State Police records. He'd spent some time in investigative services as a detective at Logan Airport. For him, though, it was a lucky bounce careerwise, to step into the leadership of a well-oiled investigative unit that was targeting Whitey Bulger. Still, I thought well enough of Jack to tell the guys in the section to get behind him. After all, he was in charge, and it wouldn't do the investigation any good to undermine him.

But the word was getting out that I had been sent to Leominster because I couldn't get along with the FBI, and O'Malley had to be brought in to replace me. I was the problem all along.

Even if I wanted to get off the case, I couldn't. It had gotten so vast and involved, with so many subpoenas and search warrants and witnesses, to say nothing of the long history of the investigation and all the players. I'd have to stay in, whether anybody liked it or not. Nobody else knew it the way I did. O'Malley didn't seem to like having me around, so he shifted over to other areas of SSS and left Bulger to me to work on as best I could with the people I had. It wasn't much, but it was something. We'd been through hell together, but we hadn't gotten to the other side.

PART FOUR

Bodies of Evidence

— CHAPTER 25 —

Judge Wolf held court in the old Post Office Square courthouse on Milk Street, a big ornate place with room for maybe a hundred seats, all of which were filled when Flemmi rose to take the stand as the first witness. I was in Leominster now, but I worked my schedule so I could be there for his testimony. In his jacket and tie, Flemmi had the look of a mid-level bank manager, and he answered questions about the affidavit in a flat, uninflected voice, as if his words about his relationship to the FBI were of no particular importance. But when he was done, the polish was off the FBI.

Stunned by the revelation about the informant status of two preeminent mobsters, Judge Wolf ordered Fred Wyshak to dig into all the evidence of all the FBI informants on the Flemmi case, even peripheral ones like Sonny Mercurio. The FBI and the Department of Justice couldn't duck it, either. They'd have to produce all the records they had or they would run the risk of being found in contempt of court, drawing still more unwanted publicity.

The news put the FBI in a vise. At least for the moment, Flemmi had shifted the focus of the inquiry from himself to the feds, and it rocked them. As an organization, the FBI was used to playing offense. It went after criminals, fought crime, attacked its enemies. On defense, it had to show that there was nothing to this idea of protection for Flemmi even as it acknowledged that it did use him as an informer despite his reputation, and that it never moved against him for any crimes.

———

Meanwhile, Salemme was in the Plymouth County House of Corrections await-ing trial on our indictment against him for racketeering and other crimes, many of which involved Whitey and Flemmi. He'd been held there for almost two years since he was arrested in Florida. Unlike Bulger and Flemmi, Salemme had never been an FBI informant. As those long years in prison for car-bombing Fitzgerald proved, he was a man who could keep a secret for as long as he had to. And he had to be seething about the other two, a pair of snitches—and wondering how much of his own troubles they'd brought on him. By now, Flemmi was in Plymouth, too. Together in the general lockup, Salemme and Flemmi had to have glowered at each other, these two Italians with such different ideas about omerta.

And where was Whitey? The feds did not want to compound their troubles by adding Whitey Bulger to the mix, backing up Flemmi's allegations, adding some of his own, and drawing attention to the whole thing as only a celebrity could. They'd sworn to hunt Whitey down wherever he was—so how to account for the fact that the Bureau had gotten nowhere trying to find him, and had spent so much time trying to keep us off the case instead? To reassure everyone, the feds called a press conference and wheeled out the FBI's new Boston office chief, Barry Mawn, to "clear up any perception," as he put it, "that the FBI is not aggressively pursuing him." And it kicked in a reward for information that led to Whitey's capture. It was $250,000, which wasn't all that much if the tip might get you killed. If the FBI got any leads for its money, it didn't share them with us. And the money didn't buy Whitey for the feds.

Rocked by the bad press, the Department of Justice decided that it had better do something to clean up the FBI's image. Under the aegis of an entity called the Office of Professional Responsibility, or OPR, the DOJ gathered a team of investigators from the FBI and the USAO and sent them to Boston to investigate the dark relationship between two of the city's most dangerous mobsters and their FBI handlers, Connolly and Morris. The team would be headed by a career agent, Charles Prouty.

It was the first time that the FBI had acknowledged that its agents might possibly have made a mistake or two here. That was something, and, despite the affiliations of the investigators, I held out some hope that

Prouty might dig in to figure out just what. But it seemed more likely that Prouty's real target was us. The feds had gone after us several times before—that was a big reason I was out in Leominster, after all, and not at SSS in Framingham. And, sure enough, as soon as Prouty arrived in Boston, he asked to interview me and my team to find out what we knew. With the FBI, I never knew what to believe, but I had almost never gone wrong believing less than all of it. Prouty's would certainly not be your usual inquiry. Was it A: really to find out about what the FBI did wrong on the case? Or B: to find evidence of our corruption that would divert blame from the FBI? Or C: to discover our own lines of inquiry into the FBI, in order to stymie them? I'd say no to A, and probably to B and C. But who knew?

I needed to stay on top of the Bulger and Flemmi investigation with troopers based in Framingham, all while doing a new day job in Leominster that was proving heavier than I expected. I had to coordinate our State Police efforts with local police chiefs in the thirteen cities and towns of our area, and deal with a ton of management issues at the barracks, from scheduling maintenance to monitoring the contraband inventory in our storage hold. Wherever you have people, you have people problems, and I had thirty people under me at Leominster. Draw your own conclusions.

With Prouty, Fred Wyshak was on the interview list, too. He was as suspicious of the FBI as anyone, but he was getting heat from the Department of Justice to help the feds out. The official line was—the FBI is finally going to get to the bottom of this, clean house, make things right, start fresh. And Fred bought it. "You have to give them a chance, Tommy," he kept telling me.

"Fred, how serious are they about this?" I'd tell him. "I just don't think they're for real."

"We've got to let them know what we know," he'd say. "Otherwise, they'll never get anywhere."

"Well, I want to see if they're serious first."

We never resolved that, but I did agree to attend the first sit-down with Prouty and some of his investigators. We sat around the big conference room table in the USAO as we had so many times before. Now it was Prouty. It was suits and ties all around.

Prouty sat at the head of the table, and, after some preliminary remarks about how we all needed to work together, he launched into it. "Now, Tom, maybe you can start by telling us why you believe that there has been FBI corruption." Me? It was Judge Wolf who said there was FBI corruption, not me. And it was the FBI that agreed, which is why you're here. But I said nothing, and all of us from the State Police side just looked at one another. I looked over at Wyshak, who looked away.

And Prouty wanted us to tell him everything we knew? Names, dates, times, background? Just hand it over? Why doesn't he ask us for our ATM passwords while he's at it?

Besides, we didn't want this to be a State Police investigation. The FBI already knew most of what we knew. The feds could act on it that afternoon if they wanted to. And we didn't want to give in to the same "State Police versus FBI" mentality that had caused us so much grief. Small-time us, big-deal them, with the pettiness and jealousy all on our side. Mawn had called that "FBI-bashing." And, behind that, of course was the inside story of an embittered and unreliable State Police commander who was off on a vendetta against the FBI, and who had been banished to Leominster. If I was going to be hung out to dry, I didn't want to provide the clothespins.

The meeting went nowhere, and afterward I told Prouty I'd answer particular questions, but I wasn't going to be the basis of their investigation.

———

Around then, I happened to go to a retirement party for an FBI special agent, Arthur Ryall, a friend who was proof of something I tended to forget, that not all FBI agents are impossible. Ryall had nothing to do with Bulger and Flemmi. He did all his work around Worcester. The party was at the Wachusett Country Club just outside Worcester, and a lot of FBI agents were there. One was Jim Ring, the pipe-smoking former head of OC investigations in the Boston office. I'd scarcely laid eyes on him since he'd retired back in 1989 in the wake of the Naimovich scandal. This was 1997, but it might have been a century later, given how much he'd changed. Once so sure of himself, puffing away so confidently, now he seemed almost fragile when he called out to me. "Hey, Tommy! Tommy, jeez, good to see you." He spoke as if we were old friends. But, of course, we weren't friends, never had been, and never would be. Not after what he did to Naimovich.

Now the worm had turned, and some heavy charges might be coming his way. By this time, in his affidavit, Flemmi had said Ring was heavily involved in the effort to protect Flemmi and Bulger from our investigation. That was outside the scope of the Prouty investigation, but it was of considerable interest to Judge Wolf. Knowing what I knew about Ring, and about what he'd done to us, I found this to be all too likely. Ring would have to testify about all this in the Wolf hearings, and the prospect couldn't have made him too comfortable.

And I knew that Wyshak was going to ask him about another nugget we'd picked up from Flemmi. Apparently, when Billy Bulger was senate president, he'd strolled into Flemmi's mother's house, which adjoined his own on East Third Street in Southie, and spent some time there with Ring, Connolly, Flemmi, and his brother Whitey—a rogues' gallery if ever there was one. That testimony could do more than just shake up the case against Flemmi; it could rock the statehouse. A pair of gangsters weren't exactly fit company for a couple of FBI agents, to say nothing of the state's second most powerful pol. And then there were a growing number of reports that Flemmi and Whitey had given Ring several gifts, including a choice pipe. They nicknamed him "The Pipe." To receive gifts, even fairly modest ones, from a criminal informant—when he'd gone after Naimovich for doing exactly that? (Ring later denied ever getting any gifts from them.)

Ring looked worried, almost panicky, but he tried hard not to let on. He congratulated me on the success of our investigation, overlooking the fact that he had done everything he could to squelch it. "You've done well with it," he told me. "Very well. I'm impressed."

I could have said any number of things back, but I let it go at "Thanks."

That could have been the end of it, but he kept pushing the conversation on, obviously probing for what I knew. He tried for that marvelous breezy tone he used to use with me, back when he was in charge. Now his anxiety showed through every syllable. The fire in his eyes had gone out, replaced by a kind of weary dullness that was lit up only occasionally by flickers of dread.

Then, of all people, Dave Mattioli, my old boss at OC, came up to us.

"Well, hello," he said to Ring as he approached. His greeting was understandably frosty, since Ring had been the big reason that Mattioli had resigned from the State Police. Ring had screwed him over in the Naimovich affair even worse than he did me.

If it was awkward for Ring to be with Mattioli and me at the same time, he didn't show it. He just kept trolling me for information as though his life depended on it, even though Mattioli was right there. Finally, Mattioli turned to me, grabbed my arm, and said: "Tommy, you better watch out here. I don't know if you can see, but Jimmy's fin is sticking right out of his back." Ring looked like he had been slapped. His eyes narrowed as he looked at Mattioli.

"You'd know," he said, trying to get back.

"I should've known," Mattioli corrected him.

At that, Ring gave a little snort of derision and swung around, turning his back to Mattioli. I thought he'd head off to stalk somebody else, but he turned back to me, unable to let go of the conversation. "It's all Connolly, you know," he told me. "All the crap at the FBI with Bulger and Flemmi was his. Connolly is the guy you should be going after."

This part I did get into, since I'd said it countless times in countless places already: "Jim, listen, if you and Connolly's other bosses didn't know, you should have known. You were responsible for everything that happened in your unit, right? I mean, cut the shit. You had no reason to suspect? Our Bulger and Flemmi wiretaps get compromised, they skip out on our warrants, their rivals disappear—and you don't have a clue? Are you shitting me? Come on!"

"I'm telling you, I didn't know, and I didn't have any reason to know."

"Whatever you say, Jim."

Finally, Ring slunk off, a sad figure making his way across the floor in search of anything that could help him. Mattioli and I just shook our heads as we watched him go. "What an asshole," we said, practically in unison.

———

While I tried to keep my distance from Prouty's investigation, I did agree to direct the investigators to relevant bits of the court records, and to some FBI agents whose testimony might be helpful. And I answered specific questions when I was asked—like when a special agent named Walter Reynolds called me up and asked me about my conversation with Ring at the Wachusett Country Club. First off, I was a little irked that he didn't come around to speak to me in person. On something like that, I like to see the guy I'm talking to. That's how we handle interviews like that, or at least I do, but apparently not the FBI.

"Who told you about that?" I asked Reynolds, referring to the conversation. Of course, he wouldn't say.

Still, I took him through the gist of the conversation, and I thought that was the end of it. No big deal.

In the course of the investigation, Prouty went through all the motions. He made a show of talking to everybody he could, and of reviewing all the relevant documents he could find. He and his team were at it for five weeks. And in the end he cleared the FBI of all wrongdoing. But I entered into his report, despite my determination to stay out, and in an unflattering context—my strained conversation with Ring. In fact, it showed me how guilty Ring was acting. But in the report, it got all twisted around to show that Ring wasn't to blame for anything. Instead, any blame went to certain State Police malcontents who were determined to smear the FBI. One malcontent in particular.

The report cited some comments of mine about John Connolly, but it misquoted them, and in a revealing way. "Foley explained to Ring that even though they have had a number of allegations made against Connolly, they (MSP) are not about to target Connolly as a suspect. Foley then told Ring 'you should.'"

That's not the way it happened. I said that we would probably not target Connolly in our current investigation, but we would certainly hold out this possibility for later. More important, *I* was not the one who said "You should." *Ring* said that. And the difference was significant. If Ring was on the record telling us to investigate, that would suggest he thought there was wrongdoing. Of course, he had thought that, and he told me so. But this document suggests just the opposite: it sounds as if he knows nothing of any irregularities. Further, by shifting that quote to me, and away from him, the document removes Ring from the list of people to pursue for further information—he knew nothing!—and puts me on it instead.

When we heard the details of Prouty's report, he did not come out and say that Connolly and Morris had done nothing wrong. He said only that they had done nothing wrong "within the statute of limitations," which is different. Since this was the summer of 1997, that would mean since the summer of 1992, five years before. John Connolly had retired two years before that, in 1990, ending his official connection with Bulger and Flemmi. And, to cover more recent crimes, Prouty added another out. He considered the actions only of "current FBI employees." Morris had retired the year before, so he was off the hook, too.

No matter how artfully Prouty avoided charging either agent with a crime, a large problem remained for a report like his. Whitey. Where was he? He was gone because he had been tipped off to the coming arrests by John Connolly, and Connolly had done that to save his own skin. If Bulger and Flemmi were gone, they couldn't testify to Connolly's crimes in protecting them. By this point, Flemmi had filed affidavits with the courts naming Connolly as the one who told them to flee. And phone records subsequently revealed that John Connolly had made several dozen calls to O'Callaghan inquiring about the status of the grand jury and the timing of the indictments. He knew—and he told Bulger and Flemmi what he knew.

If Prouty was trying to say that, while he found no corruption within the confines of his report, there was corruption outside it—nobody got it. The message everybody took away was that the FBI was clean. And FBI higher-ups appreciated this, and they rewarded him by promoting him to run the Boston office. Ultimately, Charles Prouty became the third-ranking administrator in the FBI.

— CHAPTER 26 —

When Flemmi learned that the FBI was ducking any responsibility for his crimes, he was furious, and he responded by going into ever-greater detail about the nature of the FBI's secret connection with him and Bulger, detail that made it ever harder for the FBI to deny this connection. Still, Judge Wolf proceeded with our case against Flemmi, which would begin in January 1998.

But in his obsession with getting back at the FBI, Flemmi had lost sight of something essential to his health. Just as our war against Bulger and Flemmi was proceeding on many fronts, his war to fend us off involved many, too. He had gotten the idea that he need worry only about the FBI. If he could somehow persuade the world that the FBI had permitted his crimes, he thought he'd be home free. But he overlooked the many mobsters who would be enraged to discover that as an FBI snitch, he had ruined their lives, and who would come for him, bent on revenge. He already had Salemme to contend with.

Now he had John Martorano. As a codefendant with Flemmi on the RICO conspiracy charge, he sat in Judge Wolf's courtroom for the next few weeks, after it became all too clear that Flemmi had been an FBI informant. Martorano was up in the front row with Bobby DeLuca and Salemme, who'd also been brought together by our charges. A solid, menacing figure, Martorano sat there all day every day, stone-faced, with his arms crossed. On the stand, Flemmi did not say that he and Whitey had used the FBI's protection to remove their mob rivals. But Martorano could add two and two. And it didn't take long for him to figure out how it could have been that Bulger and Flemmi had themselves avoided arrest in the race-fixing investigation, had known enough to alert Martorano to his impending arrest, and had watched Howie Winter go off to prison, ceding to them the top spot at Winter Hill. Meanwhile, Martorano had been forced to abandon his family and friends to go on the run for fifteen years.

From that first day, through weeks of testimony, Flemmi's eyes never once met Martorano's, even though Flemmi had always insisted he and Bulger were Martorano's best friends in the world. But Martorano sat dead still, his eyes going nowhere except to Steve Flemmi. If a look could kill, Flemmi would be lying in a pool of blood. Out of court, Martorano was housed at the Plymouth County House of Corrections. His cell was three doors down from Flemmi's. At night, in their beds, each could hear the other breathing. All the cells opened at six in the morning, allowing all the inmates to mingle. Martorano thought often about strangling Flemmi or slipping a shiv into him, but he never did it. He had a better way to take revenge than murdering him.

Martorano had heard good things about how we'd handled sources like Chico Krantz and the bookies Jimmy Katz, Paul Moore, and others. For us, it was simple: we did what we said we would do. No surprises, no exceptions. Plus, Martorano had been impressed by the way Steve Johnson and Sly Scanlan handled his arrest in Florida. Criminals aren't ever going to like cops, but they do appreciate professionalism, and Mike and Stevie did the whole thing by the book. It's like what they say about your reputation. It takes a lifetime to build and a moment to blow.

The first we learned of Johnny Martorano's interest in cooperating came when his younger brother Jimmy asked us to come out to his home in Quincy to talk. He didn't have to send out any feelers; I knew what it was about. Now we had to decide if we wanted to go down this road. Martorano was a stone-cold killer. He could pop you and then have a nice dinner. If ever there was a deal with the devil, this was it. I went around and around on it. We were kicking the crap out of the FBI for coddling a pair of killers. Would people think we were doing the same thing?

This one wasn't easy, and I talked it over with Wyshak, Doherty, Johnson, and others in the unit. Was this OK? Should we do it? How would it look? None of us liked it. Martorano was the devil, no question. We were all agreed on that. But what choice did we have? Besides, our dealing with Martorano was a whole different thing from the FBI's dealing with Bulger. We certainly didn't keep Martorano in business the way the FBI did Bulger. Just the opposite. We'd captured Martorano and thrown him into prison. The feds had protected Whitey from arrest, and now they seemed bent on letting him stay gone forever. Basically, they had let him kill as many people as he wanted, and maybe they were continuing to, as far as anyone knew. By taking Martorano off the street, we'd make the killing stop.

Martorano was exactly the man we needed for our plan to work. The idea had always been to start with the bookies, and keep going up until we get the full truth. The lesser charges would be enough to put Whitey in prison, and that's when we'd lay the real charges on him. But this was back before DNA, when you usually needed a body or a reliable eyewitness to win a murder conviction, and both were hard to find with Whitey. We knew he was a killer. That was his reputation, and any number of people had disappeared after seeing him. But we hadn't found the bodies that would allow us to develop murder charges, or anyone to tell us about the crimes. Whitey never left a body behind, at least none whose death could be traced to him. And no eyewitnesses ever came forward. They knew better.

That's how the FBI could play Whitey as a lowly racketeer who, despite a lot of tough talk, never actually hurt anyone. Martorano would put an end to that. He'd know all about Bulger's murders. And once a guy like Johnny Martorano started to talk, others would say some more. And then we'd start to make some inroads into the FBI cover-up, too. And whoever was behind that in the USAO, the DOJ, and anywhere else. We would follow this snake back to its hole.

And we had the families of the murder victims to consider. In a lot of Bulger's murder cases, nobody knew what happened. As far as the families knew, their loved ones were just gone. Many of them had been gone so long that the families had long since started to fear the worst. But not knowing can be agonizing, and if we could get Martorano to tell us what he knew, that could end their suspense.

Johnson and Doherty stayed in touch with many of them. The families couldn't be absolutely sure that it had been Bulger and Flemmi who had killed their relatives, but they had ample reason to suspect. Johnson and Doherty had broached the subject of our gaining solid information about what happened, since they could not legally be brought into any plea bargain, but the families made clear their views. They wanted to know the truth, however painful it might be to hear.

—————

Born in 1940, Jimmy Martorano was just eleven months younger than his brother Johnny. We knew all about them. For Jimmy was in the files, too. The brothers were in the same grade growing up, and they'd gone pretty much in lockstep through life. The family had started out in Somerville, not far from Winter Hill, but then moved out to suburban Milton, where it was quieter and the boys had room to run. Their father, Andy Martorano, had started out as a cabbie, but he went in with a bookie, Abie Sarkas, to buy a sleazy nightclub called Luigi's in the Combat Zone. Jimmy stayed in public school in Milton, but Johnny was more difficult. His parents tried to straighten him out at an all-boys Catholic prep school down in Rhode Island. One of his friends there was Ed Bradley, of *60 Minutes*. But Johnny ran away one fall to rejoin his brother at Milton Junior High, and they went on from there to Milton High, where they were cocaptains of the football team. As a hard-running fullback, Johnny was called "the milkman" because he always delivered. Jimmy went on to Boston College, but Johnny went to Luigi's.

Their dad was a gambler who liked to bet on stupid little things like whether the Red Sox star Ted Williams would hit a grounder or a fly ball. Johnny picked up some of that. He also took an interest in his father's twenty-two rifle, and proved a good shot. And Luigi's was heaven to him—all the lowlifes and wiseguys drinking and swapping tips and smoking and grabbing women and carrying on. It gave him ideas, and before long he got arrested for carrying an unregistered firearm. To escape the charges, Johnny fled, first to South Beach, then to Havana. From there, a payoff made the gun charges go away, and he returned to Luigi's. He then jumped to Winter Hill, brought in by a friend of his from Luigi's, Jimmy "The Bear" Flemmi, who was into everything. That was Stevie Flemmi's big brother. By now, Johnny's brother Jimmy Martorano had gone from Boston College to the mob, too, but the New York Mafia. The two brothers went along separate lines, but parallel ones.

We decided that we could at least see what Jimmy Martorano had to say. Johnson, Doherty, and I took a ride out to his place. Jimmy was a thinner version of his brother, with less power but more coiled energy. He sat us down in the dining room and, without any preliminaries, he got right down to it, and it was as we'd thought. Johnny wanted to talk. "He's ready to tell you everything he knows about Stevie and Whitey," Jimmy said. He brought his hand down hard on the table. "What those fuckers did to Johnny, he will do to them."

But, he added, there were "certain concerns."

"And what might those be?" I asked.

"My brother is concerned about his reputation."

"Sure."

"Johnny is no rat, you understand me? He'd never consider doing this if Stevie and Whitey hadn't done what they did. But this is where we are. Here is what I'm saying. I'll handle that. The people I need to reach will understand. You can't rat a rat. Follow me? It's as simple as that."

Jimmy expressed other concerns; Johnny did not want to be segregated in prison. He'd be in with everybody, and he'd take care of himself. And no Witness Protection Program when he got out. He'd return to his life. He was done running.

"Oh, and one last thing," Jimmy said. "No FBI. He doesn't want to talk to the FBI. That clear?"

After the FBI's role with Bulger and Flemmi, we didn't have to ask why.

"I'm sure things can be worked out OK, Jimmy," I told him. But I set down some conditions of our own: Johnny would have to tell us the truth, and nothing but. If we caught him in a lie, the deal would be off, and we'd prosecute him. End of story.

"I understand," Jimmy said. "I'll let him know, and I'm sure he'll agree."

Because such deals with witnesses are ruled on by the U.S. attorney, we had to take the idea back to Donald Stern. Stern had his misgivings, and they were mostly the same ones we had about doing a deal with a professional murderer. But in the end he went along. "OK," he said wearily. "You got it, you and DEA. See what you can work out for a proffer."

A proffer is kind of a proposal, a preliminary presentation of the things a subject is prepared to talk about. The government needs it to decide whether it will enter into an agreement. Nothing in a proffer can be used against the subject, so he is able to speak freely. But what would Martorano say? To find out, we had to take him someplace quiet and out of the way.

By now, the FBI had gotten word of Martorano's cooperation, and the feds desperately wanted in. They were worried about what Martorano might tell us, and they figured that they'd better find out. But after what the FBI did with Bulger and Flemmi, Martorano didn't want them anywhere near him. I asked Wyshak to tell the feds to forget it. Martorano was ours. We'd find a place that was completely secluded, from the mob and from the press.

———————

A couple of days more, and we had just the place. So, on one hot July after-noon, when Martorano was finished with Judge Wolf, he was not returned to his cell at the Plymouth County House of Corrections. Instead, some U.S. Marshals packed him into a black SUV and took him to the State Police barracks by the Massachusetts Turnpike in Weston. There, he was transferred to a State Police van, and we took him to a forgotten little town called New Braintree in the middle of the state. A Seventh-Day Adventist school had been converted to a small prison and then been taken over by the State Police as a training facility. It was well off the road, out in the middle of nowhere, but there was still a small holding area inside. It was perfect.

We never told anyone in the DOJ where we'd taken Martorano, but when the people in the department figured out he was gone, and in our exclusive charge, they complained to Wyshak that we didn't know how to handle prisoners like Martorano, and that we shouldn't have him. In their frenzy, they cited a recent joint effort we'd undertaken with DEA to investigate a State Police sergeant who was dealing cocaine on Cape Cod. To them, this somehow proved that the State Police were unreliable and custody should be returned to DOJ. It didn't matter that the State Police and DEA had combined to *clean up* the corruption, not to cause it. The DOJ was just mad that the FBI had been left out of the Martorano interviews, and was having a tantrum about it.

Wyshak and Kelly had to stay up several nights running to fight that one off, although it put them in an awkward position, since they were DOJ themselves.

———

With the DOJ held at bay, we began the debriefing process with Martorano. That first evening when we brought him to New Braintree, we went through the ground rules regarding the proffer and then told him we'd be back in the morning to start in.

The next morning, the tabloid *Boston Herald* came out with a big article trumpeting that the notorious hit man John Martorano had turned state's evidence, and he was being held for interviews by the State Police and DEA. I'd scarcely gotten out of bed when the phones started ringing. All of the callers had the same question: Where'd this come from?

When the courthouse opened up, Judge Wolf did what the DOJ had long been demanding: he took Martorano away from us, handed him back to the U.S. Marshals, and restored him to the custody of the DOJ. Wyshak and Kelly took our side, but almost no one else did—in the USAO or anywhere outside the State Police, for that matter. Judge Wolf appeared to believe we were the leak.

Judge Wolf had lost all patience with these media leaks and didn't really buy what I was selling. I can only guess that he saw law enforcement as a single entity. In his mind, the Boston police, the State Police, the FBI, the DEA—they were all basically one operation with several different departments. If one department screwed up, they were all to blame.

This also gave Judge Wolf a chance to make some headlines of his own, something he never minded, as he personally headed up his inquiry into the source of the leaks.

And the DOJ jumped on us now that we were down. It dispatched its Office of Professional Responsibility—Prouty's old outfit—to grill us about the leaks. The OPR would file affidavits and ask probing questions to determine what contacts people in our unit had with which reporters, at what times, and on what subjects. If the topic was Martorano, the answers were none and none, but that didn't satisfy the people from OPR. In their minds we were all guilty, and we should confess. Even though there were plenty of better candidates for leakers out there, DOJ zeroed in on us. We consoled ourselves by thinking this was a kind of praise. The DOJ focused on us because we were the only ones doing real police work. But that was small consolation.

In the course of his investigation, Judge Wolf summoned me into his chambers with some representatives of the USAO to interrogate me. Once again, I could not believe that I was on the receiving end of such grief. What was everybody thinking? Around the room were Herbert and Farmer and several other people who had done nothing but hinder our investigation, and they were delighted now to see me on the defensive.

When I told Judge Wolf it wasn't us, he'd just shake his head or grimace. It seemed to me like he wanted to make us as uncomfortable as possible. Why, I don't know, but someone was pointing him in our direction. How could he not understand? He didn't get it.

So I asked him: "Why would we compromise our own investigation? What would we possibly gain? We went to such great lengths to keep the interviews secret; why would we want to tell anyone? That would just make everything harder for ourselves."

To Wolf, it already had done that.

————

A few weeks later, the leak was found, and, needless to say, it wasn't us. It was Jimmy Martorano, along with the lawyer he'd hired for Johnny. Both of them were trying to get ahead of the idea that Johnny was ratting anyone out. That was part of the strategy that Jimmy talked about with us in Quincy. Jimmy had gone to the *Globe*, Johnny's lawyer to the *Herald*. Once the news was in those two papers, it might as well have been on every billboard in Greater Boston.

So it wasn't us, just as we'd said. But that didn't matter. The damage had been done. We'd been deemed untrustworthy, and we were still untrustworthy, regardless of the facts. Judge Wolf went ahead and gave Martorano to DOJ just as he said he would, and DOJ took him away from us to an undisclosed location that could have been anywhere in the whole country. We'd still be able to interview him at some point, but he was out of our control. So who knew? He was gone. I couldn't imagine what Martorano thought, rushed off into the night.

My breathing problems got bad again. Climbing stairs, I felt I was running a marathon, and I wasn't sleeping too well either. Whatever we did, we got slammed. Right thing, wrong thing, it didn't matter. Flemmi's testimony and the stuff Martorano was ready to give us—they were a couple of big guns aimed right at the feds. But now the feds, in conjunction with their bosses at DOJ, were shooting back with some heavy firepower of their own.

I was still in the Leominster barracks, working long hours to get everything done. This didn't make it easy to get to Boston to attend Judge Wolf's hearings or support the guys on the investigation. Wyshak was pretty beat. It was catching up to him, too. He was trying to fight off the FBI, the DOJ, and some of the attorneys in the USAO who were supposed to be his colleagues.

And by now, most of my original people had drifted away. After O'Malley replaced me as the head of SSS, he took the remaining four of them—Tutungian, Scanlan, Patty, and Gale. It made sense. He was their new boss. I could see it from their side. Our work was hard, the hours were long, and we were getting it from all sides, no matter how well we did.

We still had a strong team and stuff was getting done. We were focused and knew that we had some real good opportunities to bring the investigation to a higher level. Johnson, Doherty, and Duffy all hung in, sticking it out against long odds, and at some risk to their careers, to send Bulger and Flemmi away forever. We were in it together, but that didn't mean that they didn't get frustrated with me, and after Wolf's ruling they were pissed when Martorano was snatched from us.

"Shouldn't we be going after Connolly, Tommy?" Stevie Johnson asked me one day.

"Stevie, I know. And, Fred, I know you are frustrated with this too. But listen, if we can get going on the proffer, we'll see some movement on Connolly. For now, we've got to stay focused. Get Whitey and Flemmi on the little things, then on the bigger things. The closer we get to nailing Whitey, the more we'll get on the FBI." And I had to like the guys' spirit. They might get down, but never out. They were fighters, every one of them.

— CHAPTER 27 —

In the spring of 1998, Judge Wolf got his hearings going again, and now Wyshak and Kelly started getting seriously squeezed. They were the ones to prosecute Bulger and Flemmi, but the case was slamming them up against the FBI. The FBI was housed at DOJ just like the USAO was. The DOJ was not thrilled that its people were hacking away at the good name of the FBI. But it was increasingly obvious that there was no way to prosecute the case without damaging the FBI. If the Bureau denied that it had given Flemmi authority to commit crimes, Flemmi would scream all the louder that it had. If it admitted that it had done that, then it was facing serious penalties, since it has no legal authority to grant that sort of immunity. For the sake of the truth, Wyshak and Kelly couldn't ignore that. For the sake of their jobs, they were supposed to. Adding to the pressure, assistant U.S. Attorney Jamie Herbert, a great loyalist of U.S. Attorney Donald Stern, sat himself down right beside Wyshak and Kelly at the prosecution table.

It was an untenable situation—the government was supposed to prosecute itself—and Fred was smack in the middle of it. The case was giving him a beating. The guy went hard at everything he did, but he'd never been slapped around like this. He always looked as if he was about a week behind on his sleep. He tried to go right down the middle, arguing neither the FBI's innocence nor its guilt. Have the FBI acknowledge that, yes, there was a violation of the FBI standards here, but it wasn't a pattern of corruption, and the entire Bureau certainly should not be blamed. It was all one guy, John Connolly, who wildly exceeded his authority.

Even to acknowledge any illegality on Connolly's part was new, for the FBI had always insisted that its handling of Flemmi was completely proper, whatever Flemmi might say. After John Morris took the stand, that argument wasn't so convincing. Morris played this one far better than Connolly had. As soon as he could, he became the state's witness, testifying in exchange for immunity. With something like that, you don't want to be second in line. To maintain his immunity, Morris told all, much more than the FBI must have wanted. For example, when a key witness in one case refused to cooperate, Morris said he'd put what looked like several sticks of dynamite and a blasting cap under the man's car. Then he called the bomb squad, and they rushed to the scene and carefully removed the device. Needless to say, the witness became very cooperative after that—and he demanded to be put in the Witness Protection Program when he was done.

On Bulger and Flemmi, Morris detailed all the gifts he had taken from the mobsters to supplement his FBI salary, which was stretched when he took up with his secretary and made her his second wife. Still, the dollar value wasn't much. From Bulger, he received a silver wine bucket; from Flemmi, $1,000 toward a plane ticket for his girlfriend. He claimed about $7,000 in all. Still, the point wasn't the dollar amount but the intimacy the money suggested, the coziness of the foursome, which Morris richly detailed as he described get-togethers like the one with Joe Pistone.

Connolly had thought of himself as a guy who could schmooze so brilliantly with mobsters that he could turn them, often in a single conversation. He had no idea that Bulger and Flemmi were even better at it, turning *him*. It really didn't take much. And in return, along with Morris, Connolly gave Bulger and Flemmi everything two mobsters could possibly want—protection for their crimes, warnings about rivals, and alerts to any investigations. In a nasty line of work, they got safety. There were a million things we would have liked to ask Morris, but we never had the chance. Even though it was our case, Morris was not our witness. He was the FBI's and USAO's—theirs to get to talk, and theirs to get *not* to talk, if they could.

———

When he read Morris's testimony, Representative Marty Meehan of Massachusetts was astounded that the FBI could have handled Bulger and Flemmi like that, and he announced that he would be holding hearings on federal agencies' use of informants. It was one thing to win the attention of a federal judge like Wolf; it was another to draw congressional scrutiny. The DOJ might be able to push the State Police around, and corral an assistant U.S. attorney like Wyshak, but Congress? For the first time, the FBI started to act like maybe it wasn't on top of everything after all. Maybe the Bureau's critics had a point.

That forced U.S. Attorney Don Stern to admit that, well, maybe the problems went beyond Connolly after all. Maybe he and Morris didn't follow proper procedures, or maybe the procedures themselves were at fault. After claiming that the FBI tried to keep in place a "system" to handle informants, Stern acknowledged that it didn't work too well here. The statement was long-winded, and it needed to be, for he had to state a truth and duck it at the same time. "The FBI and attorney general informant guidelines, together with FBI administrative controls, are intended to provide the necessary checks and balances and to ensure that often difficult decisions are made at the appropriate level, based on complete and accurate information. While admittedly no system is foolproof, clearly those objectives were not met here, at least in certain critical aspects." He went on to say that these national guidelines were being reviewed by the DOJ and the FBI. It was left to Barry Mawn, the head of the Boston office, to provide the kicker. "These controls are obviously weakened and nullified if the FBI supervisor is corrupted and does not ensure complete compliance on the part of the handling agent."

Well, which was it? Was it the FBI according to Donald Stern, or the FBI according to Barry Mawn? Was this a broad system failure, as Stern was implying? Or was it simply an instance of human error, as Mawn implied? If it was just one guy, then that was it, right there. If it was a system failure, well, who else was in the system, and what was the system? Surely it was not just John Morris. It was obviously Connolly, too. And probably Ring, and who knows who else? It may have gotten deep into the works of the FBI itself, spreading throughout the Boston office, into other offices across the nation, and up the chain of command. Who knew how far this went?

The fact was that there was no functioning FBI policy on informants. No checks, no balances. Informants went over the line into criminality because there was no line. That's what I learned back in the Naimovich case, and it was still true. This was not just one guy, and the more people at the FBI said it was, the more convinced I became it wasn't.

————

In August 1998, after many months of affidavits and brief appearances in pretrial hearings and then the slow cranking of justice in his own trial, Steve Flemmi was finally going to appear on the stand before Judge Wolf in the racketeering case we'd brought against him, sending out tremors in every direction. After such a long wait, I was eager to hear how Flemmi was going to play it. I always find it gratifying to see the subject of an investigation, especially one like this, on the stand, finally forced to answer the questions that we had raised. I was also curious to see how much trouble he caused the FBI, for Flemmi on the stand was a lose-lose proposition for the feds. If he stuck to his line—"The FBI let me do it"—then the FBI had to bear some responsibility for everything he did. The feds already admitted that he'd been their informant for decades. If he abandoned the line, everyone would have to wonder—so why didn't the feds arrest him?

Either way, all the attention on Flemmi, and on FBI informants, was putting the Bureau in the spotlight at a troubled time.

To my frustration, this was when Stern wanted us to interview Martorano. Despite the satisfaction that DOJ seemed to have taken in removing Martorano from us, it must have known that we were always going to be the ones to debrief him. He was our witness, after all. As usual, Wyshak was the one to make the overture to us. The USAO knew by now that when most other people in the office talked to us, the conversations didn't go so well.

"Don wants to know when you guys are going to interview Martorano," Fred told me on the phone.

It was news that he did. "When?"

"Soon as you can."

This was wait and hurry up, but I said OK, even if it meant missing Flemmi.

It turned out that Martorano was in La Tuna Penitentiary in El Paso, Texas, near the Mexican border. A federal prison, it had a kind of high-security annex for the interrogation of federal witnesses. The Department of Justice people called it the "Valachi Suite," after Joseph Valachi, an Italian mobster who'd been interrogated there back in the early 1960s. He was part of Lucky Luciano's New York crime family and the first one to acknowledge the existence of the Mafia, which he called La Cosa Nostra. I could only hope that our conversations with Martorano would be as fruitful.

Down we went—Doherty, Johnson, Duffy, and myself. All four of us would listen. I would take notes and then write out everything of value afterward.

In summer, El Paso produces a dry, burning heat you never get in Boston, and it almost hurts to pull this heat inside your lungs. After landing at the airport, we drove a rental car about ten miles west to the prison.

The "Valachi Suite" was hardly the Four Seasons. It was more like a concrete bunker, with a meager cell off on one side, and a sad conference room with unbreakable furniture on the other. Martorano was in a prisoner's orange jumpsuit for our meetings, but it never mattered what he wore, or where he was, or what was happening. He was always the same, all business, all the time. No small talk, no humor. Just get on with it.

Once we settled into the bench around the table, he spoke in a low monotone, with no flourishes, just word-word-word. It was four of us and one of him, but it didn't seem one-sided. He wouldn't be moved no matter how hard you pushed. Maybe he was a vicious murderer, but to me and the guys, he was just someone else to interview. We were focused on the information he could give us, nothing else. And as for my safety, I figured I was as safe as I ever was, and that was plenty safe for me.

I began by going over the ground rules, explaining that we were there to obtain the basics of the proffer, which would provide the basis of the negotiation over his sentence. I reminded him of one essential point. He had to tell us the truth. Every place, every name, everything he said happened had to be absolutely accurate. If he didn't remember, he should say so. But if he did, he should tell us. If we found out he'd done anything less than tell us the full and accurate truth, the deal was off, and good-bye. I had to be firm about this. If Bulger was going away, we'd need Martorano to send him, and I didn't want to find out in court that Martorano's testimony had holes in it.

We had only three days with him, so we needed to pace ourselves. We took seats around a kind of picnic table: the benches and table were all one piece. He had a glass of water at his feet, but nothing else. No notes, no books. Just him, a thickset man with dark eyes looking back at us without emotion. We picked up where we had left off in New Braintree months before.

"So you want my life story?"

"Yes. Beginning to end."

He nodded slightly at that. I wanted to start with something neutral and easy as a way of gauging how much he was likely to tell us. If he gave us a lot of detail with that, I'd want just as much detail later. So he gave us the early bit from Somerville through Luigi's until we got to what we'd come for.

Danny and Stevie had brought many of the Martorano murder files, and later, when we got into the murders, they would be reviewing the files and corroborating his story, often showing me pictures of victims and where the bullet holes were located. When he talked about a particular murder, we'd pull out the relevant file. We'd ask, "What about 'Indian Joe' Notarangeli?" And he'd say, "Well, for that, I dressed up like a meat worker with a long white jacket, hard hat, sunglasses, and a fake beard, and I found him in a little place called the Pewter Pot. We knew he was inside using the phone. I put a bullet between his eyes and two in his chest."

And then we'd look at a picture of the corpse from the file, and there would be a bullet hole between the eyes, and two in the chest, just like he said. And there were notes in the file about the murderer being dressed in a butcher's meat jacket and all the rest. And every one of them was like that. No details were off. We continued to listen for incongruities between what he said here and what he said there, but, not finding any, we could relax.

We weren't there just to learn about Martorano, though, but to establish his credibility regarding the mobsters we wanted to get: Whitey Bulger and Steve Flemmi. They'd been with Martorano since his earliest days at Winter Hill. Sometimes Martorano murdered on his own, but often he murdered with them, and as Martorano went through his hits, we listened hard for details of Whitey's and Stevie's involvement. The two came in soon enough.

When Martorano was in his early twenties, his father—the Andy Martorano who owned Luigi's—started having an affair with a Dorchester divorcée, Margie Sylvester, who worked as a waitress there. She was not loved by everyone, though, and she ended up being stabbed to death and rolled up in a blood-stained rug upstairs in Andy's nightclub. It was like a murder in Clue: any number of people could have done it. Johnny was never suspected, but his brother Jimmy was. Johnny himself suspected an ex-con, Bobby Palladino, who'd been drinking and gambling at Luigi's that night.

This was in the middle of the first Irish gang war, the one between the McLeans and the McLaughlins, and gangsters were being rubbed out all over the city, so people started to forget about what happened to Margie Sylvester that night at Luigi's. Stevie Flemmi was nearly killed by a hit squad in Dorchester in 1964, and then he survived getting blasted by some other goons a year later. Johnny had been in Stevie's circle for some time, but now they started getting close. Stevie was the one to tell him that Bobby Palladino was putting out the word that Johnny's brother Jimmy had killed Sylvester.

As Martorano told us, "Stevie was basically telling me I had to kill this guy." That was Stevie, putting out a line to Martorano even then. What Martorano didn't figure out until much later was that Stevie wasn't concerned about Jimmy Martorano. He was concerned about his own brother, Jimmy *Flemmi*, since Jimmy Flemmi was upstairs at Luigi's the night Sylvester died. Taking out Palladino would eliminate the only witness to this fact, and, thinking it a favor to his Jimmy, Johnny Martorano was bent on doing just that. He had to hurry, and get him before Palladino got word of Johnny's plans. Late one night, so late it was also early, Martorano found Palladino playing blackjack and drinking whiskey at a club on Blue Hill Avenue in Roxbury. Palladino didn't think to say no when Johnny asked him to take a ride in his Cadillac. Johnny had a friend drive, so he could sit in the back, behind Palladino. As the friend started the car, Palladino suddenly panicked, pulled out his own gun, and fired a shot at the driver. Palladino missed. From behind, Johnny didn't. They dumped the corpse by a stanchion in North Station, trying to make Palladino look like just another victim of the endless gang wars in Boston, which in effect he was.

Martorano went on from there. Most of the early murders were like that, trying to set things right for his brother Jimmy. Jimmy would screw things up; Johnny would unscrew them. He hunted down Stu Jackson, another hood who knew about Margie Sylvester's death, and shot him, too. He popped a bruising South Boston fighter, Tony Veranis, after Veranis beat his brother Jimmy up over a loan shark debt. Plenty of people saw the killing, but such was Martorano's reputation that no one said a word. Martorano removed an eyewitness to a murder committed by a couple of other friends. Then he killed to avenge another beating given to his brother Jimmy, sending three shots into a parked car on a winter night and killing his target, plus two others. Murders came easily.

Most of these were in the late 1960s, when Martorano wasn't yet out of his twenties, and the murders were generally one-shot affairs, nothing more. Things changed later, when he got to know George Kaufman, the pal of Chico Krantz's who ran the garage in Somerville that was home to Winter Hill. A skillful mechanic who asked no questions, he'd chopped up the Cadillac after Martorano used it for the Palladino hit.

Kaufman knew that Howie Winter was always in the market for a tough guy, and that was enough for Howie. He brought Martorano into Winter Hill, and he soon went in with Winter to co-own a smoky South End nightclub that came to be called Chandler's. It was here, in 1972, that Martorano met Whitey Bulger.

Now that he was edging into Bulger we started paying real close attention. Martorano and Bulger must have seen a lot in each other. Both were survivors who would never say more than they had to. Bulger had just come from murdering Donnie Killeen; he wanted to see if Winter could help end the carnage between the Killeens and the Mullens before it claimed him, too. Martorano was the one to set up the meeting. He was barely thirty, and he was already a player.

Once Bulger was in with Winter Hill, he wanted to bring someone else in, too. John Connolly. He made the introduction to Martorano and Howie Winter in 1973 or 1974. We expected to hear about Connolly, but not from that far back. You'd think that mobsters would have been a little apprehensive about bringing an FBI agent into their midst, but no. They knew that FBI agents came in all stripes. Some played, some didn't. They just wanted to know what Connolly wanted. Whitey explained that Connolly had been talking to Billy Bulger, his friend from the projects who was then a rising state senator, and Connolly had asked if there was anything he could do for Billy in exchange for the help that Billy had been giving him. Billy said yes, there was something. Watch out for his brother Jim and try to keep him out of trouble.

Now, when Connolly came around with the offer, Whitey said sure, he'd appreciate help like that. Martorano and Winter were fine with it, too. They didn't realize that it wasn't really about them. It was about Whitey and Connolly, and it was the start of Whitey's being a top-echelon informant, with Connolly as his handler. It was the start of everything, right there in Marshall Motors. And despite Billy Bulger's claims to the contrary, it sure looked like it all started with him.

It's the kind of thing you hear in this business, when sources start telling you things from long ago. It was fascinating, and it explained a lot. It was too far back to act on, but, if we believed Martorano and if he was truthful about everything else, it did add another name to the lengthening list of the powerful who'd misled investigators to save themselves.

Connolly soon demonstrated his worth when Martorano and Winter tried to muscle in on a vending-machine business, Melo-Tone Vending. The owner, whom Martorano remembered only as Jack, had run to the

FBI. Connolly found out, and told Jack that if he wanted to push a complaint like that he should prepare to go into the Witness Protection Program and move his family to another state. Jack withdrew his complaint. In gratitude, Bulger pulled out a two-carat diamond ring from a stash of stolen jewelry he kept at the garage hangout on Winter Hill, and handed it to Connolly to give to his wife. Flemmi was there, too, Martorano told us. By then, he obviously had a special relationship with Connolly, too.

There in the Valachi Suite, Martorano told us all this in an even monotone, as if it were just data—a string of numbers, or names from a phone book. He spoke only to answer our questions; he rarely volunteered anything. So the conversation had a halting quality, as he was done talking sooner than we'd expected. "And then what did you do?" we'd ask, to keep things rolling. "So what did you do about that?"

The first time he went in with Whitey on a murder was in 1973, his first contract hit. It stemmed from a vicious rivalry between a couple of bookies that forced Boston underboss Jerry Angiulo to take sides. One of the bookies was "Indian Al" Notarangeli, a nickname left over from his days as a boxer. No Indian, Notarangeli—the brother of "Indian Joe" Notarangeli—was as Italian as his name, but he steered clear of the Mafia, and he was strictly an independent when he set up a bookmaking office near North Station, home of Boston Garden, and not far from Angiulo's headquarters on Prince Street in the North End. Being so close without being part of the Angiulo operation, he was a thumb in Angiulo's eye. Notarangeli also dabbled in larceny, drug dealing, and arson, and in 1970 he'd been sent off to Walpole—this was shortly before I got there—for a botched firebombing of a ski resort in Vermont. Another bookie who was operating downtown, Paulie Folino, saw this as his chance to peel off some of Notarangeli's customers. Unlike Indian Al, Paulie went in for full protection from Angiulo, and he was paid up on his rent, so he thought he could do this with some impunity. Still, Indian Al was outraged when he found out about it, and when he got out on furlough in August 1972, Notarangeli came gunning for Folino. With a pal named Sonny Shields, Indian Al caught up with Folino at a golf course in Andover and somehow lured Folino to his car. There they hog-tied him and stuffed him into the trunk, his neck bound so tightly to his ankles behind him that he soon strangled himself.

That caused problems for Angiulo. The plain fact was that Indian Al had killed a bookie Angiulo had pledged to protect. "So he wanted me to square things," Martorano told us. Johnny wasn't Mafia, but he was getting a reputation as one of the best hit men in the business. He would do Indian Al. His first hired hit, and the first on a target who knew it was coming. He plotted it like a commando raid. Martorano assembled a team of assassins. One of them was Whitey Bulger. He didn't have to emphasize it. We all took note.

Martorano gathered an arsenal of high-powered weapons, placed spotters around Indian Al's favorite places, and plotted out the hit: who would do what. It was like one of our own operations—a lot of preparation and then a lot more waiting. When everything was in place, Martorano and everyone else hung out in an apartment in Somerville, playing cards, cooking, joking around, and waiting for the phone to ring.

Notarangeli had a nightclub near the North Station called Mother's, and Martorano got the call late one night that Indian Al was there. He immediately set out in a convoy of three cars. The last one, the crash car—the backup in case the others crashed, or to provide cover for the shooters—was driven by Bulger. All were linked by walkie-talkie. For all the focus on Indian Al, Martorano had never actually seen him. "I really wasn't too sure what he looked like," he told us. He'd go by some details, and the car.

When he spotted Notarangeli's brown Mercedes in front of the restaurant, Martorano opened fire out the window with a machine gun. He killed the driver and wounded two passengers. But Indian Al survived unscathed. As one of the three drivers, Bulger was in on it. He was part of a conspiracy to commit murder. Legally, he might as well have pulled the trigger himself.

A week or two after that, Notarangeli was seen driving down Atlantic Avenue in the North End. He was still in his car when Martorano reached the scene, with Whitey as part of his entourage. Once again, Martorano pulled up beside Indian Al's car, and opened fire. This time, a wild firefight followed, and it left another of Indian Al's men dead and two more wounded. That was on Whitey, too. But once again, Indian Al escaped.

"So now we had to change our strategy," Martorano told us. He'd take the same approach we'd used—don't go straight at the top guy, but work your way up from the bottom. If Indian Al was now protected by a gang of soldiers, start by taking out the soldiers. Then take out Indian Al. So— bang. Down went an associate, William O'Brien, when he was stopped at a light. Whitey was there, too. Then Martorano's friend Joe McDonald tracked an associate of Notarangeli's to Florida and killed him there. Then Martorano popped Indian Al's brother, Indian Joe Notarangeli—the one he killed at the Pewter Pot, when he was dressed like a butcher.

In increasing desperation, Indian Al offered to meet Angiulo, Winter, and Martorano at a North End café in hopes of working something out that would keep him alive. He pushed $50,000 across the table to Angiulo and promised to take care of Folino's widow for life. Angiulo was grateful for the consideration, but noncommittal. After that first meeting, Indian Al sought another. This time, Martorano offered to give Indian Al a ride to the meeting place. He didn't have much choice. Martorano left the driving to an associate, while he took the seat directly behind, and let Indian Al ride up front. Once the car was moving, he reached forward with his snub-nosed twenty-two, put a bullet in Indian Al's head just below the ear, and then added another to the slumped-over corpse, just to be sure.

Martorano and the driver pulled over, rolled up the body in a moving company's blanket, and shoved it into the trunk. Then they abandoned the car. When the corpse surfaced, some Boston homicide detectives were called in to investigate what had all the earmarks of a mob hit. When they returned to headquarters on Berkeley Street, an FBI agent, newly returned to town, was there to talk things over with them. His name was John Connolly. No one asked how he'd gotten there so quickly.

———

Telling us this, Martorano seemed more to be reciting than speaking. We weren't convinced yet that he was telling us the truth. Because of the importance of consistency, we did everything we could to trip him up. We'd ask him a question, note the answer, then double back much later to ask the same question again and make sure the answers matched up. Or we'd bore in on a detail, to make sure that there really was something behind it, that he wasn't just making something up to fill out a story. Or we'd tell him he'd said something to us before, even though he hadn't, to check his reaction. And each time, he'd stay firm. "No, I didn't say that," he'd insist. "I never said that. I said this." And he was always right.

At a certain point, though, all the killing got to me. Not the killing itself, but the way he talked about it, so flat and factual. As if the victims weren't people to him. Somebody lives, somebody dies. It was no big deal which was which. It was as if he was describing the best route to Providence, Interstate 95 or Route 24. You could go either way. But these corpses had been people once, people with families, with hopes. It shouldn't have been up to Martorano to decide if these people should be dead forever, with no chance of coming back.

When he was finished telling us about Indian Al Notarangeli, about how he'd killed five people to get one, I was starting to feel it. In this job, you get used to hearing about some pretty horrendous things, but it isn't often that you get to hear from the guy who did them. Maybe I should have let it go, but I couldn't. I had to speak up.

"John, let me ask you something. You've been telling us about all these murders. I've got to ask you: Did it bother you to kill all these people?"

He looked at me as if he didn't understand the question. "Well, yeah, it was my job. It was a job I was doing for my friends, people I was very loyal to." He paused for a moment. "At the time."

"So you don't feel any remorse? No regrets? You could kill these people and just walk away and have dinner?"

He looked at me, and his eyes softened for a moment. "Of course I think about it," he told me. "I think about it every day." It was the first time he'd shown any emotion, and it hit us all hard. "Of course I do." Like it was obvious. "I'll never forget the things I did. But that doesn't change anything. I can't bring anybody back. But do I feel remorse? Yeah, I do. Every single day." Then he looked at me. "But there's nothing I can do about it now."

— CHAPTER 28 —

As the murder stories went on, Martorano gradually got into the ways that Whitey and Flemmi pulled Connolly into their schemes, or he pulled them into his. For some of it, Martorano simply wasn't in a position to know, since he hadn't been aware of Connolly's role. Later on, he would have a clearer idea. But for the Castucci murder, only we could see the full story of what went down.

Joe McDonald had been a Winter Hill pal who'd helped Martorano out on a number of his murders—including Indian Al's—as a spotter or a driver or, once or twice, a killer. But he had his own activities, and when he realized he'd been indicted for some of them, he skipped town and hid out in New York City. Since he had helped Martorano plenty, Martorano gave him the name of a hustler up in Revere who maybe could help him find a crash pad in the city.

Richard Castucci owned a few nightclubs in Revere, and he gambled and did some booking on the side. When Bulger and Flemmi heard about the Castucci connection, they freaked. They screamed at Martorano to get McDonald out of there right away, because Castucci was an FBI snitch. They never said how they knew, of course, and Martorano didn't ask. He assumed that it was just another piece of information that Flemmi and Bulger had access to because of their connections.

Once Bulger and Flemmi had acknowledged that they knew Castucci was talking to the feds, they had to make clear that they weren't in league with him, and they did it in a very dramatic way. When Castucci came around to collect some gambling debts from the Winter Hill group, Flemmi and Bulger asked to meet him in an apartment down the street.

There, Whitey asked Castucci to take a seat at a card table. He'd piled up a good stack of money there.

"Go on, count it," Whitey told him. Castucci did as he was told; Whitey pulled up a chair across from him. Castucci was still counting when Martorano came up behind him with a thirty-eight snub-nosed revolver. When Castucci wheeled around, Martorano shot him in the forehead. They shoved the body into Castucci's car, drove it to a mall in Revere, and left it there in the parking lot.

Martorano did that one. But the FBI had a hand in it, too. For we learned later that the feds had lured Castucci into informing by lying to him. Through his nightclubs, Castucci was a low-level wannabe who developed some celebrity connections, such as Sammy Davis Jr. That made him someone the FBI would like to know better. When the feds had nothing on him that they could use to turn him, they made something up. They whispered to him that his wife was having an affair with a major drug dealer, Michael Caruana. Castucci was never the most stable guy, and the FBI figured the news would throw him. Maybe he'd kill Caruana; maybe he'd shoot his wife. Either way, the FBI could make use of the results. Or the feds could simply make themselves seem like Castucci's friends, telling him important facts he wouldn't have known otherwise. Whichever, they'd get some information from him in return. And they did, and they let Bulger and Flemmi know, and Castucci paid for it with his life.

With the Martorano debriefing, the killing went on and on. There was the murder of Jimmy O'Toole in 1973, after he'd said he wanted to kill Steve Flemmi and Howie Winter for their role in the gang wars. Flemmi took him out with a carbine, Martorano followed with a spurt of machine-gun fire, and Joe McDonald finished him off with a bullet in his brain. Edward Connors talked too much about the O'Toole hit, so Bulger tracked him to a pay phone where Connors was waiting for a call, and opened fire.

— CHAPTER 29 —

And then there was the death of Roger Wheeler. Of all the murders, this one was pivotal, and when Martorano got to it on that third and final day in El Paso, we all listened in complete silence, knowing that, at last, we were hearing evidence that would bring down Whitey and Flemmi and strike back at the FBI. We'd had our suspicions about it, but no hard facts, since we'd never spoken to anyone on the scene. The cover-up proved more serious than the initial crime. For the murder of Wheeler had required a second murder to protect the secret, and then two more after that. That got the murderers in ever deeper. Also, John Connolly, having known about the first murder, encouraged the second one to conceal it, and the third as an accidental extra to the second, and a fourth to be completely sure. By the time the killing was done, Connolly's fate was pulled in so tightly with Bulger's and Flemmi's that it was virtually indistinguishable from theirs. Their crimes became his. And Martorano was able to tell us all about it, because he was in on them.

Raised in Boston, Roger Wheeler had made a fortune in high tech in Tulsa. He plunked down $50 million to make some easy money as the owner of World Jai-Alai, putting on a lightning-fast Basque version of racquetball that involved two players hurling a ball about at speeds of over a hundred miles an hour. The gambling element made World Jai-Alai lucrative, but also shady, and its operations were closely watched in the dozen states where they were allowed. John Callahan had worked for Wheeler at World Jai-Alai. He'd been at a Boston accounting firm before that, and he styled himself as a stand-up Boston businessman. But he'd also had close ties with Winter Hill that stemmed from his friendship with Johnny Martorano's brother Jimmy, who had been his roommate when he was younger. Jimmy introduced him to Johnny, and the two hit it off even better. In 1978, when Johnny had to flee to Florida to escape prosecution in the race-fixing case, Callahan visited him down there at one hideout or another, and he let Martorano in on a secret—that he was going to take over World Jai-Alai from Wheeler. Callahan had been in on the franchise, but he'd had to step down after the Connecticut state police spotted him with a number of mobsters, including Martorano, and stripped him of his license to operate a pari-mutuel. Callahan had brought in a friend from the accounting firm, Richard Donovan, to become president of World Jai-Alai under Wheeler. Now that Callahan was out, Donovan offered to tell him certain details of the financial operation that would help him buy Wheeler out at a good price. He could also fix things on the inside that would encourage Wheeler to sell. Callahan assured Martorano that if the deal went through, he'd hand off the parking lot revenues to him, and to Bulger and Flemmi, presumably in exchange for their involvement in the business later on.

That was January 1981, but despite Donovan's maneuvering, Wheeler wouldn't sell. He didn't trust Callahan, and why should he? Wheeler had noticed that ever since Callahan came back on the scene, things had really fallen apart. The place was hemorrhaging money, starving Wheeler for the cash he needed to make his payments on the original loan for the purchase. Given the rising distrust, Callahan was afraid Wheeler might try to turn him in. And then Wheeler's director of security, the former FBI agent H. Paul Rico, who Callahan hired, provided another key bit of information. He whispered to Callahan that if Wheeler "were not around" he was pretty sure he could do business with Wheeler's wife. He meant himself, but he left the impression that he meant Callahan. Rico knew Callahan well enough to know what he'd do with such information.

Back in Boston, ever since the mid-1950s, when he was keeping tabs on Whitey, Rico had always somehow conveyed the impression that he should have been a mobster. He was cold in that way, and calculating. In any situation, he always seemed to be asking—what's in it for me? And here the answer was obvious—a helluva lot of easy money.

Now, Callahan knew perfectly well what Rico was saying, and it made perfect sense. Through Flemmi, Callahan asked Whitey about it, and Whitey agreed that murder was the only way to go. Whitey also suggested the murderer—Brian Halloran. That was a rare blunder, and it would prove catastrophic. Bulger had no business recommending Halloran for anything. He was a boozer, a cokehead, and such an idiot that Whitey called him "Balloonhead," sometimes to his face. And sure enough, after Bulger signed up Halloran, and gave him a down payment of $20,000, Halloran spent the money on a car and blew town. Nobody found it funny.

So Callahan asked Martorano if he'd do it. Martorano told us he really wasn't up for it, and would do it only if Bulger wanted him to. Bulger was a hard man to turn down. Martorano almost never even spoke to him. (In all those fifteen years on the lam, he did that only twice, once when Martorano's father, Andy, died.) He called Flemmi instead, and asked him to pass his question along to "the other guy." Flemmi could never say yes on his own; only Bulger could. When he did, and Martorano got the word, he told Callahan he was in.

The purchasing group would include Rico; this would have made most gangsters nervous, but Rico's tips had helped any number of them survive the gangland wars. Martorano brought in Joe McDonald, the fugitive Castucci gave up to the feds.

It was Rico who scoped out the situation. He told Martorano where to find Wheeler and how to identify him. When the plan was set, Martorano and McDonald flew to Oklahoma City, then drove a rental car on to Tulsa. There, they waited in a motel until Whitey sent down the guns they'd need. They also checked out different sites Rico had recommended for the hit: the driveway to Wheeler's home; the area outside another business, called Telex, that he had in town; and the parking lot at the Southern Hills Country Club, a stop on the PGA circuit, where he played golf. Of these, Martorano and McDonald were inclined toward the last. Rico had let them know that Wheeler had a standard tee time on Saturdays at the club. Martorano and McDonald drove over there, and it was exactly the right spot for the job. On Saturday, after the guns arrived, the two of them stole a Ford from a mini-mall and drove to the club that afternoon. They waited among all the other cars parked in the lot for a golfer who looked like Wheeler to make his way to the black Cadillac that Rico said he drove.

Spotting a man who matched Wheeler's description, Martorano climbed out of the car and followed behind him, waiting to see if he went to the Cadillac. To disguise himself, Martorano wore a false mustache and beard and clear gold-rimmed glasses. The man stopped, turned toward the car, unlocked the driver's door, and climbed in. As the man tried to close the door, Martorano yanked it open and fired one bullet between his eyes. He left the body there, twisted in the front seat, a splattering of blood on the headrest.

They heard about the murder on the radio. It was Roger Wheeler.

———

This worried Flemmi. Flemmi and Bulger's kills didn't usually make the news. He wanted to be sure that Martorano would get out of there, but Martorano and McDonald made a hasty exit on their own and were soon back in Florida.

Through Connolly, Bulger and Flemmi found out that Balloonhead Halloran was an informant for the FBI. Supposedly, he'd already squealed to the feds about Whitey's murdering the bookie Louie Litif—the one Chico Krantz had told us about, who liked to color-coordinate his underwear. Now he was telling the feds about Martorano's role on Wheeler, and he was only minutes from giving up Callahan, too. And, if he dared, maybe Bulger and Flemmi.

Halloran had to go. Whitey did it. Wearing a fake beard in order to look like Halloran's sworn enemy Jimmy Flynn, Whitey found Halloran getting into a parked car on the Boston waterfront. After Halloran settled into the driver's seat, Whitey drove by with an automatic carbine firing right into his face. Whitey took out not only Halloran but also a passenger, Michael Donahue, who had the misfortune to be in Halloran's car.

But that didn't entirely contain the damage. Flemmi arranged for a meeting with Martorano and "the other guy" at the La Guardia Marriott to figure out what to do. The meeting was brief, and Bulger did most of the talking. Our friend has really saved our ass on that one, he said, meaning

Connolly. Bulger rarely used names, figuring he was being bugged. Now that Halloran had told the feds about how Martorano had killed Wheeler, Callahan had to go next. Connolly had assured Bulger and Flemmi that he'd checked into it, and Callahan had no special relationship with the FBI that he knew about. But Connolly still didn't trust him. The guy was weak, and Connolly was afraid he'd give everybody up as soon as the feds looked at him, which they were likely to do soon. Connolly told Bulger and Flemmi that Callahan had to go. They agreed. And then they looked at Martorano.

"Well, OK, but I don't want to do it," Martorano told them. He went a fair way back with Callahan. They'd spent a lot of time drinking together, palling around. He'd never killed a friend before, and he really didn't want to start with Callahan.

If he didn't, they were all screwed. That was Whitey's point. Plus, they wouldn't be in this mess if Martorano hadn't vouched for Callahan in the first place. And finally, Callahan was running around telling stories to all the wrong people. No, there was no question about it. Callahan had to be done, and Martorano had to do it. That was all there was to it.

It took Martorano a while to come around, but he finally did. What choice did he have?

Bulger had one last suggestion. Don't do it in Boston. There was too much heat there. Do it in Florida.

The meeting lasted maybe half an hour. When everyone was leaving, Martorano told Flemmi and Bulger he was glad that Connolly was looking out for them like that. Of course, at that point he had no idea about the full deal. He was thinking it was just Connolly looking out for Billy Bulger's brother. But he was still upset that it had come to this, choosing between killing a friend and spending the rest of his life in prison.

Martorano returned to Florida and tried to get a sense of where Callahan would be. He couldn't get anywhere going through Callahan's secretary. Meanwhile, Flemmi kept calling and calling to see where things stood. He was increasingly eager to get Callahan out of the way. He offered to help Martorano out on the hit, but Johnny said he'd rather use Joe McDonald again. Finally, Martorano found out that Callahan would be flying to Fort Lauderdale airport in a few days, and managed to reach him on the phone. He told Callahan he was coming in around then, too, and he'd be happy to give him a ride into the city. They needed to catch up, anyway. Grateful for the lift, Callahan said fine. He'd love to chat.

Martorano arrived in a stolen van, McDonald in a separate car. Martorano waited for Callahan by the curb, and when his friend arrived, he slid his bag into the rear while Callahan took a seat up front. Then Martorano reached into the backseat for his twenty-two, with a silencer, and popped Callahan twice in the back of the head. Martorano had taken the precaution of covering the upholstery with plastic sheeting, to help with the cleanup. McDonald emerged from his car to help Martorano roll Callahan into the backseat. They took the van to a garage, where they transferred the body to the trunk of Callahan's Cadillac. (Callahan had given his friend a spare set of keys.) Then they left the Cadillac at Miami International.

That murder went unsolved.

The partnership's effort to buy World Jai-Alai fell to Paul Rico. If he had an angle on Wheeler's widow, nothing ever came of it.

———

This was all back in 1981, long before I got involved with OC. A young detective in Tulsa, Mike Huff, landed the homicide case, and, while he'd never been able to make any arrests, he'd never let go of the case, either. He could not believe that Wheeler had been the victim of a random murder, not in the gangster-infested world of jai alai. About two years into his investigation, he flew to Boston to see what he could get out of the FBI. Despite the suspected involvement of Boston mob figures like Bulger, Flemmi, and Martorano, the FBI showed no interest in the case, or in Huff.

Now, seventeen years after the murder, Huff was still on it, and I thought we owed him a chance to make some progress. So, before I left for El Paso, I told him we'd be talking to Martorano, and if we got anything useful, I'd let him know. After Martorano got into Wheeler's murder in some detail, I gave Huff a call and offered him a chance to hear some of it for himself. He got all excited and made plans to fly down right away.

"But it's for you only, all right?" I reminded him. "This gets out, and we're all in deep shit."

"Understood," he told me.

As soon as he stepped into the Valachi Suite, I could see the eagerness on his face. When we got him inside and sat him down, he asked questions of Martorano, the same as we did, but his were all about clearing Wheeler. He didn't get anything we didn't get, but what he got was from Martorano directly, and it excited him. When he was leaving, he told me how grateful he was.

"Remember, though. Keep this to yourself for now. No media. And no FBI."

He gave me his assurances, and drove off.

———

That night, I got a call from Fred Wyshak that another couple of investigators wanted in, too. Jamie Herbert and John Durham.

This was not good news. Herbert, of course, was Wyshak's colleague in the USAO, and not exactly a supporter of ours, most often advocating for the FBI. Durham had been brought into the USAO to do what Prouty had failed to: investigate the FBI thoroughly. Fred knew that the idea of bringing in the FBI was a nonstarter with Martorano, but he was in a bind.

"Why are they coming?"

"To talk to him."

"But why?"

"You know how Durham is on FBI corruption. He wants to ask Martorano a few things about that. And Jamie wants FBI input on the proffer."

"For chrissake, Fred. That's total bullshit. We handle the agreement. That's our agreement with Martorano and his attorney. We do it, and nobody else. Certainly not the FBI. Are they crazy?"

"I know, Tommy, but they wanted me to call you on this. They want you to hang in until they get there. They're coming. Maybe you can hash it all out when they get there."

I didn't like any part of it. We'd been there almost a week, and were set to leave. What was Martorano going to think? Could he still trust us? "These aren't real good questions for Martorano at this point."

"I hear you," Fred told me. "But you know how it is. There's no saying no to these guys."

"They don't really want us to close a deal with Martorano, do they?"

He had to laugh at that. "You could say that."

"By the way, did they even get Martorano's attorney's OK to meet with him?" I asked.

"Nope."

"And they're going to fly two thousand miles down here without it? Christ, if we tried that, they'd be all over us."

"Yeah, but they're them."

They came the next night, Herbert and Durham. All four of us stayed on an extra night to wait for them, irritating as that was. And we drove over to greet them at the airport—and to tell them the whole effort was wasted. "Martorano isn't going to talk to you," I told them.

"How do you know?" Herbert asked me.

"I know."

We drove back to the prison facility the next morning, all six of us crammed into a rental sedan. Not much conversation. And we went straight in to Martorano. He scarcely looked up when Herbert and Durham came into the room and explained who they were.

"We would like it if the FBI could get involved with the proffer, maybe," Herbert said weakly.

"And I'm here on the FBI corruption task force," Durham added. "We thought you might have a few things to say about that."

Martorano looked both men dead in the eye, first one, then the other. "I really don't want to talk to either of you about anything."

So the trip wasn't really about the proffer. No surprise there. That was just an excuse. As had happened so many times before, they were simply trying to find a way to bring the FBI in to our interview—so they could figure out what Martorano was telling us, and how to limit the damage. From the top to the bottom of the FBI, information is power. Whatever the feds' plan was, it didn't work. Martorano refused to speak to them, and they flew home. It had to have been an embarrassment for them. They'd flown two thousand miles for twenty minutes of no. Stern may not have abided by our agreement, but Martorano had certainly lived up to his. No FBI meant no FBI.

———

When we returned to Boston, we found out that the FBI had gotten most of Martorano's testimony, and so had the newspapers. And much of it was verbatim. How'd they get it?

I was terrified that—again—Wolf would think it was us. I knew that Herbert was itching to see that it *was* us. I knew it wasn't, but I couldn't think who would do such a thing. Herbert and Durham had been in with Martorano only briefly. And that left only Mike Huff, but it seemed inconceivable that he would have run to the newspapers with secret testimony.

After the story broke, he tried to deny it, but then he admitted it was true. In his excitement, he'd told a Boston FBI agent about his interview with Martorano, and word had gotten out to a reporter.

With someone like Martorano, you have to do everything you can to make him feel you are in complete control of the situation. There is nothing you don't know, and no trouble you're not ready for. That was not the case here. Martorano would have every reason to think that we'd lost the handle on this case.

If Martorano had told us to go screw, I would have understood. But he didn't. We still offered him the best chance of punishing Bulger and Flemmi, and of managing his sentence so he'd see his son again within a reasonable period of time. Plus, it was us or nobody. So he hung in with us, and we with him.

Because his testimony would be so critical to the prosecution of the murder case against Bulger and Flemmi, we wanted to be absolutely sure of all the details. The following April, Doherty, Duffy, Johnson, and I flew back to Tulsa, this time with Martorano, who was accompanied by federal Marshals. We wanted him to walk us through his movements in his week down there with McDonald, so we could see where he said everything happened, and compare it with the actual landscape. It had been nearly twenty years, and Tulsa had changed a lot, adding high-rises, sprawling a little farther out into the desert. But all the places that he described initially were still there, although obviously they had changed some over the years. Despite the length of time, he had little trouble directing us to the motel where he and McDonald stayed; to the office building that had once housed the other company of Wheeler's, Telex; to the Wheeler house, and finally to the country club parking lot. It was all just as he said.

When we went to the country club for our last stop, it was a cheerful afternoon, with a bright blue sky overhead, but I felt uneasy as we made our way down the parking lot where Martorano had followed Wheeler in those last few minutes of his life.

"Here," he said, gesturing to a space by some low bushes. "The Cadillac was right here, facing in." The spot was empty now. And then he went through it—where Wheeler sat, where Martorano stood as he pulled the trigger. It was all like it was happening right now.

————

After that, Martorano relaxed a little, and on the way back he told us a few stories about a life in crime. He told us about a couple of close calls in Florida, when the cops came within inches of catching him, once when he was hiding in a Winnebago. In Hawaii, he was catching some sun when the actor Tom Selleck asked if he'd be an extra on a *Magnum PI* episode he was filming. When Martorano said no, Selleck said he was stunned. "I've never been turned down before." But his favorite story was from the Sugarshack, a bar in Boston, in the summer of 1962. Knocking back a few drinks there one night, Johnny realized that the man getting lacquered on the stool next to him was Earl Wilson, probably the best pitcher the Red Sox had that year. The two of them stayed up all night drinking and telling stories, and they were both thoroughly potted the next day. Wilson was due to pitch the next afternoon, and Martorano dropped him off at Fenway, and then laid down the biggest bet of his life on the Angels, who Wilson would be pitching against. And lost it all when Earl Wilson threw a no-hitter and added a long home run to beat the Angels 2–0.

By the time he was done, Martorano had provided testimony on nineteen mur-ders that Bulger or Flemmi had participated in. Most were in and around Boston, but several were elsewhere, as in the Wheeler case, where the killings took place in Tulsa and Miami as well as in Boston. As representatives of the State Police, we had worked with the district attorneys of the various Massachusetts counties where so many of the crimes had been committed. But we had held no meetings out of state. And all the prosecutors would need to be on board if we were going to make a single deal with Martorano for his testimony.

To work everything out, we called a big meeting of representatives of all jurisdictions. In deference to the USAO, which would handle the federal case against Bulger and Flemmi, we had it in the USAO's boardroom in the handsome new courthouse named for Congressman Joe Moakley down by the Boston waterfront. There must have been about twenty people there, some of them from other parts of the country.

In setting up the meeting at the USAO, we made it very clear to everyone that the FBI would not be included. Martorano had insisted on that. We'd be revealing a good bit of his testimony, and he would never have spoken to us as freely as he had if he'd known the feds were listening in. And the different prosecutors and investigators needed the freedom to speak their own minds, too.

At the USAO in the federal courthouse, we were all getting ready to go into the conference room when Wyshak came up to me with one of those hangdog looks of his.

"Hey, Tommy," he said. "The FBI is going to sit in on this meeting."

Obviously, it wasn't Fred's idea. Still, I practically exploded. It was El Paso all over again. "Fred, are you kidding? We made it clear to everyone that the FBI would not be attending. Come on, we talked about this."

"But they want in, and Stern wants them in."

"This is not our agreement, Fred. They said they'd stay out." I couldn't believe it—when does it end?

He moved away from me, and I thought that was the end of it. We all stepped into the conference room and took our seats at the big table. The meeting had just started when the door suddenly opened wide, and in walked Jamie Herbert and Stan Moody, the FBI case officer assigned to watch over us on Bulger.

The place went dead silent; there was shock on everyone's face. This was the opposite of what everyone had agreed would happen. What part of no did the FBI not understand? I wanted the feds out of there in the worst way, but that wasn't going to happen. Herbert and Moody both grabbed seats, and they stayed there for the whole meeting. They didn't say a word. I could think of almost nothing else.

I was furious with Fred, but I couldn't really blame him. It was the situation. He was in the USAO, he had to do what he was told, and that's just how it was.

In frustration, I wrote a long letter to U.S. Attorney Stern, laying out how I thought the State Police and the USAO should work together on Bulger. I probably should have kept it to a page or two, but I went on for almost twenty. I was a lieutenant stationed out in central Massachusetts as troop operations officer, and that was still a pretty humble position from which to address a U.S. attorney at such length.

I shouldn't have taken the risk, but I was sick of all the runarounds, the butting in, the deception, the politicking, and basically all the *crap* the FBI was dropping on us. I wanted Stern to know that, whatever he might have heard, or whatever he might think, we were trying to do our jobs. I wasn't trying to be difficult. We had no vendetta against the FBI. We were trying to put Whitey Bulger away. The FBI and the State Police might be locked in a bad marriage, but I was still committed to working on it.

"Some would like to portray us as being uncooperative," I wrote. "But I believe we have gone above and beyond normal expectations in trying to make a relationship work." I took him through the history of everything since I signed up with OC in 1984. I tried to play it straight, just the facts, but I am sure he could smell the anger on the page. And then I came to the point. The FBI was trying to kill us off, and I gave all the examples. I trod lightly, for fear that if I laid it out the way it really was, he'd think I was laying it on too thick. All I asked was that the USAO be an honest referee here, and not in the tank for the FBI. The FBI was dangerous when wounded, and Stern was the only one in Boston who could tell the FBI to back off before people got hurt. "We all know that politics is a fact of life, however in this case it should not and cannot be the governing and deciding fact," I told him. I was sending copies of the letter to my two commanding officers, Lieutenant Colonel Regan and Colonel Hillman, too. "I feel that due to my extensive experience in this investigation that I must bring this matter to the attention of my superiors," I concluded. "There is nothing left to do." *

_____

I never heard back from Stern, but I later found out Farmer's reaction. "I bet we'll see it in the paper someday," he said.

_____

And that's the way things were in those days. It almost made me miss inves-tigating Whitey and Flemmi. They were evil men who did evil things, and it was clear: catch them, convict them, and send them to prison. That was the drill. But the FBI? The corruption was like a radiation leak. It's dangerous, maybe lethal, but it's invisible, and you never know exactly where it's coming from. With the FBI and Bulger, you couldn't tell who was actively in on the plot to aid Bulger and Flemmi, who merely supported it, who knew about it but didn't do anything about it, who did not want to know about it but did, and who was completely innocent although not to the point of blowing any whistle.

_____

The Wolf hearings had created such a furor that the Department of Justice realized that it could no longer sweep the matter under the rug as the Prouty investigation did. The DOJ couldn't leave it to the FBI to clean house but needed to go up a level, and it turned over the investigation of the FBI to a freshly minted assistant U.S. attorney, John Durham, the

* See Appendix for the full letter.

one who dropped in on us when we questioned Martorano. Despite my suspicions of Herbert and some of the other assistant U.S. attorneys, I was somewhat hopeful that Durham might get somewhere, largely because he wasn't FBI, and he wasn't from Boston. He'd been a prosecutor from Hartford, Connecticut, who had handled OC cases; and Dan Doherty, a straight arrow if ever there was one, vouched for him.

He would now be a special prosecutor, so he couldn't just write up a report and walk away. This was a criminal matter, and he was expected to charge individuals with crimes. He would use FBI agents for the investigation, but they'd be drawn from all over the country, a tacit admission that FBI agents from Boston were not to be trusted. Still, given his efforts to be independent of the Boston office of the FBI, it wasn't encouraging that Durham set up shop right across from One Center Plaza, the feds' new quarters downtown.

— CHAPTER 30 —

A few months after I wrote to U.S. Attorney Stern, I got some good news. Colonel Hillman, the one who'd sent me to Leominster, was being replaced by a new superintendent, Colonel John DiFava. A short time after that I made captain, and DiFava returned me to headquarters to serve as chief of staff for Lieutenant Colonel Jack Cunningham. He was in charge of Field Services, which covers most of the State Police activities. He'd done some investigation, and he believed in the Bulger case. I still couldn't work on the case full-time, but I could watch over it more closely than I could in Leominster, and I had the support of the colonel and my lieutenant colonel. And I was back.

———

And then there was Kevin Weeks. If Martorano knew the Whitey of the past, Kevin knew the Whitey of the present, right up to the time he fled in 1995, and even since.

Weeks was a real Southie type—tough, street-smart, humorless, and loyal. He would never have made a move against Whitey if Martorano hadn't. Like both Bulgers and John Connolly, Weeks had grown up in the Old Harbor housing project. He was one of six children; his father changed tires for a living. He'd been a decent boxer in his teens, and after graduating from South Boston High, he'd turned semipro as a middleweight. He'd taken a job at Whitey's bar, the Triple O's, and Whitey liked the way he'd handled himself, dispensing punishment only as needed. Whitey didn't like many people, but he liked Weeks and let him hang around. People said that they were like father and son, that they looked out for each other. As it turned out, the concern went only one way.

Kevin was one of the thugs I'd seen frantically dashing about Southie that last night when we were both trying to find Whitey—they wanted to warn him about us, and we wanted to arrest him. Since then, we'd gotten the earlier info from the counterfeiter suggesting continuing ties to Whitey as a fugitive, but we never had enough to move on Weeks.

We eventually got to Weeks with the help of a terrific agent named Dave Lazarus at the IRS, plus Johnson and Doherty and Tom Reilly's attorney general's office. After months of legwork, we hit Weeks with a serious package of indictments. Teams of troopers fanned out over South Boston to get him. Mike Scanlan, Trooper Nunzio Orlando, and Lazarus were the ones to spot Weeks on N Street as he was returning to his car.

"Kevin," Scanlan called out to him. "You got a minute?" Weeks didn't recognize him but said he was headed to the Rotary Variety, Whitey's old store, and could meet him there if he wanted. Then Scanlan identified himself and told Weeks to stay right where he was.

Then Johnson, Doherty, and Duffy swooped in to help out, and Doherty arranged to bring Kevin back to his DEA offices near City Hall. There, they handed him the indictment. It was long and involved, with twenty-nine counts in all, including extortion, racketeering, money laundering, conspiracy to distribute drugs, and several others. These were serious charges that had taken us months to put together. Weeks's head dropped as he read through all of them.

This was November 1999, long after Whitey's flight and Flemmi's revelations. By now, Weeks knew that Whitey Bulger was not what he seemed. Later, he told us exactly when he found out. It was back when Flemmi was testifying. Weeks had the TV going in the background while he read a book. The ten o'clock news came on with a report about Flemmi's relationship with the FBI. Weeks lurched out of his seat, sending the book to the floor. He stormed around the house screaming, *"What the fuck? What the fuck?"* He couldn't believe it. He was so sure he'd misunderstood that he watched until the eleven o'clock news came on and he realized he had it right. Steve Flemmi was an FBI informant, and probably Whitey Bulger was, too.

Weeks was full of arrogance. You could see it on his face, and in the way he carried himself. As many charges as there were, and as detailed as they were, he figured he could beat them. No prosecutors would ever outsmart Kevin Weeks.

But a couple of veteran mob lawyers set him straight: even if he did get rid of most of the charges, which he probably wouldn't, he'd still spend a good twenty years in prison. And there was something else to consider. Now that everyone knew Flemmi and Whitey had been federal snitches, they might think Weeks was one, too. And that might not be healthy.

But he had the example of John Martorano. Weeks had never met Martorano, but he admired him. A lot of hoods did. Not flashy, not loud, but solid as anything. Others might think that Weeks was Bulger's son, but Martorano would have been a better fit as a father to him. Both of them told it like it was, and briefly. Neither ever wanted to be a legend, or the boss. They just did what they had to do, and no more. If Johnny Martorano turned state's evidence, then Kevin Weeks could, too. As Jimmy Martorano said, you can't rat a rat.

When Weeks was first arrested, he wanted to make clear to everyone that he was never going to give up his friends. That was the end of November. Early in December, Weeks told his girlfriend, Janice Connolly (no relation to John), to get in touch with our man Duffy and let him know that actually he'd like to talk about cooperating with us. (One columnist calculated that the turnaround from "cooperate never" to "cooperate now" took exactly fourteen days, and said that Kevin should be renamed "Two Weeks.")

As soon as Weeks said he wanted to talk, though, he stopped dealing from strength. He was still a tough guy, but a tough guy who needs something from you isn't quite so tough. On our side, we had nothing to lose. If Weeks could produce information that made it worthwhile for us to consider cutting his sentence, then we would. If he didn't, then he got nothing. It was pretty simple. On Kevin's side, the question was—when was he going to see that he needed us more than we needed him? The sneer on his face said never; it seemed welded on. But he loosened up eventually.

He wasn't the warmest guy, but I could work with him. I didn't care about any of the macho; I cared only about what he could give us. And if he could hand us Whitey, that was sure good enough for me. Because of Weeks's efforts to help Bulger secure fake IDs, I'd hoped that he might help us find Bulger. He'd been gone for almost five years, and nobody seemed to have a clue about where he was. There was talk that he was overseas, maybe in England. Or he could have been in Florida. Who knew? Not the FBI, anyway. A current alias, a location, a car. Anything that would jump-start the manhunt? Unfortunately, Kevin shook his head. He had no idea. While he'd been in touch with Whitey weekly for the first year or two, as Whitey called in from pay phones to see what was going on in Boston, the contact had fallen way off a year before, and Kevin said it was totally dead now. He didn't know where Whitey was.

Weeks was able to fill us in on why Whitey had fled. As Flemmi had told us, Connolly had tipped him off to the coming arrests at the end of December. Weeks said that, unlike Flemmi, Whitey had immediately left town, going to New York with Theresa Stanley. He'd holed up there in a hotel, and Weeks had gone down to see him, meeting them there outside the New York Public Library. But when the arrests didn't happen, Whitey had figured it was September all over again, and he started back to Boston on the evening of January 5. Driving up through Connecticut, though, he got news of the indictments over the radio. He immediately made a U-turn back to the city, and the two hunkered down there, just two more faces in a big city, for several more weeks. At one point, Weeks drove down to see them. Whitey asked him to meet them "at the lions," meaning outside the New York Public Library. Stanley soon got sick of life on the run with Whitey, who was never the most cheerful companion. She missed her kids and wanted to go home. Whitey drove her back to Southie and dropped her off with Weeks in a parking lot. He said he'd call her, but he never did. Weeks then picked up Catherine Greig.

If we couldn't use Kevin to find Whitey, I hoped that we could at least use him to tear down some of the legends that had sprung up about him.

Martorano had gone a long way toward implicating Bulger in Wheeler's murder, but there were others that we wanted to get him for, and we needed Weeks's help. Despite the revelations about Whitey's illicit relationship with the FBI, and his drug dealing, extortion, and racketeering, a lot of people around town continued to believe that Whitey wasn't really all that bad. If he was an informant, this line went, wasn't that a good thing? And if he was a gangster, so what? There are always gangsters.

But it was more than that. In media interviews, the FBI was promoting Whitey as a Robin Hood, supposedly keeping drugs *out* of South Boston.

And in Southie, the politics of forced busing still hung over everything. Even though that issue was from the 1970s, it created a "Southie against the world" mentality that had never gone away. Whitey had played into it back then, shooting out windows at the *Globe* offices late one night because he was infuriated by its pro-busing line. And he represented the harsh Southie approach to life, the attitude best expressed by a middle finger. The more that people elsewhere in the city were shocked by Whitey Bulger, the more they liked him in Southie.

But Kevin Weeks would change all that. He would lead us to the bodies.

When the year rolled over to 2000, on top of everything else we had to deal with the Y2K hysteria, preparing for a host of possible public-safety crises that, thankfully, never happened. By now Colonel DiFava had promoted me to major and assigned me to command the 230-man Troop A in Danvers, toward the North Shore. DiFava was still a believer in the Bulger investigation, so I was free to devote as much time to the case as I could spare.

On New Year's Day, Kevin Weeks was in the custody of the U.S. Marshals. With Weeks, even more than with the others, you never knew quite where you stood. But at bottom, working with informants is all about trust, and that has to go both ways. You expect them to tell the truth, and they expect you to honor your promises.

And that trust can only be developed one-on-one, or as close to one-on-one as you can get. Certainly, it can't be developed in a room full of people with different agendas firing off questions. But with Weeks, guess what. Once the FBI learned that we had flipped him, the feds wanted in. And they did the usual: they leaned on the USAO, this time on Durham.

In December 1999, we finally brought Weeks up to the new federal courthouse for the first of a series of formal interviews. He was represented by a former federal prosecutor, Dennis Kelly. On our side, it was me, Johnson, Doherty, and Duffy—and John Tutungian, of the original five, who'd been working for O'Malley and managed to get reattached to the Bulger case, at least for the time being.

All witnesses, even the most hard-boiled of them, tell stories. They're human, and that's what humans do. They give their version of the truth. But there are certain facts that are so monumental that there is no getting around them, no matter what anyone says. And those are the facts on which you can build your case. And, finally, Weeks gave them to us. He gave us the murders. Ones he saw and could describe in detail. And once he did, and we could confirm them, the legend of Whitey Bulger was over.

Still, before we could get anywhere with Weeks, we had to test his veracity. And we had our chance when he told us about the guns. He said that Bulger and Flemmi had stashed a small arsenal in an outbuilding in back of Flemmi's mother's house, the one pretty much next door to Billy Bulger's place.

Weeks told us exactly where to look: behind one wall in a little guesthouse that the Flemmis used primarily for hanging out and drinking beer, in back of the main house. They had everything there, Weeks told us. Handguns, semiautomatics, silencers. At least thirty guns altogether.

That was it, the perfect test. Either the guns were there or they weren't. So either he was telling us the truth, or he wasn't. We needed to move on that right away before those guns disappeared. Wyshak drew up the paperwork for the search warrant. That would take a day, so, while we waited for it, we turned Weeks back to the murders.

We went out to Mrs. Flemmi's house a few days later. It was a freezing Janu-ary day, with biting winds and several inches of dusty snow on the ground. Doherty, Johnson, and Duffy went with me, and I brought along some State Police crime scene personnel to do the special forensics of such a site, if we found it. Photographing everything, pulling off any fingerprints, mapping out the location. When we knocked on the door, Mike Flemmi answered. A shorter, wider version of his brother, Mike was an officer in the Boston police department; he and I had worked on some fugitive cases together. The third brother was the oldest, Jimmy "The Bear" Flemmi. Like his two brothers, Mike was an edgy guy, and I'd never felt comfortable around him. Having two mobsters for brothers will do that when you're in law enforcement. It was dizzying—here we had Stevie, Jimmy, and Mike Flemmi all together in one house, and Whitey's brother Billy Bulger next door.

We showed Mike the search warrant we'd obtained to look for the guns. Weeks had told us they were hidden inside a wall in a small cottage beside the house. Flemmi looked at the warrant, but he didn't seem too surprised, and he said almost nothing. This was revealing. If he'd showed up at my house with a search warrant for thirty guns on the premises, I'd have plenty to say. He found the key to the cottage and led us around to its front door. The place was basically just a rec room with a couch, a TV, some chairs, and a kitchenette. Weeks had told us that the guns were hidden inside the wall behind the refrigerator. While Flemmi stood by, arms crossed, radiating irritation, we pulled the fridge back from the wall. The wall was paneled, and the nails weren't gouged or dented as if they'd been pulled and re-hammered. Everything looked neat and tight, as though it had never been touched since it had been installed. But when I rapped on it with my knuckles, it sounded hollow.

We dug into a tool kit, pulled out a couple of hammers, popped the nails, and peeled the panels back. There was a shallow closet in there, with several shelves. We didn't see any guns. But we did find several gun racks— holders for what looked like a range of firearms, from handguns on up to automatic rifles, maybe even submachine guns. There were spaces for at least two dozen guns altogether, and maybe more. But the racks were all empty. Somebody had obviously cleaned them all out.

I glanced back at Flemmi and asked him if he knew anything about this. He shrugged, said no. But he was a poor actor, and it was plain he knew all about the guns, and had probably removed them himself. When we probed around inside with a flashlight, we found some boxes of bullets of various calibers, and a gun silencer or two. I glanced back at Mike, and he just kind of shrugged, as if to say: I don't know anything about that.

Finally, Johnson took the flashlight, peered down behind a strip of paneling we couldn't remove, and thought he saw something. He put on a pair of clear plastic gloves, reached all the way down, and came back up with a handgun.

I turned back to Mike. "Any idea how that got here?" I asked.

This time, Flemmi looked panicky. "Shit—I don't know," he said. "I've got no idea how that got there."

———

This time, it wasn't the FBI, at least not directly. We found out later that when Stevie Flemmi learned that Weeks was talking to us, he'd told Mike and Flemmi's stepson Billy Hussey to clean the gun locker out. They opened up the paneling, scooped out all the guns—machine guns and automatic weapons, just as we'd thought—stuffed them into some duffel bags, and drove them down to a storage facility in Florida. We found them all there later.

———

Staring at the handgun he missed, though, Mike had to wonder—had this gun been used in a murder? By his brother? In that case, would it convict Stevie of murder? And was Mike now an accessory?

The raid produced more than the gun. It showed that we could trust Kevin Weeks.

———

It was fairly late by then, maybe seven, and we were tired and hungry after a long day, so we went down to a dinner place called Farragut's for something to eat. We'd hardly started in when Stevie Johnson got a call on his cell. He listened for a few minutes, then shut off the phone.

"Hey, Tommy, that was a trooper. They're about to start digging."

"Shit, no. At Florian's?"

"You got it." Weeks had showed us the spot earlier, but we hadn't had a chance to get in there because we were so busy with the guns.

"Now?" It was freezing. The plan was to do Florian's tomorrow.

"O'Malley wants to get it going tonight," Stevie told me. "He's got the heavy machinery, the crime scene people, everything."

———

Guns were one thing, bodies another. I knew that, and obviously O'Malley did, too. After he took over from me as head of SSS, he'd pretty much ignored the Bulger investigation as a losing proposition. We'd been hitting roadblocks with USAO, had some bad luck with court rulings, and had trouble getting the witnesses we needed. So O'Malley had gone off and done his own thing with SSS, and that was OK with me.

Now that things were finally heating up on Bulger, and we were close to getting the bodies that would prove Whitey to be the murderer we all knew him to be, everything changed. Now O'Malley wanted in. I can't blame him—human nature. It was flattering, in its way. We had something desirable.

———

In law enforcement, you can pile racketeering charges up to the sky, but they'll never match a single count of murder, let alone several counts. Florian's could deliver us those, and we'd have Weeks's testimony to prove that Bulger and Flemmi had done it. The discovery would finally bring closure for families wondering what had happened to their loved ones. And it would make irrelevant Flemmi's belabored argument that the FBI had allowed any crimes up to murder. Well, this was murder.

Lots of times, murders are just part of the mobster business. Kill or get killed. But the murder of Debbie Davis was different, and Kevin Weeks had told us all about it. More than any of the others, this was the one that showed the savage side of Bulger and Flemmi. By all accounts—and plenty of other people knew Debbie—she was a sweetheart, gentle and trusting. The girl next door, the kind who'd babysit for your children and call you Mrs. or Mr. She looked like Farrah Fawcett, whose pinup was everywhere back then, because of the big blond hair, the radiant smile, and the curves. But there was still a lot of little girl in her.

Although Flemmi still had a wife from his days as a paratrooper, he lived with Marion Hussey, the mother of the Stephen who owned Schooner's and of Billy, who'd removed the guns, in that nice house with a tennis court out back in Milton. But he loved girls like Debbie, had loved several like her, and would love several more. He'd sneak around with them, act all excited about them, right up until they got into their twenties, when womanhood set in, and he'd lose interest. Davis had been Flemmi's girlfriend since she was seventeen. He met her in an upscale jewelry store in Brookline, one town over from Boston, where Davis worked at the counter after school. She was a high school junior. Flemmi was in his forties, and she was perfect for him.

It wasn't long before Stevie Flemmi and Debbie were tooling around town in his Jaguar, and he'd installed her in a love nest he rented in Brookline. He'd bought her stuff, too, like a Maserati. She must have loved the attention and the money, and maybe she was impressed, too, with the worldliness of a man like Stevie, who acted as if he knew everything and everyone. But she must have been aware of the sick rumors about another pert beauty who'd captured Flemmi's attention and with whom he had dallied for some time. This was Marion Hussey's own daughter, also named Debbie. That Debbie was his stepdaughter, and Flemmi had been abusing her since she was in grade school, if not before. Strung out on all the weirdness of being regularly molested by a mobster stepdad, Debbie Hussey was a mess. She did drugs, stripped in the Combat Zone, did anything to get by. It was both incest and sexual abuse, but nobody ever said anything about it, or at least nobody said anything that made a difference. No one ever said anything when it came to Stevie Flemmi. If a problem came up, he laid a little money on it. And if it kept coming up, it disappeared.

Debbie Davis stuck by him, seduced by the fast life. She knew that Flemmi ran with Whitey Bulger, that he was in with other mobsters, that he had a lot more money than he could account for, and that he never mentioned a legitimate job. She even knew about Connolly. Knowing anything about Connolly was knowing too much, and she knew a lot more than that. She was OK with all the craziness with the FBI, but it started to bother her that she was losing Stevie's attention. He seemed stressed all the time. (This was 1981, after all, the year of all the Wheeler murders.) Plus, she was sure there were other women. To show her he cared, he finally divorced his first wife, but that wasn't the point. She had to have wondered: What's the use? That summer when she turned twenty-six, she decided to take a little break from him and flew to Acapulco. There, she met a handsome young Mexican businessman who was respectable, was fun to be with, and genuinely adored her. He wasn't like Flemmi at all. She returned to visit him again a few months later, and stayed longer.

Flemmi must have seemed to be understanding, an older man who knew how things are. Because when she got back from Mexico the second time, she did something that was otherwise extremely risky. She tried to get clear with Flemmi. She wanted to break up. She loved her new man. Flemmi got angry, but that was to be expected. He didn't go crazy. He said she should come over to his parents' new house, the one where we later found the guns on East Third Street, to talk it over. Flemmi had just bought the house for his parents, and he wanted to show her around. She'd figured she'd be fine if Flemmi's parents were around. A couple of days later, after she went shopping with her mother, she dropped by the place as they'd arranged.

That was September 17, 1981. Debbie Davis had never been seen since.

Her disappearance was never investigated. No one in law enforcement ever asked Flemmi about what went on that afternoon. Everyone took Flemmi's word for it that she was a screwed-up kid who'd decided to blow town and get away from everything. She had her Mexican, after all. And she'd talked of wanting to go to California. In retrospect, it was obvious why no one in law enforcement pursued it: thanks to Connolly, the FBI had persuaded everyone to back off. The feds would handle it. But, of course, they never did, and the mystery of Debbie's disappearance was never solved. Despite the heavy suspicions of the Davis family, who knew plenty about Steve Flemmi, the matter was treated as a routine missing person case, nothing pressing. Eventually, just about everyone except her family and friends forgot that Debbie Davis had ever lived.

————

That was everything that was known about Debbie Davis until we talked to Kevin Weeks, and he told us the rest, because he'd gotten the lowdown from Bulger. When Debbie stepped inside that door, Whitey and Stevie were waiting for her. It was only them. Flemmi's parents weren't around. Neither of them had any plans to work anything out with Debbie. She knew too much, and she had to go. Bulger grabbed her and tied her to a chair, and then wrapped duct tape around her head, sealing her mouth. Then, when she was immobilized, Flemmi loomed over her. As she looked up at him in terror, he leaned down, kissed her on the forehead, and whispered she would be going "to a better place." Then Bulger leaped toward her, brought his hands around her neck, and squeezed. She must have struggled and kicked; strangle victims never go easily. But Bulger was unrelenting, and she soon went limp. Later, Flemmi claimed that he was so angry at Bulger that he nearly shot him right there. But, of course, he did not. He let it be. "His ego got in the way," Weeks told us with a shrug, as if it was no big deal. "He couldn't take her leaving him for another guy, especially a Mexican."

Weeks said that Whitey and Flemmi stuffed the body into a plastic garbage bag, threw it into the back of a trunk, and then buried it somewhere along the shore of the Neponset River, on the Quincy side. He didn't know exactly where. He just knew it was down there with the body of Tommy King, a mobster Whitey had dispatched in 1975. As Weeks told it, King had made the mistake of making a fist at Whitey after the two had words. Later, Whitey made King think that he'd forgotten all about it, and they should all go out in the car when Whitey was, as Weeks said, "looking for someone to kill." King had stuffed himself into a bulletproof vest, thinking he was going out on a hit, and sat in the passenger seat, the death seat. Whitey was behind, in the murder seat. King got it in the back of the head. Because Weeks couldn't be sure about the exact location of those graves, our plan had to be to start with other grave sites he was sure of and work our way up.

That afternoon, before we went to Flemmi's mother's house, Doherty, Duffy, and O'Malley, along with a few U.S. Marshals, brought Weeks out in handcuffs to point out the spot where he'd helped Whitey and Flemmi bury the bodies. Even though Weeks probably hadn't been out to this part of Dorchester in years, he directed them to Florian's as if he came out every morning. Turn here, turn there, and there it was.

Florian's is a function room owned by the Boston firefighters' union, a modest place for a dinner dance or a banquet. A driveway passes in front of it, and then there's a thicket of trees and some low bushes across the street, which settle down into a gulley that must drop five feet off road level.

It was not the most obvious place for a mass grave, and that's probably the reason Whitey chose it. Just a dumping ground, the bones of the dead all heaped together, Weeks said, about eight feet down. The whole idea was hideous, a burial ground just off the road, right where banquet guests would come out. And the three bodies joined together forever, like a family: Bucky Barrett, John McIntyre, and Debbie Hussey. This was the wreckage that Whitey left behind.

Bucky Barrett was the first to die. He was a safecracker, drug dealer, jeweler, and bank robber who'd failed to cut in Whitey on a $1.5 million bank heist in nearby Medford. Instead, he'd handed Frank Salemme $100,000 to protect him from Whitey. That did not sit well, and two years later, Whitey lured Bucky to a friend's house at 799 East Third Street to take a look at some hot diamonds. When Bucky arrived, Whitey thrust an automatic rifle in his face and told him to sit down at the kitchen table. Stevie shackled his legs to his chair while Whitey trained the gun on Bucky's face. He complained about Barrett's deal with Salemme and demanded compensation. Bucky told Whitey where he'd stashed money around town, and Whitey and Stevie drove around collecting what they could while Weeks watched Barrett. The two came back with $50,000. Bucky said his prayers. Exhausted from the ordeal, he asked to lie down. Stevie led him downstairs for a nap, and Whitey shot him from behind. The basement had an earth floor, and, with a small military shovel, Flemmi dug a shallow grave for Barrett. Bulger and Flemmi stripped the corpse, chopped off the fingertips and yanked the teeth, and dropped Barrett into the hole. They spread lime over the body before covering it up. Afterward, Bulger started calling Flemmi "Dr. Mengele."

————

Then came the deckhand McIntyre, who had been buried in the basement at 799 as well.

————

And finally, it was Debbie Hussey. She was never the steady that Davis was, but then, Flemmi had to do his best to conceal the relationship, considering that he was living with her mother and regarded her as his daughter. Like Davis, she was twenty-six when the fun went out of the relationship for Flemmi. He'd turned his attention to other girls, younger ones, and that made Debbie furious. But she knew too much, and he could never just let her go.

Before she broke with him, though, Flemmi asked her to meet him one last time. At 799. He'd bought her a fur coat first, to let her know there were no hard feelings. But as soon as she was inside the door, Whitey was on her, slamming her to the ground, then hooking his legs around her waist and groping for her neck with his hands. Debbie was small, barely five feet, and weighed nothing. She didn't put up much of a struggle. He squeezed furiously, relaxed his grip only to see her surge back to life, and then squeezed again. Finally, she lay still, her lips and face a faint blue, her eyes bulging. Flemmi bent over her and put an ear to her chest. He insisted he heard a heartbeat.

Weeks was watching, horrified. He was sure she was dead. "But Stevie and Whitey sometimes got into this thing, where they competed with each other to see who could be tougher when it came to killing people." Stevie took some clothesline, looped it around her neck, and twisted it ever tighter with a stick until he was sure it was over. Together, Whitey and Flemmi yanked off her clothes and removed her identifying details. Then they carried her downstairs and dropped her into a ditch that Weeks had dug for her there. But he'd miscalculated, and Hussey ended up almost on top of McIntyre.

That was 1984. A year later, Whitey and Stevie learned that his friend was planning to sell 799. They thought of buying the house themselves, but ended up enlisting Weeks to help them dig up the three bodies and move them somewhere else. They did it on Halloween weekend. Bulger chose the Florian's site, and the three of them—Whitey, Stevie, and Kevin Weeks—set to digging a deep hole in the gulley to receive the bodies. At 799, the work was far grislier, as the bodies released such a horrible stench when they were uncovered that Weeks had to rush upstairs to an open window. Flemmi remained with the bodies, and when Weeks returned, he said Flemmi had "a wild look."

The bodies were hideous beyond belief. The lime had eaten them away, and Barrett's skull had snapped off at the spine, so that it rolled loose when the three tried to lift his corpse free. Hussey was wedged in on top of McIntyre, so that when Weeks tried to pry her loose with a pickax, he accidentally drove it into her chest. Finally, though, they were able to pack the remains into three body bags, and then carry them to a station wagon that Whitey called the Hearse and drive to Florian's. Because it was Halloween weekend, Whitey pointed out, no one would pay much attention to them. Working in the dark, they settled the bodies into the open holes, and then packed the loose soil down on them.

———

With the officers guarding him, and his wrists handcuffed, Weeks directed everyone to the spot, thick with underbrush, across from Florian's. "There," Weeks said, pointing. The Marshals took Weeks back into custody, and we obtained warrants to search the site and the outbuilding at Flemmi's mother's house. Since it was getting late, and cold, we decided to hunt for the guns first. We'd come back to search for the bodies the next day.

It was nearly evening, darkness was falling, and the temperature was down in the single digits and likely to fall lower. But O'Malley insisted on going after the bodies anyway. He'd called in earthmoving equipment and a six-man crime scene unit, and he set up a State Police command post—an RV with radio equipment, conference room, and heat. He set the superbright lights going to light the whole scene like a movie set. People started pulling in to see what was going on, and soon the media people with the TV trucks were there, with satellite feeds.

A backhoe was grinding away when I got there. I found O'Malley standing in the driveway. When he saw me, he gave off an icy chill that was far worse than anything winter was doing. At the time, I outranked him—I was a major and he was a detective lieutenant—but that was nothing compared with the fact that I had put in ten years on Bulger and he'd put in about ten minutes. His boss, Rick Fraelick, Deputy Commander of Investigative Services, and Lieutenant Colonel Paul Regan, head of the Division of Investigative Services, were planning to come by shortly, and probably for the same reason.

"What's going on here, Jack?" I asked O'Malley, as genially as I could.

"We're going after the bodies. Weeks says they're down here."

"It's pretty cold out, and it's only going to get colder."

"No point waiting."

I didn't tell him the bodies weren't going anywhere.

"We found that arsenal hidden at Flemmi's mother's," I told him. "Weeks was dead-on there."

"Good. Let's see if he's right about this." Then he turned his eyes back to the deepening pit, ending the conversation.

As the machinery continued to grind away, O'Malley stayed on, but Regan and Fraelick came around only long enough to look everything over, and then returned to the warmth of their cars. We stayed all night, and clear through until morning, even though it got brutally cold and an icy breeze came up. We'd put a tent over the dig to keep out some of the cold, but it didn't do too much. It was better at concealing us from the increasing number of media people who were crowding around.

In the depth of winter, the permafrost is like concrete, and it went down about a foot. So it took a while for the teeth on the bucket of the heavy backhoe to cut through it and peel it back. Grinding and scraping and clanging, the big yellow machine made a huge racket that seemed all the louder at night. The deeper it went, though, the more delicately it had to work. This was a crime scene, but also a burial site, and we had to be respectful of the dead, and of the living who would grieve for them.

Dr. Anne Marie Miers, from the medical examiner's office, was there working with us. She was an expert in recovering buried bodies, and after each scrape of the backhoe she'd check for any change in the color or consistency of the dirt that might indicate it had been dug up and replaced at some point. But down and down the backhoe would go, and there was no change.

Finally, about four or five feet down, we spotted something poking up out of the earth, something slim and knobby. At first it looked like a piece of a tree branch. It was a brownish-gray, as dark as the soil it was embedded in. But it was bone. Femur, Dr. Miers said after she'd had a chance to spoon away the dirt and then brush the bone off. "We're there," she said.

With that, the backhoe pulled back. Despite the cold, the forensics people in their blue State Police jackets went at their work patiently, piece by piece, scrap by scrap. It was like an archaeological dig. Everyone had to shovel gently to work around the bones, then dust them off with fine brushes, and finally sift the dirt for any tiny fragments that might have been missed. Bone, tissue, hair, clothing—everything had to be photographed on-site, removed, bagged, labeled, and mapped. It was an elaborate, exhausting procedure, made all the more difficult because the bodies were buried right on top of one another and the remains had intermingled as they had decomposed.

Despite the elements, we all kept on through the night. It was like the old days, when it was us against everybody. By the time the sun broke over the horizon, it was clear that we'd uncovered three bodies, and we had nearly finished the complicated task of removing them from the ground. Because they were just crumpled skeletons with shreds of cloth, it would take detailed analysis and DNA testing at forensic laboratories to make an official determination. And to prove what we already sensed was true: that we were looking at the remains of Debbie Hussey, Bucky Barrett, and John McIntyre. Everything fitted with what we knew of their physiques, the way they'd died, and how the bodies had been mutilated.

It was an exhausting night, one filled with a sense of accomplishment but also of terrible tragedy. When we were finally ready to leave, I was asked by a reporter to comment on what had gone on. "We're conducting an investigation into organized crime," I said, deliberately limiting myself to the obvious. "And we've just uncovered the remains of three victims."

———

From the reaction I got, you'd think I'd taken a potshot at the governor. Even though we had pulled three bodies out of the earth to confirm our worst suspicions about Bulger and Flemmi, and even though I was the ranking officer for the State Police on the scene, the only topic in law enforcement circles was: What the hell is Foley doing? The USAO declared I had no business commenting on a federal case. Others in the State Police thought I should butt out, since I was only a troop commander.

Making it personal, Major Fraelick drove out to see me at my office in Danvers. Fraelick had been involved in the Lancaster Street surveillance of Bulger for the State Police back in the 1980s. That surveillance hadn't gotten anywhere, for reasons that were very familiar to us. You might think that Fraelick saw us as colleagues and was coming to congratulate me on seeing his work through. Actually, no.

"Tommy, I'm here to remind you that you are out of OC work and you're to stay away from the Bulger investigation."

"On whose orders?" I asked him. He had no authority over me, as we both knew.

"On the orders of Colonel DiFava."

"Rick, I've been working this case since 1990. I've stuck with it when everyone said it was going nowhere. And you want me to walk away? I don't think so. And if Colonel DiFava thinks I'm done, he can tell me himself. Not you."

"It's not your place, Tommy. You're up in Danvers, not Framingham."

"Doesn't matter. I take my orders from Colonel DiFava. Not you."

Before I could get to Framingham to see DiFava, though, Fraelick called Fred Wyshak and tried to recruit him to push me off the prosecution of Bulger and Flemmi.

But Wyshak would have none of it.

When I got in to see DiFava, he told me that he didn't know what Fraelick was talking about. "I never said anything like that. I think you're doing great work and you should keep it up." He specifically mentioned the dig at Florian's, and Flemmi's guns. It reflected well on the State Police, and there was no reason for me to stop.

It was the same old thing, except it wasn't. Fraelick wasn't trying to bounce me off the case for all the usual reasons: because the FBI was pressuring him, or because I had run afoul of the USAO, or because I was stepping on someone's toes. He wanted me off because the case was going so well. He wanted me off because others wanted in. In their own twisted way, Fraelick and O'Malley did believe in me. I knew because they wanted to take our case.

———

That sentiment became unmistakable a few months after the discoveries at Florian's. I got a call from Colonel DiFava at my office in Danvers. It was one that, at that point, I thought would never come. "I'd like you to come back to headquarters, Tommy," DiFava told me. "I want you to be the deputy division commander of investigative services here." Just as I had gotten used to barracks life in Leominster, I'd adjusted to it in Danvers. A tiny part of me wanted to stay right where I was. But the rest of me was ecstatic. I knew what it meant: that I could go back on the Bulger case full-time, and just as all our work was coming to fruition, too. I'd be serving under Lieutenant Colonel Paul Regan, and alongside Major Fraelick. That wasn't going to please Fraelick. He would be in charge of the Special Service Section, SSS, my old organization, but it didn't include Bulger anymore. But this didn't matter nearly so much, now that I had the colonel's support. I would be free to work on the case from headquarters unhindered, with ready access to the resources we desperately needed to push the case forward.

— CHAPTER 31 —

Although Weeks's information was yielding major discoveries, we certainly had not forgotten about Martorano. We continued to work him and did him whatever small favors we could to keep his trust in us going. At one point, Martorano developed a terrible toothache. At the time, he was with the Federal Bureau of Prisons in Florida, and its people weren't helping. He was back up for a debriefing when the Marshals called: the interview was going nowhere because he was in such pain. I got him in to see my own dentist, Dr. Jeff Maher, in Worcester. A security contingent of U.S. Marshals and troopers brought him to the dentist's office, and then stood guard while Maher attended to Martorano in the dental chair.

The whole thing probably took an hour or two. Afterward, Maher wanted to know why all the security. "Who was that guy?" he asked.

There was no reason not to tell him. "A hit man named John Martorano. He's up from prison in Florida."

Maher whitened slightly.

"He's probably killed thirty or forty people." I kept it casual, but this was only getting Maher more distressed. "But I don't think any dentists." I waited a beat. "But you filled that cavity, right?"

———

It was toward the end of the debriefing that Martorano told us all about State Police Lieutenant Dick Schneiderhan. Even as I gathered an ever-greater understanding of what had really happened with Whitey, the FBI, the USAO, and all the other agencies involved, I had the sense of sinking into ever-deeper levels of depravity that I'd never wished to reach. The mangled corpses, the betrayals, the vicious murders.

I'd known Schneiderhan, but only as someone to say hello to, not much more. He was tall and pale, with hair that went white early. He had a stiff, formal manner that I associate with Germans, and he was proud of it. He wanted people to call him "The German," as if that were his name, not Schneiderhan.

He was retired by now, in 2000, from any work, but he'd been a career State Police officer, leaving the job in the early 1980s. Martorano told us he'd gotten to know Schneiderhan in the late 1960s, when he was working on OC cases out of the attorney general's office in downtown Boston. After work, Schneiderhan would often grab a bite at a restaurant downtown called Enrico's. So did Martorano—not that Schneiderhan knew that.

Until one night, when some bikers came in, and someone said the wrong thing, and it was pandemonium. Fists, chairs, bodies—everything was flying around. Although they operated on opposite sides of the law, Martorano and Schneiderhan were united against the bikers, and they both did some damage. When the fight finally died down and the bikers shoved off, the criminal and the cop must have had some warm words for each other, for they hit it off. They were both tough guys who happened to work on opposite sides of the law.

They started to eat together, and to hang out. Eventually, Schneiderhan thought he might make something of the connection, and he asked if Martorano would be interested in being an informant. Martorano said no, he was no rat, but no offense taken. The two remained friends.

A decade passed, and Schneiderhan developed a heart condition that kept him out of work for about six months. Cooped up at home and worried about money, he was annoyed that nobody in the State Police came by. Had everyone forgotten about him? Martorano hadn't. He visited, talked about old times, and, before he left, slipped his old friend a few thousand dollars to help him out. Schneiderhan shouldn't have taken the money, obviously. But he did. It was one of those moments when your life takes a turn, and you can't quite turn it back.

Martorano let Howie Winter know about things with Schneiderhan, and Winter saw the opportunity. Together, they decided to make a pitch of their own to Schneiderhan. Martorano arranged for Schneiderhan to get together with him and Howie Winter at the Holiday Inn outside Harvard Square. Schneiderhan must have known that just to show up was to say yes to whatever they asked. And he was right about that. The mobsters said that all they wanted was a little information from time to time. Things like which independent bookies might be brought into the Winter Hill fold, or if anyone wanted to kill them. And advance word on any investigation might be useful, too.

No problem, Schneiderhan said. This all seemed doable.

The mobsters slipped him $1,000.

After Bulger and Flemmi persuaded Martorano to flee the state, he fell out of touch with Schneiderhan. That was twenty years ago. It was interesting, but nothing we could use. But then we started talking to Weeks, and he told us about a source he had in the State Police *now*. Schneiderhan.

"Shit yeah," Weeks told us. "Schneiderhan's still in it. He's still in touch with Stevie." When Weeks used to see Flemmi at the Plymouth County House of Corrections after his arrest—but before Flemmi had revealed his FBI status, and long before Weeks started talking to us—Flemmi had told him to get in touch with "Eric." That was code for Schneiderhan, although it took a while for Weeks to figure it out. Flemmi added another code word like "eagle" to use when Weeks was calling Schneiderhan for Flemmi.

Flemmi needed Schneiderhan to let him know which guys were informants. But he also told Schneiderhan when he heard Martorano had flipped. He said Schneiderhan should cut off all contact right away.

The last contact that Weeks had with Schneiderhan came in September, about two months before Weeks himself decided to cooperate with us. Weeks received a coded letter from Schneiderhan, telling him to warn Billy Bulger, now the president of the University of Massachusetts, and his brother Jackie that their phones were being tapped. Weeks did as he was told, getting the word to both brothers through Jackie.

Hearing all this, I finally got it. For some time, the FBI had been giving me veiled warnings that my department had "a problem" of its own. I had assumed that this was the feds' usual bluster, but more pointed now that we were doing so well. I kept telling them, "Look, if we have a problem, tell me what it is, so I can address it." No dice. They didn't want me to fix a problem; they wanted me to have a problem.

Now it was clear: the problem was Schneiderhan. And he was a problem. It was Naimovich all over again, but worse.

And the feds were all over it. Once Weeks told us about Schneiderhan, the feds pounced. They had Connolly; we had Schneiderhan. Tie score. We were no better than they were. See?

Well, not exactly. With the FBI, the corruption was systemic, widespread, and unending. With us, it was confined, as far as we could tell, to one individual operating alone for a set period of time. The FBI did everything it could to stymie any investigation into its misbehavior; we were the first to undertake ours. Totally different—but not to the FBI.

The fact is that corruption is part of human nature. It's inevitable, in law enforcement or anywhere else. For an organization, the important thing isn't so much what happens, but what you do about it when it does happen. We would do our best to make it right. Could the FBI say the same?

And, despite everything else that was going on that fall, we swept into action. The feds wanted in on this, so they could be the clean ones for once. But we wanted to do it ourselves, and not just because Schneiderhan was one of our own. It was the same old thing with the FBI. We knew the territory, and the history. And I had the feeling that Schneiderhan would talk to me, cop to cop, in ways that he never would with the FBI. John Durham was working on FBI corruption by now, and to his credit, he agreed to let us take our shot at an interview. In exchange, we agreed that if Schneiderhan would talk to the feds, we'd help set it up.

I'd known Schneiderhan from my first days on OC, back in 1984, and, although I'd lost touch with him, he'd followed what I'd been doing since.

He had a little ranch house up in a quiet neighborhood in Randolph. When I showed up at his door and asked to speak to him, I got the sense that he was relieved to find someone he knew, but also ashamed, for the same reason. I'd brought Duffy along. He invited us in, and we settled ourselves in his living room.

"So, what's this about?" he asked. He rubbed his hands together nervously and looked around for a face with some warmth in it.

I kept it open. "There's something that isn't fitting together in a case we're working. I wonder if you can help us."

"Well, I'll try." He kept fidgeting on the couch, taking deep breaths.

He started to ramble about how he didn't trust the feds, didn't even like them. Then he added that he didn't trust any institution very much, including the Massachusetts State Police. It sounded like he was dodging this way and that, trying to find a way out of the interview, even as he knew, as a police officer, that he'd look guilty if he ducked it.

"Listen, Dick, all we want is the truth here. You know what it's like in these investigations. You talk to this person, talk to that person, and it takes a while to add it all up. Now we need a piece from you."

He looked at me for a moment. "OK," he said. "If that's what you want." He touched my forearm. "But no notes, OK?"

"You know we've been investigating Steve Flemmi," I began.

"Yes," he said. "The Rifleman."

I nodded.

"You know him."

"I did. Slightly."

"Have you been in touch with him?"

"Recently?"

"Since he's been in prison."

He glanced at me. He had to be wondering: How much do I know? What's going to catch me out?

"I wrote him once or twice. I had cancer. I wanted him to know."

"Were you friends?"

"God, no. I'd just gotten to know him a little through the years."

"And Weeks?"

He nodded. "Flemmi sent him to see how I was doing with the cancer, that was all." As the evening went on, Schneiderhan kept looping back to Flemmi and Weeks, trying to limit the damage. And then to Martorano, too. But he just made it worse, going back and back. He wanted us to think he was just doing his job as a cop, checking up on criminals. But he must have known how hollow that sounded.

"Don't worry," he told me. "I cut all that out. My wife . . ." His voice trailed off. "She didn't want me into anything like that. If she'd found out, she'd have kicked me out of the house. Things haven't been so great between us, I might as well tell you. I didn't need the stress."

"Dick, I have to ask. Did you ever take any money from Martorano, Howie Winter, or anyone from Winter Hill?"

"Shit no! Tommy, come on. You know me. No, never!"

"Never?"

"Never."

"Have you ever given them any inside information?"

"No." He said it quietly.

"Not at Lancaster Street? When the State Police put in that bug in 1983, and Whitey stopped talking that same day? That wasn't you?" We'd heard from Martorano it was.

He looked a little panicky. "God no!"

"We have also been told that you dropped off a letter to Kevin Weeks warning him about the electronic surveillance we were doing in South Boston." I could have said it was on Billy and Jackie Bulger, but I wanted to leave it open.

With all the questions, Schneiderhan was starting to squirm in his chair. "Who's saying these things? I didn't do anything like that. I didn't know about any of that."

The conversation went around and around some more, with us asking and him denying, all the more desperately. He was in a leaky boat, and the water was rising. It was getting late, and he was obviously getting tired of ducking accusations and questions that seemed to be coming from all directions. At one point, he doubled back to the question of the electronic surveillance, as if to dismiss that one once and for all. "Listen, Tommy, guys, I didn't know anything about Billy Bulger's phones being tapped. You've got to believe that."

The room went still for a second. Duffy and I looked at each other. "Dick, no one said Billy Bulger's phones were tapped. We just said electronic surveillance in South Boston, and you said you knew nothing about that. Let me ask you now: How did you know Billy Bulger's phone was tapped?"

At that, Schneiderhan remained silent except for the sound of his hands rubbing together.

———

It was a harrowing interview. There is nothing more agonizing than investi- gating one of your own, and then finding him guilty. You're pleased to get answers, but you're disgusted to discover what those answers are. I was all worked up when we finally left Schneiderhan's place. Mad, sad, everything. It infuriated me to have the questions coming at us just when the questions were finally going *away* from us.

———

Duffy and I went back to Schneiderhan a couple of days later. This time, his wife was there when we talked to him. "Dick? What is it?" she asked him, obviously distressed. "What did you do? Please—just tell the truth." And he did: he admitted to telling Weeks all about the taps on Billy and Jackie Bulger's phones. He'd found out about them from a niece who worked at the phone company. And he corroborated the rest of what Martorano and Weeks had told us, too.

We'd kept John Durham, of the Justice Task Force, abreast of the developments, and when we were finishing up, he came in with a crew to search the house, and he came away with a number of documents.

The next morning, Schneiderhan left an urgent message asking to speak to me. When I called him back he sounded very agitated. "Tommy, those shitheads from the FBI took some letters from me. They're personal, OK? Really personal. They're mine, and they have nothing to do with the case. They were sealed up, and I want them to stay that way. Those fuckers had no business taking them, and I want them back. Do you hear me, Tommy? I want those letters back!"

I told him I would do what I could, and I passed on the request to the FBI. But no one was about to return any criminal evidence to a suspect, no matter how urgently he wanted it. Duffy and I opened them ourselves. They dated back to September 1994, around the time that the first round of indictments against Flemmi and Bulger was expected.

All three had a valedictory theme, as if it was all over for Schneiderhan. But the first one summed it all up. It was to his son, Eric. It was written as a final farewell, as if Schneiderhan were dying, even though he wasn't; it also has the quality of a will, instructing Eric about how Schneiderhan wanted things to be when was gone. He wanted Steve Flemmi to take over, in effect, as Eric's new father. If he hadn't fled in anticipation of the indictment, Flemmi should be invited to sit with Eric "as family" during Schneiderhan's wake. If Flemmi needed to flee, Eric should stay in touch with Flemmi by coded letters, as Schneiderhan had been doing. "TRUST HIM," Schneiderhan added in capital letters, referring to Flemmi. "He is one of the few people in this world you can trust." And then, again in capital letters, Schneiderhan made clear that he knew where he was headed, and deserved to be, just as Flemmi did, and he wanted Eric to pass the news along to his friend. "TELL HIM I SAID THAT I WILL SAVE HIM A COOL ROCK TO SIT ON WHEN HE GETS DOWN AMONG ALL THE FIRE AND BRIMSTONE. HE'LL HAVE AT LEAST ONE FRIEND DOWN HERE."

A tormented soul, obviously, but the letter reminded me where mobsters take people who get too close to them. They don't send them to hell. They make a hell for them on earth.

———

The indictment of Dick Schneiderhan came down in November 2000. Along with a few FBI agents who insisted on being involved, Duffy, Doherty, Johnson, and I made the arrest. The lead FBI agent, someone named Bald, had wanted us to do it the FBI way, and he asked us to review the FBI arrest policy and "operational plan" beforehand. "Washington requires it," he told us. The four of us had seventy-five years of experience with arrests, and we told Bald we didn't need his operational plan.

The arrest made a grim scene, as if we were escorting him to the gallows. His wife wasn't there, so Schneiderhan was all alone when we showed up to cuff him, led him outside to the cruiser, and took him to the federal courthouse for booking.

Afterward, the FBI and USAO issued a press release that once again somehow failed to mention our involvement in the case.

— CHAPTER 32 —

Even after we'd retrieved the three bodies from in front of Florian's, I knew that our work would not be done until we'd found Debbie Davis. She'd become symbolic of something important for all of us on the investigative team, and for many others besides. We wanted to do right by a young woman who didn't deserve the horror that had come to her. It was too late to protect her from that, but at least we could give her to her family for a proper burial, and allow her friends and family to grieve for her privately and honor her memory.

All Weeks knew was that Davis had been buried somewhere in the vicinity of Tommy King, on the shore of the Neponset River in Quincy. Catherine Greig's town house had been just two hundred yards or so from there, close enough that Whitey could see the spot from her window. Weeks said Whitey sometimes stared out pensively toward the river shore, but he never spoke of either victim, and Weeks doubted that Greig ever knew they were there.

Weeks remembered that once, when Bulger was driving north with him on the Southeast Expressway, he pulled over onto the breakdown lane, and said "Paulie" was buried down below, in line with a flagpole near the University of Massachusetts campus on Columbia Point. "Say hi to Paulie," he'd said, looking down.

That was Paul McGonagle, the leader of the Mullens, whom Whitey had executed over a quarter century before. Whitey had dispatched Paul's brother Donald first, back in 1969, but that one was a case of mistaken identity, and then he'd come for Paul a few years later to straighten it out. A third brother, a barroom brawler named Robert, survived. Southie being the tangle it is, Robert had gone on to marry Catherine Greig when she was in her twenties. She dumped him for Whitey, while Robert moved on to Catherine's twin sister, Margaret McCusker.

Tenean at least offered a shorter piece of beach than the stretch of the broad shoreline of the Neponset River by the expressway half a mile to the south, where Tommy King and Debbie Davis supposedly lay. The flagpole wasn't much help, since it didn't line up with anything that we could see. But Weeks was sure that McGonagle was down here. In mid-September 2000, we reassembled the team we'd used to dig up the three bodies near Florian's and brought them to Tenean Beach in Dorchester. It's a noisy spot, close to the expressway, where so many cars roar by, but it looks out over the widening Neponset River to the Boston campus of the University of Massachusetts, where Billy was ensconced as president. The gleaming Kennedy Library stood across the water, and Vice President Al Gore and Governor George W. Bush would soon debate there, drawing viewers from around the world, few of them aware of the gruesome excavation going on a few hundred yards away.

We concentrated on the corner of the beach nearest the highway over-head. Back in the 1980s, the area had been thick with brush, but it was much less so now. Was the corpse ever here? Was it still? We were afraid that the surging tide might have hollowed out the shore enough to dislodge the body and wash it out to sea. Or possibly Bulger had noticed the erosion and had come back some night to move the body somewhere else. We wouldn't know until we dug.

When we got started, nine months after the dig at Florian's, it was a hot September day, more summer than fall, with strong light that made the chilly water of the bay sparkle. With all the heavy equipment, and the police cars, and the uniformed officers standing by, work like this can quickly create a scene, just as it did at Florian's, and it didn't take long for a crowd to gather, and for gawkers to pull over on 93 and stare down at us over the side wall, backing up traffic. At one point, a surveillance camera up on the highway that was supposed to monitor the traffic flow swung around on its pole to watch us instead.

We got started just before noon. As at Florian's, we had to work the beach gently, using the backhoes to rake the sand, with their teeth digging just a few inches down with each pass. Slowly, carefully, they raked maybe a hundred feet of beach, running their scoops back and forth as spotters watched for anything emerging from the sand. For this one, we got lucky. About an hour later, one of the forensic people gave out a yell. "Stop! Wait! Wait! See that? Look—there!" Everyone converged on the spot where a furl of clothing caught the sun, maybe a couple of feet down. When the forensics people climbed down into the shallow trench to look closer, they found the furl of cloth, with some cracked bone poking through, just splinters. But Dr. Miers confirmed that it was human bone, possibly a tibia. The tide was still out, and the site was maybe halfway down from the high tide line; it would be several feet underwater when the tide was up. We threw up berms of sand to try to keep out the advancing water, which puddled in all the same, and the forensics team quickly extracted all the bones it could, carefully labeling and bagging them as before. Nothing would be definitive without DNA sampling, but no one had any doubt this was McGonagle. The skull had been punctured by a bullet from behind.

By now, Debbie Davis's three brothers had heard about our progress. They'd come to watch from behind the police tape, maybe fifty yards off, sure we were trying to find their sister. But the search had served only to remind them of their outrage about the way Debbie's case had been handled. The youngest brother, Victor, who was worn out from the strain, almost got into a shoving match with a trooper, demanding to know if it really was Debbie we were looking for down at the beach. "She was murdered by those pieces of shit," he shouted, meaning Bulger and Flemmi. He kept acting up down there, screaming and pushing, so I brought him back to the command post we'd set up, and I told him that he'd have to cool it or we'd be forced to arrest him and nobody wanted that.

"Do you fuckin' know what my family has been through for the past twenty years?" he screamed at me, tears streaming down his face. "Do you? Do you have any fuckin' idea? That piece of shit killed my sister!" He buried his face in his hands. "My mother has not been the same since.

Sleepless nights, crying, it's all she thinks about." Then he bent over in his chair, his head in his hands, quaking.

I told Victor that we weren't looking for Debbie there, but we hoped to find her at another location fairly soon. It was more than I should have told him, and he was grateful. It was probably the first time that anyone in law enforcement had gone out of the way for him.

I got another visit that day, too. From an FBI agent. He trudged through the marsh and banged on our trailer. When I opened the door, I knew exactly who, and what, he was. There was no need to show a badge, as he was inclined to do. He wanted to know if we needed any help.

"Help?" I asked blankly, as if the FBI's actually providing help was inconceivable to me.

"With the digging," he said.

I didn't even answer him, but turned away as if he didn't exist and busied myself with something else. And the agent got the message, for he had disappeared by the time I turned back to look for him. I hadn't even heard him leave.

————

Then we shifted our operation half a mile south to a narrower section of the Neponset. There, on the southern shore, it was time to look for Debbie Davis. I kept thinking of Whitey at Catherine Greig's, gazing out at the beach where he'd buried the two bodies.

This time, we set up the command post in the parking lot about a hundred yards from the shore, and brought in a couple of State Police vehicles to help cordon off the area. Here, Weeks didn't know exactly where the bodies were buried; he knew just that they were in there somewhere. That left us with almost three football fields of waterfront to comb, from the beach up fifty yards to the thick marsh grass, and another three hundred yards along the water. We deployed a pair of backhoes from public works to work it all, and maybe half a dozen troopers to pitch in with shovels, too.

We'd pulled tidal charts, terrain maps, architectural plans, MDC records—anything we could find to give us an idea where to look. Nothing was much help. It was such a wide area, and the expressway bridge overhead might have dislodged the bodies when it was put in a few years after they were buried. We didn't know how deep to dig, although we figured that, after what we'd found at Tenean, shallow graves were more likely. Plus, so close to the sea, we couldn't be sure that the tide hadn't worn the bones down, or scattered them, or maybe taken them out to sea.

All we could do was search. We used the backhoes to pull back the sand very slowly, making grooved strips in the square matrices we'd marked out along the beach. A number of us from the State Police joined in with shovels, all of us keeping our eyes peeled as we worked. It was mid-September now, and the sand was warm under the sun. Clattering away, the backhoes skimmed off a few inches with each pass, working their way down deeper and deeper into the matrices we'd set out. A couple of long days went by like this, and we found nothing.

As the days passed, everyone on the team was starting to feel the strain. A lot of media people had gathered behind the police tape to watch what was going on, and they in turn attracted a larger crowd of onlookers. A few politicians had come by, including Congressman Bill Delahunt and the Norfolk County DA, Bill Keating, who'd led a failed coup against Billy Bulger when he was a state senator. As at Tenean, all the attention slowed the traffic on the bridge overhead, causing long backups in both directions. Debbie's three brothers were there every day, up on the bluff that was reserved for the public.

After our encounter with Victor, the family members seemed more understanding; they knew who we were looking for. The oldest brother, Stephen, was especially grateful for our efforts. We were all grateful to see the tensions eased.

———

While we managed to keep the FBI off the site of the dig, the Bureau was horning in on our investigation in other damaging ways. When the FBI realized that Kevin Weeks had been so forthcoming, agents from the Bureau's fugitive task force on Bulger were dispatched to get what they could from him, too. We never provided the FBI with any of the fake names that Weeks and the counterfeiter gave to the Bulger. But Weeks did. He produced part of a name, which the feds used to get the whole thing. Concerned about the counterfeiter's safety, we refused to give the feds any more information, but they demanded details about the false ID that Weeks had provided Bulger. When I wouldn't budge, they turned to John Gartland, a friend who headed up the DEA in Boston and was a close ally of ours through Dan Doherty. Feeling the pressure from the FBI, Gartland asked me about the phony IDs.

"John, I'm sorry but I can't give you that."

"We've got to work together here."

"Well, yeah, but the FBI has to work with us, too. If this stuff gets out, Whitey won't have any trouble figuring out how we got it, and our guy might get killed."

Danny Doherty had become an irreplaceable team member. Without him we would not have had the success we had. Not only had I become a professional admirer of his, but I considered him a close and loyal friend. I appreciated the DEA's help in giving us Danny, and all the support the DEA provided. When Gartland asked me for this favor I felt I couldn't say no. He assured me that he would keep it quiet: not to worry.

The next thing I knew, I was watching TV and saw a promo for *America's Most Wanted* trumpeting "new information" in the search for James "Whitey" Bulger. The new information? The name that Gartland had assured me would never be made public.

We rushed to notify the source and offer protection, before Whitey got to him. Gartland called up in a panic, assuring me he had nothing to do with the leak. The FBI had demanded the name from him, and, not seeing the harm, Gartland had given it up. The feds had put it up. And so we wondered: was this indeed an attempt by the FBI to capture Whitey, or was it the feds' way of tipping him off, so that he stopped using that ID?

———

But then some good news. When we dug deeper into the heavy clay of the marsh, a trooper spotted what looked like a round rock rolled loose from the edge of a dig. The backhoes immediately shut down, people gathered to look, and the forensics people confirmed that it was a skull. The crime scene team stepped down into the trench, and they got to work extracting the rest of the skeletal remains. The body was definitely King's. What was left of the torso was encased in the bulletproof vest—soggy and much decayed—that he wore that last night, when he thought he was headed out to do a kill for Whitey. The punctured skull told the story of what happened to him instead.

Because of the crime scene team's follow-up work—carefully photographing, bagging, and mapping all the King remains—I couldn't get the hunt for Debbie Davis going again for several more days. Weeks couldn't tell us if Debbie's grave would be near King's or far from it—or whether it would be farther along the beach or up in the marsh grass. Or if it was even here.

We started back in on a Monday, and the dig ran that whole week. We had the two backhoes going, and in places we sent them deep. We came up empty. Wherever we looked, we were looking in the wrong place. Had we covered a wide enough area? Were we digging deep enough? Had the body gone out to sea?

In desperation, we brought in sonar equipment to scan the entire dig site, and added dogs from the K-9 units to sniff along the beach. At night, when the beach was quiet, we let loose some cadaver dogs—German shepherds that have been especially trained to detect decayed bodies—to roam the beach. But they couldn't find anything.

Weeks hadn't been wrong before. On the strength of his recollection, we'd pulled out five bodies. But that was not to say we'd get a sixth. Maybe our luck had run out. Afraid that we might quit, the Davis brothers would sometimes call out encouragement to us as we were coming or going to the site, to keep up our spirits.

Much of this was marshland, and I was afraid that any day now, the conservationists would close us down for disturbing it. Money was a problem, and, out in the hot sun day after day, my troopers were getting drained. Johnson, Duffy, and Doherty were going hard on this, as always, almost from dawn to dusk. The case had been like this all along—digging,

digging, and digging some more. But this was it, the last piece. If we could get Whitey on this, then he was done.

When we turned into the second week of hunting for Debbie, and we still hadn't found her, I knew we were reaching the limit. We couldn't keep at this forever, clawing away at a long, wide beach that might not hold her. I decided that if Debbie didn't turn up by Friday, I was going to have to close the search down for a couple of weeks so we could regroup and reassess our information.

I didn't like the looks on the Davis brothers' faces when I told them. "We know you're doing your best," said Steve Davis, sadness in his eyes. "You guys are for real. We know that."

That Friday passed without discovering her, so I reluctantly called a halt. But we came back, as we always came back. Two weeks later, we were there with the equipment early Monday morning, and we were digging once more. Up and down the beach, peering into the long trenches that the machinery opened up. It didn't go any better. By now, we'd gone way beyond the area we'd assigned ourselves. And we'd gone deeper too. Nearly two feet deep all across the beach, four feet in some places, and six in some others. In a couple of places, after people thought they'd seen something down below, we went down a full twenty feet. It was agonizing. I'd given us only another week, and when the days added up and we reached Friday, we were at the very end of the road. When the light started to darken that fall afternoon, turning the blue sea something closer to black, we were done whether we found her or not. If she didn't turn up, Debbie Davis would have to remain an unsolved mystery, a torment to her brothers, and a frustration to all of us who had worked so hard on the case.

All through that day, the backhoe kept grinding and grinding to no avail. Finally, the sun was dropping behind the big hulking bridge that took the expressway over the Neponset, sending long shadows across the beach. The crowds had gone, and it was practically just the Davis brothers maintaining a lonely vigil behind the police tape, their eyes trained on our efforts from fifty yards away. It was time.

I thought I'd pick one last spot, and decided on an area much closer to the water, below high tide level, and closer to the great hulking bridge. It didn't seem likely that Bulger would leave a body to lie under the sea for hours a day. But the tide was out now, beckoning us to this stretch of beach, and we'd looked just about everywhere else. So I marked out with rocks the last square where we should look, and then headed back to the trailer to start putting out the word to various officials that we were closing up shop.

The backhoe got right to it, and, from the trailer, I could hear the usual grinding of the heavy machinery on the beach. I'd left Johnson and Doherty to supervise. The operator was down to one last scoop before shutting down forever. For it, Johnson had kicked aside one cornerstone so the backhoe could dig underneath it.

Down came the bucket for the last time, and when it was lifted up, Stevie could see that its teeth had snagged a green plastic bag, which broke open as the bucket rose. Inside it, Stevie could see something sand-colored and vaguely round. He kept staring.

It was a skull.

He couldn't believe it. The last bucket of the last day. It was Debbie; it had to be.

"Oh my God!" Johnson started shouting. "We found her! Guys! God! Look!" He pointed frantically, then he charged up toward the trailer, screaming for me. "Tommy! Tommy! We found her!"

With another trooper, I broke out of the trailer and ran to the scene, my shoes sloshing across the sand, until I got to the plastic bag that was now resting on the lip of the pit that had been dug into the beach. Forensic people hovered around it. The backhoe operator had killed the engine and jumped down from his rig, and he was standing next to Stevie, and they were all staring at the skull. It shone dully in the fading light. It was small, with hollowed-out eye sockets, and it was shrouded in strips of plastic bag, and resting at an angle on the sand.

It was Debbie Davis. There she was.

I yelled up to the Davis brothers, who were still by the perimeter, and waved for them to come down. And they ducked under the police tape and came down closer, but troopers still kept them a distance from the site, since it was now a crime scene. All three of them started shouting madly, happy beyond belief, but also inexpressibly sad. It was a wonderful moment, but it was a terrible, absolutely terrible one, too. She should never have died, not like that. And then we were all in tears—them, us, almost everyone. After three exhausting weeks, we'd found Debbie.

"We knew you weren't going to give up," Steve Davis said, his cheeks wet. "Thanks for finding our sister."

Whitey Bulger took so much away from so many people—money, lives, peace of mind.

That Friday evening, we finally put something back.

———

On the strength of the first five bodies we had unearthed from the shores of the Neponset and in front of Florian's, supplemented by the eyewitness testimony of John Martorano and Kevin Weeks and several others, we put together a superseding indictment against Bulger and Flemmi. It would take the original racketeering charges and add the other, more serious ones. The new indictment ran to eighty-two pages and included thirty-two counts, of which by far the most weighty were eighteen counts of murder for Whitey Bulger and ten for Steve Flemmi. That was on September 27, 2000. If convicted on all counts, Bulger and Flemmi could be sentenced to many lifetimes in prison. We added the murder of Debbie Davis when she was found, and then the slaying of Indian Al after that. Six months later, grand juries in Tulsa, Oklahoma, and Dade County, Florida, returned their own indictments against Bulger and Flemmi for the murders of Wheeler and Callahan. The action in Tulsa and Dade County was noteworthy, because in those jurisdictions, unlike Massachusetts, judges were still empowered to impose the death penalty for the crime of murder in the first degree.

PART FIVE

The Big Picture

— CHAPTER 33 —

John Connolly had always carried himself as if he had everything under control, what with the nice threads, the big smile, and the whole living-large attitude. He'd kept it up through his career in the FBI and well into his new job as a lobbyist at Boston Edison. He was confident enough that after he left the Bureau he briefly considered making a run at becoming police commissioner in Boston. Then came Judge Wolf's hearings into FBI informants, the revelations about Steve Flemmi's status, and the disclosures about John Connolly as the handler who let two murderers run amok, and life for him wasn't quite so good anymore.

Judge Wolf could not have expected to veer off into such topics when he drew Flemmi's case. He'd assumed it would be standard mobster fare—an array of racketeering-type charges to be matched against the evidence produced by eyewitnesses, documents, and electronic intercepts. But when Flemmi said he was innocent because the FBI—meaning Connolly and Morris—let him do it, that changed everything. Before Wolf could get into the charges we'd brought against Flemmi, he had to resolve the legal questions that Flemmi had raised.

I give Judge Wolf a lot of credit. There weren't too many federal judges who'd let a matter like that take over the way Wolf did, but he was an unusual judge. In the end, his investigation took more than six years and included witnesses on every side of the issue: the FBI agents involved with handling Bulger and Flemmi, and the agencies handling them; those of us in the State Police who had to fight through the FBI to get at Bulger and Flemmi; USAO personnel, past and present, who'd tried to arbitrate between us and the FBI; the administrators who set policy for these different organizations; other law enforcement officials who'd faced similar cases in the past; and on and on. There were forty-six witnesses altogether, and seventeen thousand pages of transcripts. Judge Wolf didn't care how long it took, or how many people he pissed off. He was going to skin this apple all the way down to the seed.

To him, it was a matter of determining the FBI informant status for Whitey and Flemmi, then of considering exactly how much license that gave them, then of determining whether agents could legally offer such immunity, and finally of determining where the corrupt agents stepped over the line.

Connolly was the man at the center of everything, largely because, with his personality and temperament, he'd made it so. Given his top-of-the-world air, it was all the more striking when he was finally called to the stand, and for once he had absolutely nothing to say. Special prosecutor John Durham handled the interrogation, and in response to almost every question he posed, Connolly took the Fifth. This did not endear him to Judge Wolf, nor did it fit the image of a man with nothing to hide.

Once he was off the stand, Connolly thought he was done with the Wolf hearings, and nothing would come of anything he said. So he immediately went on a media tour, including a sit-down with *Dateline*, in which he expounded on his role as a handler of informants, which he likened to being a lion tamer. (More likely, he was the one being tamed.) He lit into his former boss John Morris for betraying him, and he expressed nothing but gratitude to Whitey Bulger for providing the information that helped bring down the Boston Mafia—although his own records showed that Bulger had done very little of that.

Actually, there was still time for Wolf to put Connolly back into the witness chair. And he did. This time, under oath, when asked to address those same topics, Connolly again invoked the Fifth over and over and over again. Judge Wolf was plainly furious. All the unanswered questions hurt him. The peacock's plume seemed to wilt a little after that.

In the end, Judge Wolf issued a 661-page report that one columnist called the "Rise and Fall of Bulger's Empire" because it was so sweeping. Most of those pages described areas of questionable activity in the FBI's handling of Bulger and Flemmi, but ultimately the report was termed a "nondecision." It raised all the issues, identified potential culprits, outlined areas of possible malfeasance, but didn't bring any specific charges. Perhaps Wolf was leaving that to Durham, who was running his separate USAO inquiry for that purpose.

More alarming to us, Wolf declared that, misguided as the idea was, the FBI had indeed offered immunity to Flemmi and Bulger, and the feds were obliged to keep their promise. Flemmi and Bulger could not be prosecuted for the crimes. That was terrifying, and, if it stood, would mean the end of the case for us. It must have brought a huge smile to Flemmi's face—and some serious looks of annoyance to the faces of his many co-defendants who hadn't struck any such deals. Wyshak assured me that he'd beat it on appeal; he quickly took the case to the First Circuit of Appeals and managed to get a reversal on the grounds that FBI agents aren't authorized to offer such immunity. That power remains with prosecutors. For all Wolf's fear of getting second-guessed, that's exactly what happened here, and thank God.

Judge Wolf fingered Connolly more than anyone else in the Boston office of the FBI. He discovered that Connolly had warned Bulger and Flemmi about the hazard posed by Brian Halloran, Wheeler's would-be assassin, and by John Callahan—a warning that led to their executions, the first done by Bulger, and the second by Martorano. Connolly improperly sanitized his FBI files to get rid of incriminating documents. He took thousands of dollars in bribes and gifts from Bulger and Flemmi. He socialized with them inappropriately. And he tipped off Bulger and Flemmi to our pending indictments, causing Bulger to flee. Morris had committed many of these same crimes, of course, but since he had immunity, Connolly was left to face the music alone.

Connolly responded with typical bluster. "I did not tip Bulger, Flemmi, or anyone," he insisted in a prepared statement. "Judge Wolf has engaged in irresponsible speculation on a matter involving my integrity."

By then, relying on evidence we'd developed, Durham had executed a warrant to search Connolly's office at Boston Edison. Among other things, Durham found stationery from organizations around town, including the *Globe*, that Connolly had used to punish enemies. One example was Sergeant Dewan, whose integrity Connolly had savaged in an anonymous letter to Dewan's superiors. Frank Dewan was a lone wolf who'd taken it upon himself to investigate Bulger and Flemmi largely on his own, for years. He was not in a position to conduct a proper investigation, let alone to make an arrest. But he had been outraged that Bulger and Flemmi had been able to operate with impunity for so long, making a mockery of the Boston police, just as they had of the State Police and the FBI. At this point, Dewan knew nearly all there was to know about Whitey and Flemmi without being in their inner circle. But his pursuit of Bulger and Flemmi had irritated the FBI, as it challenged their idea that Bulger and Flemmi weren't worth worrying about. All we knew originally was that someone wrote to the Boston police commissioner, William Bratton, a letter on *Boston Globe* stationery questioning Dewan's emotional reliability and loyalty to the department. It closed by demanding that Dewan be fired immediately.

You'd think a letter like that would be ignored, but not at the Boston police department. It sparked an internal investigation, which ultimately revealed nothing. But the claim remained in Dewan's file, a permanent mark against him.

The results weren't much, but the search itself turned the tables on Connolly. The investigator was being investigated. I'd love to have seen the stunned look on his face when they came through his office door. That would have said everything about the rise and fall of John Connolly.

And then the hammer came down. Relying entirely on our investigation, Durham prepared a federal indictment against Connolly for tipping off Whitey and Flemmi to the coming 1995 indictment, and much more. Later, other jurisdictions would have to weigh in on other crimes, like the murder of Wheeler and the ensuing murders. One count summed up all the others—the combined racketeering charges against Whitey Bulger, Stevie Flemmi, and John Connolly. Connolly was a mobster, too.

When it came time to make the arrest, the FBI insisted on handling it alone, as if the investigation of Connolly was the feds' idea, and their doing. Once again, we were in no position to say no, and we certainly wouldn't miss the prospect of seeing another law enforcement official go down. So John Durham, the special prosecutor who was now leading the investigation into FBI misconduct, took charge of the group of agents who drove up to Connolly's conspicuously lavish house in the northern suburb of Lynnfield to take him. It was a couple of days before Christmas in 1999. Worn out by all the stress, Connolly was home alone with the flu, and he went quietly.

He must have known the arrest was coming, but it took a lot of the starch out of him all the same. He was no longer the Dapper John; now he was just another defendant facing hard time. He was brought into court handcuffed, wearing a sweatshirt and jeans, his hair uncombed, his eyes empty, and his face gray. After he pleaded not guilty, the judge released him on $200,000 bail.

You'd think we might have celebrated to see an adversary in handcuffs. But I didn't take any joy in it. I don't like seeing anyone in law enforcement take a fall. To me, it was like Naimovich or Schneiderhan all over again. When a cop of any stripe is accused of serious crimes like these, all of us in law enforcement take the hit. The situation blurs the line between the good guys and the bad guys, and it gets confusing to people. The next time they read about an FBI investigation, they may stop to wonder: Are they on the take? But it was encouraging to finally see justice done, and to see investigators working to make wrong right.

––––––––

Shortly after we finally found the remains of Debbie Davis on the Neponset shore, we received an unexpected visitor at the command post. It was U.S. Attorney Don Stern, and he was bringing us a box of doughnuts. Cop cliché aside, it was a nice gesture, and, even though Stern had caused nothing but trouble for us, we welcomed him inside to join in the celebration of what we'd accomplished.

He clutched my arm. "Tommy, I'm here to tell you something I thought I'd never say."

"And what's that?"

"You were right all along."

I just looked at him.

"Absolutely. You were right to keep going on this thing. But I am proud of you and all your guys for seeing it through. And I really mean that. You guys did a great job."

That meant a lot to me, and to the guys on the team. It was big of him to say that—he was the only one at DOJ who did. And I was grateful, and I never thought I'd miss him when he left, as he did shortly afterward, but I did. People can change, and change for the better. It was rare on this case, but it definitely happened.

———

Of course, that didn't keep the higher-ups at DOJ from going after us. Ashcroft was the attorney general then, under Bush. It was ridiculous. Those guys would not stop. We could have found the Unabomber, and they'd still have demanded to know if we were up-to-date on all our vaccinations. Once again, there were some media leaks, and once again DOJ was sure they'd come from us. No matter that we'd been through this exercise before and we'd come clean, and no matter that there were plenty of other more likely suspects, they came down on us, insisting on the equivalent of a strip search of me and my men. Extensive interviews and polygraphing all my troopers who might have been responsible. Colonel DiFava and I both called bullshit on this and we roared down to DOJ to get the people there to stop the nonsense, but they refused. I said: Well, at least have some other non-FBI agents in on the interview. No. Then a neutral witness. No. Then tape-record it. No.

Colonel DiFava said: Forget it. The DOJ returned with a threat to take us before a grand jury. DiFava said: Do, we'd feel far more comfortable there. The DOJ people fumed, then summoned us to a meeting in Washington to hash out the disagreement. DiFava held his ground, refusing to submit his troopers to the kind of treatment the DOJ was proposing. His position was unchanged: a grand jury or nothing. The Massachusetts attorney general, Tom Reilly, backed up DiFava but pushed to resolve the dispute. The DOJ told him to stay out of it. The back-and-forth went on through the summer and into the fall.

The stalemate didn't ease until a new U.S. attorney was named to succeed Don Stern. It was Mike Sullivan, the former Plymouth County DA. I was pleased about that, since a lot of troopers down there thought well of him. He thought he would start his tenure off on the right foot if he could resolve things between us and the DOJ. To show Sullivan I could meet him at least halfway, I agreed to let my troopers be interviewed if he'd have his assistant sit in. To that, finally, the DOJ said OK. The interviews were conducted, and, needless to say, nothing was found. The source never was located. But it wasted a lot of valuable time.

———

In the late stages of all this, in early September, Colonel DiFava asked me to come into his office, shut the door behind me, and sit down. I was a little apprehensive when I asked him what was up.

"As I think you know, I am set to retire from the State Police later this fall."

I knew that, of course. Everybody did.

"I thought you'd want to know I've settled on my recommendation for my successor. I'll be forwarding the name to the governor."

"Oh? And who's that?" I really didn't know.

"You, Tommy. I'd like you to succeed me."

Few things in my life have surprised me more. I'd never set my sights on the top job; all I'd ever intended was to do the job I had as best I could. I didn't know what to say.

"I've been watching you. I like the way you operate, Tommy. These are difficult times, but I think the State Police will be in very good hands. I am recommending your appointment to the governor." Naturally it was an honor to be considered.

To say I was flabbergasted would be an understatement. After all the trouble I'd caused? I was the most hated man in law enforcement! And now I was being recommended to run the whole Massachusetts State

Police. It took a little while to get used to the idea. I thanked him for his faith in me. But I still had trouble believing it.

————

A few days later, on September 11, Al Qaeda assaulted the nation. Domestic law enforcement departments all across the country were thrown into high-alert security mode, and the Massachusetts State Police was no different. Since the hijacking team had passed through Logan, we scrambled to close down the airport and flooded the place with troopers. When it could be opened again, we put in extra security details, all while we were guarding bridges; protecting the water supply; supervising high-rises like the Hancock Building and the Pru; supervising historic monuments, like the one at Bunker Hill, that might be terrorist targets; and doing a ton of other things. Obviously, the State Police would have to adapt to a new kind of threat.

A couple of months later, in December, there was a ceremony in the statehouse, at which Governor Jane Swift announced my appointment. Before she did, however, she had a request for me. "Try to get along with the FBI." She knew, as I did, that all law enforcement agencies would have to cooperate if we were to fight terrorism effectively.

"I'll try," I told her.

Now I had a 2,300-person force to run across the Commonwealth, and I'd be going in twelve directions at once. I'd be pushing to get our fair share of the budget from the governor's office and the legislature, fighting over policy issues, working out personnel questions, and deciding how best to address the different levels of security issues after 9/11.

Still, with everything that was going on, my heart remained with the Bulger investigation. Just as I had from the beginning, I worked on that case every day, thinking about strategy, worrying about our witnesses, helping Wyshak and Kelly, digging up money (this was a little easier now), and deciding how best to deploy my energies and those of my men. But now I was doing it as the colonel of the Massachusetts State Police, a title that I will admit sounded pretty good.

— CHAPTER 34 —

Judge Wolf's hearings did not go unnoticed in Washington, where a large number of congressmen were shocked to see what the FBI was involved with. Were agents really in league with mobsters? It seemed inconceivable. To me, the revelation, no matter how late in coming, was immensely gratifying. Finally, somebody with political clout saw things our way. In 2001, Tom Davis, the Republican from Virginia who chaired the Congressional Committee on Government Reform, opened hearings on what its final report would call "Everything Secret Degenerates: The FBI's Use of Murderers as Informants," a title that lays it out pretty well.

While its efforts had been provoked by the Wolf report, the committee drew heavily on our investigative work, just as Wolf did; but it went into areas that we had been unable to reach. One area was the involvement of Billy Bulger. For me, he was one of the last unknowns in the case. Even now that he had moved on to the presidency of the University of Massachusetts, he was still a supremely powerful political figure in the state—and the only man on earth whose loyalty to Whitey was matched by Whitey's loyalty to him. The committee couldn't help noting that both brothers used their muscles so as not to have to flex them, and it zeroed in on the familiar incidents in which Billy did to people's careers what Whitey did to their lives—the Billy Johnson case from Logan airport, the matter of the State Police from the surveillance of Whitey at the Lancaster Street garage, and several other instances.

But with Billy, as with Whitey, there were layers to the icy secrecy in which he encased himself, and, even though Billy was as public as

Whitey was private, he was no more available. When asked to testify about his brother, Billy pleaded the Fifth in response to every question, no matter how innocuous. The committee had no choice but to grant him immunity, but even then, Billy wanted to be interviewed behind closed doors, off the record. To that, finally, Representative Davis said no.

Finally seated before Davis's committee, Billy was obliged to answer questions about what he knew of Whitey's activities, or risk being cited for contempt of Congress. Most of the questions were obvious—how much he had used his position to protect his brother, in what ways he might have retaliated against those who had sought to bring his brother to justice, etc. He answered none of them. Even as he sat before the congressional panel, with a horde of spectators behind him, he went instead on the attack, blaming John Morris for trying to get his brother killed by leaking Whitey's informant status to the *Globe* back in 1988. "Morris's leak had one purpose plain and simple—to bring about the death of James Bulger," Billy said. That was fourteen years before, so any such plan had obviously not succeeded.

If the committee members had hoped for candor, they shouldn't have. In a typical exchange during a full day of testimony, Representative Dan Burton asked Billy what his brother did for a living. "Well, I know that he was for the most part—I had the feeling that he was in the business of gaming and—" He stopped. "Whatever. It was vague to me but . . . he wasn't doing what I'd like him to do."

Burton asked Billy if he knew that Whitey was "involved in murder."

"Never, no, I do not. I did not."

"Narcotics trafficking?"

"No."

"Did you know anything about the Winter Hill mob?"

"The what?"

Burton brought up Martorano's testimony to us that Billy had delivered Connolly to Whitey, for Whitey's protection. "Did you ask Connolly to protect James, saying something like, 'Just keep my brother out of trouble'?"

"Whatever was done by Connolly would not have been done at my urging," Billy replied.

"Did you ever ask any law enforcement officer—state, local, federal, Mr. Connolly, anybody—to assist your brother in any way?"

"Never."

"None?"

"I don't believe ever in my life."

To almost every question, Bulger replied that he either didn't know or didn't remember. And that included such curiosities as how it was that Connolly and Morris had been the ones to investigate Bulger on the 75 State Street scandal, when Morris had just received a $5,000 bribe from Whitey. Billy had no idea about any of that. He claimed he hardly knew Connolly, and had never met Morris.

Billy didn't intend to provide the perfect example of why it's so foolish to rely on top-echelon informants regarding major crimes, but he did it all the same. He'd been enlisted by the committee, in effect, to rat out his brother, and guess what. He took immunity to save himself, thank you, and gave the government the finger. He chose loyalty to his brother over loyalty to the government. So do all such top-echelon informants, starting with Billy's brother.

One line of inquiry did reveal something about the intimacy of the relationship between the two brothers, and about the darkness in which they existed. It had to do with that phone call from Whitey to Billy in late January, about a month after Whitey fled. Kevin Weeks had told us about it, but Billy had never revealed what the call was about, and would not reveal this until it came up before a grand jury in 2001. Because Whitey and Billy were both sensitive to our wiretaps, Billy said now that he had arranged to receive the call at the home of a friend in Quincy, Edward Phillips. By Boston standards, Quincy is a long way from South Boston, maybe five miles.

That alone is suspicious, as is the fact that Billy had never mentioned the call to anyone. The other congressmen had gone fairly easy on him, but Shays let loose. He told Billy that seeing a public official take the Fifth was "disgusting," and he went on from there.

Shays: Let me ask you, when you received the phone call, you
received—your brother fled in December 1994 and you received
the phone call in January of 1995, correct?

Bulger: Correct.

Shays: OK. Your brother broke the law and you were a public official.
Did you go to the authorities to say that your brother had
contacted you?

Bulger: I informed my attorney just about immediately.

Shays: Did you go to the officials?

Bulger: No.

Shays: Why not?

Bulger: I told my attorney, and he in turn . . .

Shays: Well, big deal.

Bulger: And he in turn told the officials.

Shays: OK. And who interviewed you after that? Why wouldn't you—
just offhand—why did you have to tell the attorney, why don't you
just—I think you're a senator, correct?

Bulger: Pardon me?

Shays: You were a state senator at the time.

Bulger: Yes.

Shays: Why wouldn't you have just gone to the officials? Why do you
need to speak through your attorney to tell the authorities that
you spoke to your brother? Why are you looking at me . . .

Bulger: I have a right to do. I exercised my right to . . .

Shays: But why? You have a right to do it, but why would you do it?
Why wouldn't you just pick up the phone and say, "My brother
who's fled contacted me." And by the way, I'd like to know why
you just didn't speak to the authorities directly, why did you speak
through an attorney.

Bulger: That was my preference.

Shays: OK. Let me ask you this. . . . Whose house did you go to?

Bulger: Edward Phillips.

Shays: Did Mr. Phillips know you were going to receive that call?

Bulger: I can't remember whether he knew.

Shays: Why not?

Bulger: I don't know whether I informed him that I was receiving . . .

Shays: So you came to that home and you said, I'm going to receive a phone call from somebody, or, I need to come to this home. Tell me how that's logical.

Bulger: No, when I go to this home—very frequently, I'm receiving phone calls wherever I am. And it would not be unusual at all for me to receive a phone call while at his home.

Shays: But you knew that when you went to that home you were going to receive a phone call from your brother.

Bulger: I expected that I might.

Shays: Right. Why did you think you would receive it there? Why was your brother calling that . . .

Bulger: That was his request. I'm sure he would like a private conversation.

Shays: Did the FBI ask you why you received the call there?

Bulger: Yes. In 2001.

Shays: Isn't that amazing? You receive a call in 1995 and nobody wanted to have details of why you went there and whether or not that individual knew you were receiving the call and so on. It didn't strike you as kind of interesting?

Bulger: I think the U.S. Attorney's Office knew about it far in advance.

Shays: Yes, the problem is that there is a suspicion, which you obviously don't agree with, that the FBI and others were intimidated in interacting with you because you were a powerful political person, and you know you were a powerful political person. Did the FBI ever try to question you, and did you refuse to talk to them or answer them? Did you ever shoo them away? Did you ever suggest that maybe they should go somewhere else? Did you ever do that? Under oath. I'm asking you under oath if you did that.

Bulger: I don't recall meeting the FBI. I really don't recall it.

Shays: Did the FBI ever come to your home?

Bulger: I've told that they did, but I do not recall it.

Shays: Did the FBI ever come to your office?

Bulger: No, I don't think so.

Shays: Did any other law enforcement people come to your home?

Bulger: I don't think so.

Shays: Did any law enforcement people come to your office just to ask you questions?

Bulger: I don't believe so.

Shays: Do you think the FBI felt that if they asked you questions about your brother that you would cooperate?

Bulger: I have no idea what the FBI is thinking. They're not too friendly to me, Congressman.

Shays: I'm not friendly because I'm outraged at this whole case.

None of Billy's explanation made the least bit of sense. Surely, it was unusual for him to arrange to take a phone call at a friend's house five miles away. It was far more logical that he or Whitey was afraid his own phone was tapped. And it made far more sense for him to tell the authorities himself if he expected his lawyer to. And if he was relying on the lawyer, surely he would check to make sure the lawyer had actually followed through. Besides, wouldn't he have wondered when nothing came of it? The only sensible explanation was that he'd made up this whole story about a lawyer because lawyer-client conversations are privileged, so no one could ask about it.

All very smooth, but his testimony put Billy in a rare bind. Always before, he'd been able to dodge such pointed questions about his brother with a joke or a stare-down. Now, though, there was no obvious way out. If he said too much, he'd risk his brother's freedom. If he said too little, failing to meet his legal and moral obligations to tell the full truth, he'd risk his job as president of the university. And this time he'd said too little.

To me, Representative Shays had it right: Billy Bulger was obliged to tell the truth about a fugitive in a murder case, whoever that fugitive might be. And Governor Mitt Romney of Massachusetts felt the same. After the hearings, he went after Bulger as few people in the political establishment in Massachusetts had ever dared to. Romney had chosen a fat target, but that didn't mean he would bag Bulger. Few people in the state were better protected than Billy Bulger. But when the Democratic attorney general, Tom Reilly, who'd been so helpful to us against Whitey, joined in the effort to bring Billy down, Billy realized there was nothing for it except to bring his forty-two-year career in public life to a close.

———

The committee did not explore the Bulger case much beyond that, recogniz- ing that, between our investigation and the Wolf report, it wasn't likely to uncover much more. Instead, it went deeper into the history of the top-echelon informants policy to determine how Bulger could have happened in the first place. The very phrase "The FBI's Use of Murderers as Informants" gives you a pretty good idea of where the Committee was coming from. They could see that blame went past Connolly and Morris to the supervisors who failed to keep them in check, and to the systems that either didn't exist or didn't work to keep this stuff from happening. And those systems, or lack of them, went back decades, back to the very beginning, when the top-echelon program was created by J. Edgar Hoover himself in the early days of the Kennedy administration.

It sounded good, a top secret program to shield the criminals who'd risen so high in the crime world they were in a position to see everything that was going down—and then to tell the feds about it. But it was a disaster from the start. Martorano showed us that, for he took us way back to the beginning, to the Deegan case of 1965. At its simplest level, it was a murder mystery involving the back-alley killing of a low-level mafioso, Teddy Deegan. It would have been nothing, just another gangland slaying, except that the explanation of who killed Deegan and why it kept shifting about until there were as many versions of what happened that night as there were people to tell them. But the full truth didn't emerge for over three decades, when Martorano sat down with us again after El Paso.

Basically, the Deegan story was like Bulger, but long before Bulger, a tale of corrupt FBI agents, informants who exploited FBI protection, an FBI hierarchy that was up to its hips in treachery, innocent lives ended or ruined, a court system blind to what really went on, honest prosecutors left in the dark, and the FBI at the center of it, unable to take blame or to learn anything from it, and a stench rising up off the whole thing.

Everything in Bulger was in Deegan, and so it's probably no coincidence that it, too, took place in Boston, in many of the neighborhoods that Bulger made famous, and the key characters overlapped. For the FBI enlisted none other than Steve Flemmi as a top-echelon informant on the case, starting him on the career as a secret G-man that would run thirty years and ten murders before we captured him. That plot of his with Frank Salemme to blow up the mob lawyer John Fitzgerald's car, the one that sent Salemme to prison but allowed him to join up with Whitey and emerge as the New England Mafia boss? This came out of an effort by the feds to keep their biggest Deegan informant in line. And the agent who signed him up? The Boston office's H. Paul Rico, the John Connolly of his day, and the one who did security for Roger Wheeler at World Jai-Alai, and then brought Bulger and Flemmi into his operation on the sly.

Hoover went after the Mafia like he had gone after Communism, obsessively, with more than a little paranoia thrown in, like it was total war, and to hell with proportion and good sense and the Bill of Rights. And in this war, the top-echelon informants were the ultimate weapon. If there were problems, so what? To Hoover, and to his FBI, the ends always justified the means, but history shows they don't, not in Bulger, and not in Deegan. And besides, what ends? The FBI would be hard pressed to find a single piece of information that it got from the many top-echelon informants in Bulger or in Deegan but couldn't have gotten by legitimate means. But it did produce a lot of innocent dead. The top-echelon informant policy and the abuse of that policy were inseparable, for the whole idea of using murderers to stop crime is a fantasy. Why would a criminal want to do that? Murderers murder. For the FBI to expect any different is ridiculous.

Deegan went down in an alleyway in Chelsea riddled with machine-gun bullets. For years, it was unclear who did it, even after four low-level mafiosi were sent away on the strength of court testimony by a Mafia hit man who admitted that he himself had been there. That was Joe "The Animal" Barboza, probably the most prolific killer in Boston until Martorano came along. Barboza won his nickname after he chewed the ear off a stranger who'd been mouthing off at him in a bar. Unknown to both the prosecution and the defense, Barboza was an FBI informant soon to go top-echelon for his lies on Deegan, even though his handler Paul Rico had described him as "a professional assassin" and "the most dangerous individual" in greater Boston. He was central to the case. The feds had already signed up a close pal of his, Jimmy "The Bear" Flemmi, Stevie's older brother, a holy terror with five kills to his credit. As an informant, he would kill ten more.

Thanks to Barboza's phony testimony, as coached by the FBI's Rico, one of the convicted received life imprisonment, the other three got the electric chair. Fortunately for them, Massachusetts eliminated the death penalty before they could be executed, and they received life sentences instead. Two of them died in prison, but the other two survived until 1997, when Martorano revealed to us that all four men had been framed.

Why did Barboza and the FBI want to eliminate these four men? The answer goes back to the matter of who killed Deegan in the first place, and why. But call it a case of misplaced loyalties, first to his pal Jimmy Flemmi, who was in on it, and then to the FBI, which was using him to get at the New England Mafia boss Ray Patriarca, whom Hoover had it in for. (Because the feds had planted an illicit bug in Patriarca's office, they knew all about the Deegan murder plot long before the guns came out but never lifted a finger to save an innocent man's life.)

For their work on a case that wrongfully convicted four men, Rico and his partner Dennis Condon were hailed as heroes within the FBI, and rewarded with lavish raises and praise. J. Edgar Hoover personally sent them letters of commendation. Barboza got a year and a day for his role in the murders, but he could serve it concurrently with a parole violation sentence he was already in for at the time.

When he got out, he entered the Witness Protection Program, the federal disappearing act that had been contrived expressly for him, and moved to California. At one point his conscience gnawed at him, and he wanted to recant his testimony, but the feds kept him in jail on another charge until the last Deegan appeals were finished. Thinking he was safe from the law, he returned to his old ways, and fell in with a chiseler named Clay Wilson, who'd boosted $1 million in bonds, and then boasted he had rare powers, saying he'd sent away four innocent men back in Massachusetts, and he could do more. "He said he had the government wrapped around his little finger," as one law enforcement report put it.

Sure enough, in a tussle over the bonds, Barboza shot Wilson in the head in front of his horrified girlfriend. For that one he was arrested, and this time he had to stand trial. Rico flew to California to stick up for his informant, hailing his service to the nation, but it did no good. Barboza did seven years, and shortly after his release he was mowed down in San Francisco. No one was ever charged, but law enforcement believes the shotgun hit was the handiwork of Joe Russo, one of the wiseguys we monitored at Vanessa's. Small world.

———

When Martorano let us know what really happened, we passed the informa-tion to Durham for his corruption investigation. I don't think Durham wanted to do anything with it, since it went beyond the scope of what he thought he had to deal with. But a WBZ TV reporter, Dan Rea, had been looking into the case for years, and when the FBI finally released the information, Rea jumped on the story, and other media outlets quickly picked it up. By then, only two of those who had been falsely accused—Peter Limone Sr. and Joseph Salvati—were still alive, the other two having died in prison some years before. The two survivors immediately asked to be released. After brief hearings, both were immediately freed to return to their families, who'd endured decades of bitterness and poverty without them. When Louis Greco Sr. died in prison in 1995, his son, Louis Jr., poisoned himself. All four families sued for emotional, physical, and financial damages stemming from the wrongful incarceration.

Charged with putting a dollar figure on these horrors, Nancy Gernter, the federal judge on the case, could scarcely begin. "Candidly," she wrote, "the task is a staggering one." In the end, she awarded the plaintiffs and their families just over $100 million, divided up as roughly $25 million each. By 2012, however, none of the families had seen a penny of it, as the

Department of Justice has mounted a series of objections, even though the delay has added over $13,000 a day to the award.

By then, a number of other lawsuits had been filed by the families of other victims in the Bulger and Flemmi case, including Brian Halloran, who was mowed down by Whitey Bulger on the Boston waterfront; Halloran's friend Michael Donahue, who was sitting with him in the car; and John McIntyre, the deckhand Bulger shot after failing to strangle him with a rope. Those awards have not been so generous, however, running only to a few million each. And others have since come forward as well. Because of the hearings and the fresh appeals by the DOJ, scarcely any of the families have received any money now, decades after the fact.

— CHAPTER 35 —

The Davis committee wanted to know whatever came of the FBI's secret deal with Jimmy Flemmi and Barboza. Did Rico and Condon ever even consider revealing the truth to the defense attorneys of the four men who were convicted of murdering Deegan? Did the Bureau ever tell anyone about the illegal bug in Patriarca's office that had picked up the critical exchange with Flemmi? Is there any solid evidence that the conspiracy really was limited to just Rico and Condon? Did anyone at the FBI ever acknowledge that Flemmi had helped kill Deegan—and that Barboza had vowed to keep him free from prosecution? Did the FBI ever tell local prosecutors that Barboza and Jimmy Flemmi were federal informants, and that Flemmi was in the top echelon?

It was pretty obvious that the answer to all these questions was no. And the FBI gave the same answer when the committee members asked it to share critical documents with them. *No* to the Patriarca transcripts, *no* to the name of another informant who had been an eyewitness to much of Barboza's intrigue and who contradicted Barboza's account, *no* to the original FBI memos on the Deegan murder, *no* to evidence of misconduct by FBI agents. The FBI did make Paul Rico available to the committee, but he took the Fifth in response to virtually every question the congressmen posed. One he answered was whether he felt any remorse.

"What do you want from me," he scoffed. "Tears?"

It took a year of pounding before the DOJ even agreed to discuss the matter, and then it declared that it had no intention of handing over the materials being sought. The committee continued to press, and the DOJ to resist. The few documents that it did provide were so heavily redacted that many of the pages were unreadable. It promised to produce others but never did. The more the committee persisted, the higher the matter rose in the George W. Bush administration. It came to the attention of two assistant attorneys general, to that of the White House counsel, and then to that of Attorney General Ashcroft. Ultimately, it reached the desk of President Bush himself, who wrote a memo to his attorney general saying that to release these documents on the Deegan case would endanger "candor" within the DOJ, damage the "national interest," and "politicize" the process. That was ridiculous, and the decision raised a furor, and not just within the committee. A sweeping declaration like that could justify holding back almost anything. The committee kept at it, and eventually the White House decided it didn't need the grief; it finally authorized the release of some of the documents, although it continued to hold on to others.

A lot of what came was too little, too late. Still, the committee was able to determine the substance of what had happened in the Deegan murder and the subsequent cover-up. And from there, it was able to see a pattern of FBI deception that we knew all too well. With Rico and Condon, as with Connolly and Morris, FBI informants were protected, not just from the law and other individuals but also from reality. They could do whatever they wanted, just as Barboza said. And, of course, that first top-echelon informant, Jimmy Flemmi, became a model for all the others, starting with his brother. He saw this as his big chance to fulfill his ambition to become the "No. One 'hit man'" in Boston, as one FBI report put it. Obviously, his brother Stevie and Whitey Bulger were bent on a similar course, to be "No. One" in their fields, too, and they saw the FBI as their ticket up.

It wasn't just in Boston. This happened all across the country. The FBI would routinely intervene to keep its informants from being indicted; or, if indicted, from being arrested; or, if arrested, from being convicted; or, if convicted, from serving their time. The FBI will do almost anything to protect its top-echelon informants. As former U.S. attorney Jeremiah O'Sullivan testified, "If you go against the FBI, they will try to get you. They will wage war on you. It would have precipitated World War III if I tried to get inside the FBI to deal with informants. That was the holy of holies, the inner sanctum."

According to the final report of the Davis Committee, Director Mueller was supposedly working to "reengineer" the FBI so there would be no more Bulgers. He was centralizing administration, identifying risk factors for bad informant outcomes, and developing a checkoff system that drew on wider input for decisions regarding informants, and on a more reliable overview on the part of supervisors. The Office of Professional Responsibility, Prouty's old OPR, was to be upgraded to monitor the program, security was to be beefed up, and sharper guidelines for informants' behavior were to be established.

All of this sounded reassuring, and, reading it, I was pleased to think that our efforts in the Bulger case might help to reform the FBI. But the "reengineering" scheme went nowhere. Olds ways die hard. In 2005, just two years after the implementation, the DOJ's inspector general checked in and discovered that it was still the same old FBI. In virtually all of the cases—87 percent—reviewed by his staff, the agents failed to follow the new guidelines.

And it's the same old same old today. A Boston Mafia case from 2011 involving capo Mark Rossetti showed that the FBI hadn't changed a damn thing. Once again it gave a top guy, Rossetti, informant status, and it promised to protect him from prosecution for his crimes, and lo and behold he committed more crimes, allegedly including six murders and running a heroin and loan-sharking ring. Once again the state troopers found out about this only by accident, because they ran their own wiretap on Rossetti and picked it up. The feds didn't breathe a word about him to them. This runs directly counter to the DOJ's 2006 guidelines, the next iteration after Mueller's, which forbid an agent to "authorize" serious crimes like those. Rossetti told his handler that he knew he'd be protected, whatever he did. It's Bulger all over again, just as Bulger was Barboza all over again. When does it stop? Right now, the FBI decides for itself how it's going to do things, and it will continue to do them that way regardless of how they turn out, and regardless of what anybody says.

———

The FBI-first culture has yielded other unfortunate results, outside the realm of OC. The FBI has learned to buttress its power with information, which can be deployed to intimidate anyone it views as a threat. I'm convinced that's why it investigated us so many times on this one. If it had ever found anything amiss we would never have heard the end of it. The FBI sometimes reminds me of the runaway computer HAL in the movie *2001: A Space Odyssey.* HAL is supposed to guide the ship, but instead it uses its data and intelligence to follow only its own interests, all the while talking in that syrupy voice. The classic example from the Bureau itself is Deep Throat, the informant Woodward and Bernstein relied on to break the Watergate investigation. Deep Throat was hailed as an American hero for bringing down the Nixon administration—until it turned out that he was actually Mark Felt, the FBI number two, who was furious that Nixon had passed him over as director in favor of an outsider, Patrick Gray. So Felt did what FBI guys do. He used his inside information to retaliate, in this case by bringing down Nixon and his administration—anonymously, of course. It had nothing to do with patriotism. It was spite.

It happens time and again. Two examples are the disastrous siege of the Weaver family compound at Ruby Ridge, Tennessee, and the massacre of the Branch Davidians in Waco, Texas. Messy and embarrassing screwups, yes, but the errors were compounded by the FBI's refusal to acknowledge them, which only inflamed the passions of the victims, and their followers, all the more. They sparked the militia movement, and seem to have spurred Timothy McVeigh to blow up the federal courthouse in Oklahoma City. There are plenty more: the FBI laboratory "bad science" scandal; the false arrest of the supposed Atlanta bomber Richard Jewell; the revelation of an FBI mole, Richard Hansen; and on and on. All of these follow the same pattern that we encountered in Boston with our pursuit of Whitey Bulger. The FBI's we-know-best culture leads agents to make mistakes that occasionally cross the line into outright criminality; that behavior has to be hidden to preserve the Bureau's image; those who seek to expose it are hit with embarrassing leaks of personal information and then slammed with an exhaustive FBI investigation into their own actions and personal life; in defense, the Bureau stonewalls, then produces a trickle of irrelevant information, then stages a phony internal investigation that ends up blaming underlings for tiny infractions and other organizations and individuals for large ones. Meanwhile it claims that any external inquiries pose a threat to ongoing internal investigations, and drags everything out until everyone loses interest. Then the FBI declares that it has been exonerated and the whole matter is "ancient history." I know this all too well. That's what it did with us.

— CHAPTER 36 —

And then there was Connolly. By the time he was up for trial in 2002, I wondered why it was just him. I knew the corruption went deep into the FBI, but he was the only one who'd face charges. Why not Morris, Ring, Quinn, Gianturco, and so many others? When the DOJ threw its weight against the Davis committee, bringing in the power of the presidency to knock down the investigation—well, that just showed the firepower it can bring. The feds brought plenty of that against us, and we were just a band of about half a dozen people with precious little power, and with a commander who was under pressure from within his own State Police, and from outside, too. We could not do this by ourselves. If we were going to get anywhere in prosecuting the guilty, we needed help from the FBI, from DOJ, and from the USAO; but except for Wyshak and Kelly, we got the opposite. The FBI had decided that it was going to stick with the "one rogue agent" strategy, making this seem like an isolated case, even if that meant just adding more lies to the lies it had already told. And the other two organizations had little choice but to go along. So no one but Connolly would be held accountable; that seemed to be the message. If he was going down, he was going down alone.

Chief Justice Joseph Tauro would preside over the case. A no-nonsense judge, he was like Wolf in that his biggest obligation was to the truth. Happily, he was a little easier to get along with. In keeping with our general strategy of starting with a small winnable case and then working up to the larger, more difficult one, Durham was going after Connolly this time largely on racketeering charges. For the trial, Connolly relied on theater along with the law. But then, there was always a lot of show in John.

Rather than take a defendant's usual place with his defense team, he sat instead with his second wife and their three young sons. The idea was that he was just an observer here, not a participant. Maybe he was even a victim. A family man, in any case. If you take him down, you take down his family, too.

But that didn't hold up very long. One of the first witnesses was his first wife, who testified to receiving from Connolly the diamond ring that Whitey had pulled out of his jewel collection at Marshall Motors in Somerville; and Morris told the court how Connolly had passed on to him money from Whitey and Stevie for an airline ticket for his girlfriend even though Morris was still married to his wife. The cash value may not have been very much. But the point wasn't how much money Connolly took; it was that he took any at all.

As the trial went along, a lot of the air started to go out of Connolly's balloon. It took the jury just a few of hours to convict him of four of the five charges. At the sentencing four months later, Tauro sent Connolly to prison for ten years. It was serious time, and it staggered Connolly for a moment. His body dipped as he was standing there. But he rallied, blowing a kiss to his wife and children before leaving the courtroom to board the van to his new life behind bars.

And there was more, much of it stemming from what Martorano told us about the Roger Wheeler murder, and Bulger and Flemmi's flailing attempts to cover it up. Even though Connolly was long retired from the FBI, he'd had to remain vigilant about his former informants. He would always be their handler, and he had to be. If they went down, they'd take him with them. After the Wheeler hit, he'd been the one to tell them to target Callahan and Halloran if they wanted to keep the truth about Wheeler a secret.

That trial would come in 2008, and by then I wasn't in a position to help out nearly so much as before, and it frustrated me. I'd retired in 2004. It is customary to have only a brief term for a superintendent, but mine was a little shorter than it might have been, because of my health. Maybe it was the stress of running the whole show, but my breathing was causing me problems, and I was having some heart trouble, too. But even in retirement, I stayed closely involved in the Connolly prosecution, and was down for the trial and testified at length, all the time wishing I could do more. In many ways, it was back to what it had been at the very beginning. Just a small group of guys up against long odds.

The big question on Connolly was where to begin. With the murder of Callahan and Halloran? Or would it be some common conspiracy with Bulger and Flemmi that covered those two and Wheeler, too? The Dade County prosecutor, Mike Von Zampt, wanted to get Connolly for Callahan, since he thought that was a clear win. That made sense, but we weren't so sure it would be easy. The Connolly-Callahan connection went back to South Boston, and jurors in Miami might not get a feel for it. Besides, what are they going to make of names like "Cadillac" Frank Salemme, "Whitey" Bulger, and Steve "The Rifleman" Flemmi? To them, the names might sound less like deadly mobsters and more like cartoon figures. And would they take the word of a killer like Johnny Martorano, or a creep like Stevie Flemmi, over that of a retired FBI agent like Connolly? Finally, as murder cases went, this one was hardly straightforward. We weren't claiming that Connolly had killed anyone himself, but rather that he had designated someone to be killed. This was harder to prove, but in the eyes of the law, it's almost as bad as pulling the trigger.

To tip the scales toward believing the hit man over the career agent, we needed to make full use of the backup material Fred Wyshak had accumulated over the twenty years he had been working on the case—all the FBI reports, police records, court documents, and wire transcripts, and a thousand other things. He planned to back up Martorano's account with a solid wall of paper.

But it isn't easy to drive a small legal library like his from Boston to Miami, and not just because of the logistics involved. Fred Wyshak housed everything on the Bulger case in what we called the War Room, an unused office down the hall from his own in the federal courthouse, now located on the South Boston waterfront. He had the only passkey. The FBI knew that the War Room existed, and the feds wanted in. Understandably, Wyshak wanted them to stay out.

This irritated the FBI to no end. The feds were relentless in demanding access, but Wyshak would not give in, knowing all too well what might happen to his precious documents if he did. Finally, after months of frustration, the feds came up with a winning stratagem. They persuaded another assistant U.S. attorney that she needed that space for herself, and they got the War Room shifted to an all-FBI building to which they had the only key. Legally, they couldn't keep Wyshak, an assistant U.S. attorney, away from his own documents, but they could keep out Johnson and Doherty, and did. Wyshak raged as only he could, but it did no good.

Since the War Room had federal documents, Wyshak had taken the precaution of requesting formal permission from the FBI to move the documents that were absolutely essential for the Connolly case from the War Room down to Miami. For months and months, he got no response—until the afternoon before the move. No. They could not leave the FBI building. In this, the FBI invoked something called the Touhey Regulations, which required the FBI to review any federal documents that might be used by state prosecutors in a local court. The fact that Wyshak was not a state prosecutor but an assistant U.S. attorney didn't seem to matter.

By then, Wyshak had already ordered a U-Haul to drive the documents down, along with Johnson and Doherty and an agent from the inspector general's office, Jimmy Marra, who'd been immensely helpful to us in organizing everything we had. He had the four of them swiftly load all the Connolly documents into the U-Haul, and then went roaring out of there and onto Route 95 south before anyone from the FBI had any idea what had happened. As the thousands of documents were bombing down the highway for Miami, Wyshak got a call from the FBI. The feds had heard about what he'd done, and they insisted he drive the papers to the FBI building in Washington, D.C., and they'd sift through everything there. Wyshak knew this was crazy, and he told them he simply was sorry, but he couldn't stop. That almost cost him his career, but he got the papers to the trial.

Even though I was supposed to be retired, I still kept my hand in. I was deposed at some length by Connolly's lawyer, Manuel Casabielle, and I'd be a witness. But mostly I did my best to provide the historical context for the case. It was strange to be in a Dade County courtroom on a Boston case. With the air-conditioning going, it was actually cooler than any Boston courtroom ever was, and there was nothing ornate or historic or particularly grand like what you'd find up north.

The courtroom was low-ceilinged, with all the usual flags. The judge, Stanford Blake, was a firm, energetic character who kept tight control over the proceedings. He was especially solicitous of the jurors, knowing they were likely to feel overwhelmed by all the details of the interaction between the FBI and the Boston mob, and how these interactions had led to a murder of a shady Boston businessman in Miami.

The trial lasted two months, and it meant a lot of time away from home for Wyshak, Doherty, Johnson, and Marra, who were the real heroes on this one. By this point, Connolly had been in prison for almost six years, and it had drained him. The flamboyance was gone, and his hair had grayed. He seemed like just another guy. During this trial, unlike his trial in Boston, his family was rarely present.

This time, Connolly sat with the defense, toned down his wardrobe, and whispered frequently to his defense team, sometimes sharply in response to testimony. I was thinking that if he took the stand, he'd be our best witness. Even deflated by his years in prison, he still had enough of his smugness to kill him with a jury in Miami, as it did in Boston.

Wyshak and the state attorney, Von Zampt, were the lead prosecutors on the case. They started with Jimmy Marra from the office of the inspector general in Washington. I'd gotten so used to being disappointed by federal officials that I was blown away by Marra. The guy saved us. He'd supplemented our own investigation of Connolly, dug out a lot of fresh evidence, helped us secure key reports from the FBI that we'd killed ourselves trying to get, and arranged everything into a kind of fat encyclopedia on the case. All of this was key to putting Connolly away. I don't know if it was luck or justice, but we were really glad to have Jimmy Marra on the team. Now it was through his testimony that we got the key pieces of written evidence into the record, since all that material has to be linked to witness testimony.

A lot of the case hinged on Martorano. He was the one to testify to the central fact that Connolly had told Bulger that Callahan was not to be trusted, and had recommended that Bulger get rid of him before Callahan could spread the story around about what Bulger's people had done to Wheeler. And Martorano was in a position to know, too, since he'd been in on the discussion at the La Guardia Marriott, and he was the one to put the bullet in the back of Callahan's head. Testifying, Martorano was a big rock up there, no emotion, hardly moving, his words a steady monotone. The big question was: would the jury trust a man like that to tell the truth?

After Martorano, Wyshak brought up the other two key witnesses we had developed on the Bulger case, and, together, they made quite a threesome. Martorano, Flemmi, and Weeks. There could hardly be three less appealing characters, but we were asking the jury only to believe these guys, not to go drinking with them. They were there to tell the jury how Connolly was in so tight with Bulger and Flemmi that he ended up being a mobster himself.

Connolly's defense team tried to make him the victim here. He was not the mobbed-up, above-the-law FBI superagent at all. That was a fabrication of the press. No, he'd been the pawn of the DOJ, the USAO, and the FBI, just as we had. He'd done his job, nothing more. He was supposed to do everything he could to wipe out the Mafia. This had been the charge of the FBI since Hoover in the 1960s, and look, the Mafia in Boston had pretty much been wiped out. Ever since Angiulo went down, it had not been able to establish a steady leadership.

The defense tried to fight back by challenging the motivation of our key witnesses, starting with Martorano, whom they accused of lying to cut his sentence. It never addressed the key accusation, that Connolly had fed Callahan to Bulger. Instead, it brought out character witnesses who swore to Connolly's sterling reputation, and found a judge who, remarkably, saw nothing wrong with FBI agents' taking gifts from criminals.

As the defense wound up, all eyes were on John Connolly. What was he going to say about all this? The answer was nothing. For years, he had claimed that he was going to rip the prosecution to shreds, that our witnesses were all lying, and that whatever anybody said, he was a by-the-book agent. But, just as he had in Boston, he saved this talk for the media. He did not rise to his own defense, and once again this hurt him. If he offered no defense, how was the jury to believe there was one? The trial lasted for two months, but the jury deliberated only two days before convicting Connolly of second-degree murder. The jurors agreed with our central premise, that Callahan would never have been murdered if it hadn't been for Connolly. When Judge Blake revealed the verdict, I'm told Connolly didn't flinch. I'll give him that.

I wasn't there for the verdict. Danny Doherty called me right afterward.

"Guilty!" he shouted. "We got him, Tommy! Guilty!"

I spoke to all the guys, congratulating them and carrying on a little. And then I gave Wyshak a call. "You're incredible," I told him. "Congratulations."

It was Wyshak. We would never have gotten a single conviction without him. We probably wouldn't have gotten any warrants. No, he was the man, and there is no telling me otherwise.

There wasn't much of a celebration beyond that. You'd think there'd be more, since this was the culmination of over a decade of effort. Flemmi was gone; Bulger would go away as soon as he was caught, as we had no doubt he would be; and now Connolly. But mostly, we were relieved that the jury saw the case as we did. The truth now was out. And we were all exhausted. But beyond that I'll admit to an odd sort of sadness similar to what I felt with Schneiderhan and Naimovich. Maybe this has to happen, but I didn't want to see it. I didn't want to think about FBI agents who betrayed the public trust and arranged for people they feared to be shot in the back of the head by professional killers. I didn't want to think either of the wreckage Connolly's actions had left behind—not just the dead, but the families of the dead, and his own family, with three sons who would grow up without a father, and a wife who would not have a husband. The wound would take a long time to heal, and the scars would never go away.

When it came time for the sentencing, several months later, we were in for one last surprise. Connolly's attorneys argued that the conviction for second-degree murder should be tossed out because of an error by the judge: Florida provides only a four-year statute of limitations for a case of this type, and that time had long since passed when Connolly was arrested. The prosecution countered that the four-year limit is waived if the accused was carrying a gun during the commission of the murder, and Connolly had his FBI-issued handgun in his possession. Connolly's lawyers said maybe so, but Connolly was out on Cape Cod when Martorano shot Callahan in Miami, and no gun was going to do any damage from there. The judge said he would need awhile to think about that.

Finally, in January 2009, the judge offered his ruling. He began by acknowledging that the defense had made a strong point about the statute of limitations. But he said that another deadline mattered more: the appeal would need to have been filed much nearer in time to the close of the original trial than it had been. So, no. Blake declared that Connolly remained guilty of murder in the second degree, and now he asked Connolly to rise. This time, Connolly seemed to brace himself as Blake imposed the sentence: forty years in prison.

Under Florida law, Connolly would be eligible for parole after serving a third of that time, and he was credited with the three years he had already served. But if you add the full ten from Massachusetts, he would end up serving twenty-three years at least, a serious term. Connolly deserved to be punished for his actions on the Bulger case, no question. But so did others. The fault lay not in the individuals so much as in a system that encouraged FBI agents to wander down the wrong path, and then required yet more agents to cover for them, and finally created an atmosphere of deceit—which I knew all too well and which was the last thing you'd want at a place like the FBI. But Connolly was the fall guy, so fall he did.

———

And then there was Whitey, as there would always be Whitey. Over the weeks of the trial, we got to know a lot of the spectators in the gallery. Many of them were media, and many more of them crime buffs. But there was one woman nobody could place. White, a little heavy, fortyish. There every day of the two-month trial. No one got a name, but she said she was a freelance writer—not that she mentioned a publication. This mystery woman had attracted a good deal of curiosity from the media people by the time the trial was over. When Doherty, Johnson, and Wyshak flew back to Boston, they used the Fort Lauderdale airport, and they noticed her there, standing beside an FBI agent we all knew from the Boston office, Todd Richards.

Curious, Danny went up to her, engaged her in light conversation, and asked her who she was.

She gave her name, which I won't mention here.

"From?"

She glanced over at Todd. "The FBI."

"Not a freelance writer."

"No."

"What brought you down here?"

"I'm with the Bulger fugitive task force."

"Tracking Whitey."

"Yes. That's right."

The conversation didn't go much beyond that. Back in Boston, we called around, and found out that she was from Maine and that she'd been assigned to the task force purely to attend the trial. And why? To offer Connolly a deal after his conviction. If he provided information on Bulger's whereabouts, the FBI would see to it that the award, then up to $2 million, would go to his family. And she'd see to it that no one from the Bulger investigative team would find out.

Connolly's lawyer turned her down. It probably wasn't the best time to ask, given that Connolly had just been sentenced to forty years in a federal prison for the Bureau's sake. But the feds must have found the refusal a surprising breach of loyalty all the same. Despite everything— all the rebukes from judges, the bad publicity, the $100 million in damages—the FBI was still bent on doing things the same old FBI way. Operating undercover, under false pretenses, and making inside offers, all to manipulate an outcome that it would only make worse by trying to manipulate. It was remarkable, really. Had it learned nothing? After all this time, and everything it had done, the FBI still went ahead and made this underhand offer to the most disgraced FBI agent in its history. And it showed that John Connolly, at least, had learned something. He knew enough to refuse it.

— EPILOGUE —

Where Whitey Was

After he learned of our pending indictment in late December 1994, Whitey Bulger fled south with his girlfriend Theresa Stanley, ending up in the French Quarter in New Orleans, where they stayed at Le Richelieu Hotel through the New Year. Then they drove on to Clearwater, Florida, where Bulger scooped up the cash that he'd stored in a safe-deposit box—one of many he'd filled with money across the country, and in Europe. When there was no further news about the indictments, he and Stanley ventured north once more.

It was when they were passing through Connecticut on January 5, 1995, that Whitey heard on the radio that Flemmi had been arrested. He pulled off the highway and found a hotel for the two of them. A week later, they continued on to Hingham, on Boston's South Shore, where Bulger dropped Stanley off in a parking lot. He then swung around to pick up Catherine Greig at Malibu Beach in Dorchester, where Kevin Weeks had delivered her. Greig brought no luggage, only her purse, and left her two black poodles behind with her sister. "She smiled when she saw him," Weeks testified later about the meeting. "And he came walking out of the dark and walked up and then shook my hand and gave her a hug." Then they climbed into the car and drove off.

Bulger and Greig drove down to Long Island. He called himself Thomas Baxter, and he drove a Mercury Marquis, two significant details that Theresa Stanley later told the FBI, but that the feds concealed from us and made no use of themselves. From there, they drove all the way down to Grand Isle, Louisiana, on the Gulf of Mexico, to lie low for a couple of months. Then it was on to Sheridan, Wyoming, where Bulger was stopped by local police for a routine traffic violation. Not having anything against someone named Thomas Baxter, they let him go. There, Bulger and Greig spent some time on an Indian reservation. Toward the end of 1995, the two returned to Grand Isle, this time settling in a beachfront duplex that bore the sign "It's Our Dream." Greig was sometimes seen strolling along the beach by herself.

On the move once more, Bulger bought some prepaid calling cards from a store in Oklahoma in May 1996, and he and Greig used them to place several calls to Massachusetts in the next couple of months. From Oklahoma, they returned to Grand Isle one last time, for a couple of months. Over the summer they traveled by Amtrak from Chicago to New York, this time as Mark and Carol Shapeton. Bulger stayed for a while in New York City.

After that, the next Bulger sighting wasn't for another two years, in 1998, when he was spotted in a convenience store in Sloan, Iowa. And it was another two years before Greig was seen having her hair dyed at a salon in Fountain Valley, California, while Bulger waited in the car outside. Two years after that, the *Globe* reported that Bulger had been spotted in a bunch of places in Florida including Jacksonville, Kissimmee, and Daytona Beach. I'm not convinced about any of these sightings, which were unconfirmed; to me it just seemed like more stuff from the FBI, to make it look as though they were on the job when they weren't.

After the Florida "sightings," Whitey was not seen again as a fugitive.

Meanwhile, back home, many of Whitey's pals and two of his brothers were either getting arrested, or cooperating, or both. Theresa Stanley in 1996, John Morris in 1997, John Connolly and John Martorano in 1999, Kevin Weeks in 2000, Jackie Bulger in 2001, Billy Bulger in 2002. Each one eliminated an important source of information and of help.

And the FBI was steadily upping its reward, from the initial $250,000 in 1996 to $1 million in 2000 and $2 million in 2008, the highest reward ever offered for a domestic fugitive. And Bulger was making regular appearances on *America's Most Wanted*. Not that it was doing the feds, or us, any good.

Finally, on June 20, 2011, the FBI shifted its focus from catching Bulger to catching Greig, and two days later a tip from a former Miss Iceland directed them to the Princess Eugenia apartment building on Third Street in Santa Monica, a few blocks from the sea. The source had had a memorable chat near there about dogs with a woman matching Greig's description. The agents immediately staked out the place, and they soon spotted Bulger. Then eighty-one, he was gray and halting. His hair was gone, and he had that monkish white beard. But the fierce eyes gave him away. The feds called the building manager to ask the tenants to meet in the garage, claiming someone had broken into a storage locker. When Bulger showed up, the feds converged on him and took him into custody. Greig was arrested shortly afterward. Neither resisted.

Whitey had lived there under the name Charlie Gasko, although authorities found fifteen other aliases in the apartment, and he told neighbors he was from Chicago, despite an obvious Boston accent. Bulger had rented the two-bedroom apartment, paying cash, for over ten years. They'd obviously done a lot of traveling, but despite all the talk of their having fled to Europe, they'd been based in the United States virtually the whole time. It made me wonder, once again, just how hard the FBI had been looking for him.

In the apartment, Whitey Bulger and Catherine Greig slept in separate bedrooms, Bulger's with the windows permanently blacked out. Hidden behind one wall was a space with thirty weapons, including an assault rifle and shotguns, plus a hand grenade and a set of handcuffs, all to fight off an arrest he never saw coming. Behind another wall was $822,000 in cash, in case he needed once more to flee.

Neighbors found Whitey quarrelsome and a little hard to know, but Greig was approachable, particularly on the subject of dogs. Bulger had become something of a dog fancier, too. One of his neighbors, Denise Walsh, recalled that Bulger loved to pet her bull terrier, Joey, who returned the affection. "I guess he's not a very good judge of character," Walsh said.

Back in Boston, Whitey has made several appearances in federal court, but he is otherwise held in solitary at the Plymouth County House of Corrections, with few visitors allowed. One visitor he has requested is the actor and director Mark Wahlberg, presumably to discuss a movie of Whitey's life as a mobster. Because of the complexity of the case against him, Bulger is not likely to be tried until 2013. If convicted on all charges, he could face multiple life sentences. These would guarantee that Whitey Bulger would die in prison, just as we always intended.

— APPENDIX —

The Crimes Allegedly Committed by James J. "Whitey" Bulger While an FBI "High-echelon" Informant

Drawn from the Superseding Indictment of Bulger and two other defendants, based on evidence produced by the Bulger unit of the Massachusetts State Police and DEA, and filed in the United States District Court, District of Massachusetts, on May 23, 2001.

One count of racketeering conspiracy, including extortion, loan-sharking, book-making, trafficking in narcotics, attempted murder, and murder.

The following twenty-six murders, committed by Bulger and the others in the conspiracy, all occurred in and around Boston, unless otherwise noted.

From the 1973–1974 war on "Indian Al" Notarangeli:

Michael Milano, Dianne Sussman, and Louis Lapiana, killed in the first attempt on the life of Notarangeli, on March 8, 1973

Al Plummer, Hugh Shields, and Frank Capizzi, shot to death in the second attempt on March 19, 1973

William O'Brien, the top Notarangeli associate and protector, killed March 24, 1973

Ralph DiMasi, another Notarangeli associate, murdered March 24, 1973

James Leary, a third associate, killed April 3, 1973

Joseph Notarangeli, the brother of Al Notarangeli, shot April 18, 1973

Al Notarangeli, the ultimate target of the war, assassinated on February 21, 1974

Other perceived threats, 1973–1984:

Jimmy O'Toole, an enemy of Bulger, killed December 1, 1973

James Sousa, a witness to a botched Bulger robbery, eliminated October 1974

Paul McGonagle, a member of the rival Mullen gang, shot November 1974

Edward Connors, knowledgeable about the death of O'Toole, killed June 12, 1975

Thomas King, an irritant to Bulger, murdered November 5, 1975

Francis "Buddy" Leonard, to divert attention from the disappearance of King, murdered November 6, 1975

Arthur "Bucky" Barrett, the bank robber and jewel thief who crossed Bulger, shot July 1983

Richard Castucci, thought to be an informant for the FBI, murdered December 30, 1976

John McIntyre, informant against Bulger, shot October or November 1984

The murders related to Callahan's attempt to take over World Jai-Alai, 1981–1982:

Roger Wheeler, owner of World Jai-Alai, shot in Tulsa, Oklahoma, May 27, 1981

Brian Halloran, possible informant about Wheeler's death; and Michael Donahue, his passenger, killed May 11, 1982

John B. Callahan, to protect the secret about Wheeler, shot in Miami, August 1, 1982

Steve Flemmi–related, 1981–1985:

Debra Davis, a former girlfriend of Flemmi, strangled late 1981

Deborah Hussey, another former girlfriend of Flemmi, strangled early 1985

Further Allegations of Racketeering:

In the context of his racketeering activities, the indictment also alleges that Bulger used his real estate properties, such as the South Boston Liquor Mart, to hide income obtained from illegal sources; kept an arsenal of weapons at the homes of George Kaufman and of Flemmi's mother; concealed the remains of some murder victims; provided the fugitive John Martorano with financial assistance; and maintained surreptitious contact with law enforcement personnel to defeat electronic surveillance.

Other charges:

One count of a pattern of racketeering that affected interstate and foreign commerce

One count of extortion and demands for rent from bookies and drug traffickers Paul Moore, William Shea, Richard O'Brien, and many others

One count, extorting Kevin Hayes

One count, money laundering conspiracy

Twenty counts of money laundering through Bulger's liquor business

One count of money laundering that affected interstate and foreign commerce

One count of possession of firearms to commit violent crime

One count of possession of machine guns for the same purpose

One count of possession of unregistered machine guns

One count of transfer and possession of machine guns

One count of possession of firearms with obliterated serial numbers

One count of money laundering forfeitures pertaining to real estate property

Thomas J. Foley's Letter to Don Stern at the Department of Justice, January 1999

Frustrated by and concerned about the developments in the case, I decided to send a letter to U.S. Attorney Stern. Knowing that at this time in the investigation we had little support from higher-ups and concerned by the many attempts made by the U.S. Attorney's Office (USAO) and the FBI to insert the FBI into the day-to-day developments in the investigation, I felt that the events that occurred to this date in January 1999 should be documented. At the time I was only a lieutenant serving in the uniformed branch as the operations officer for Troop C in the central part of Massachusetts. It was not common practice for a lieutenant of the State Police to send a letter of this type to the U.S. attorney, but I felt that there never had been an investigation of this magnitude and complexity in Boston. I sent a copy to Colonel Hillman and to Lieutenant Colonel Paul Regan of Investigative Services. (I never received comment from Colonel Hillman.) Even though many shocking developments had occurred in the case that had proved and expanded upon what we had alleged, we still were not receiving the support of the U.S. attorney, and in fact he continued to support the FBI and its involvement. I was concerned about the future of the investigation and about whether we could continue to peel away the layers of obstruction. I felt it was time to send a letter to Stern detailing our concerns, and I hoped to get Stern to take a closer look at what was happening. Not knowing how the investigation would proceed, I felt it was important to document the events that had occurred up until that time. The letter as written and sent to Stern is as follows.

Dear Mr. Stern,

In submitting this copy of the report on the interview of John Martorano, I feel I must also submit this correspondence to you detailing my concerns during this investigation and most recently the events that have occurred surrounding the actual interview process. I am not only concerned but also confused and bewildered about this process that your office has enacted and endorsed. I will be more clear about my concerns in the body of this letter.

This investigation has been difficult and demanding upon all involved to say the least. It would not serve the purpose of this letter to you to dredge up every negative aspect that has occurred during this investigation. I believe that as part of your position as United States Attorney that you are not always aware of the day to day decisions that occur during these investigations. Maybe some of the comments made in this letter will enlighten you; or maybe not. I feel that it must be said however.

I would like to provide you with some background to our relationship with your office and the FBI. I feel it is important for you to be aware of the history of this relationship. Neither yourself nor Mr. Mawn were present during some very significant time periods during this investigation. Some would like to portray us as being uncooperative but I believe we have gone above and beyond normal expectations in trying to make a relationship work. What is contained in these initial paragraphs I hope will show you that we have continued to try to develop a strong working relationship in spite of some very serious problems that have arisen. Contrary to what some have said this is not a case of professional jealousy, however it has much to do with professional courtesy.

My relationship with the United States Attorney's Office began in 1984 when I was transferred to the State Police Intelligence Unit and assigned to work closely with the FBI and the Strike Force investigating Organized Crime. I quickly developed a close relationship with both AUSAs and Special Agents of the FBI due to several successful "joint" investigations. At times I was working more closely with federal prosecutors and agents than I was with my own agency. My trust in the federal government went so far that I risked my career and lost friendships based only on the information that the federal government provided me. I am referring to the investigation of Tpr. John Naimovich. During that investigation, I mistakenly believed in the FBI and the Strike Force and felt that as difficult as it was to investigate another Trooper, it was the "right" thing to do. I knew at the time that this was a very high profile investigation and that to some degree the investigation into a corrupt State Trooper was also a very "political" decision that would enhance the careers of several highly placed federal officials. I made my decision based upon information that I was provided and that I believed correct at the time. I can live with my decision knowing it wasn't made for "political" purposes. To the contrary, it put me into a very difficult situation within my agency. I took the unpopular position of defending federal officials to those in my own agency who criticized the investigation. At the same time, I was accused of lining up with the FBI against my own agency. I did what I thought was right and what was my duty. Looking back at it now, I must admit I was somewhat naïve to place so much faith in the intentions of those federal officials. I later found out that the State Police was not provided all the information in the investigation of Tpr. Naimovich and that there was an attempt to cover up information that would have hurt the case against him. Adding insult to injury, when the truth was uncovered and it was disclosed that the information being leaked to organized crime members was coming from a clerk in the FBI Boston office, not Tpr. Naimovich, the FBI took administrative action against this clerk and deliberately decided not to gather evidence against her. It was a "political" decision to investigate and indict John Naimovich and it was a "political" decision not to pursue criminal charges against the FBI clerk. I want to emphasize to you that I am bringing this incident and other incidents to your attention for several reasons. As I continue with this letter I hope that by the time I am finished, my position and reasons will be clear. I want to state at this time that I am not speaking from hard feelings or vendettas like I have been accused. I am speaking from experience. Experience that has been accrued over fourteen years and experience that I do not believe you have been exposed to.

Even though the investigation into Tpr. Naimovich was very distasteful and extremely disappointing, I didn't sever my relationship with the FBI or the Strike Force. I never liked the way the investigation was conducted and I made my feelings known. As I stated earlier, we had several very successful joint investigations with the FBI and the Strike Force and I believed that the most successful way to attack organized crime was on a cooperative, unified effort. Relationships and friendships that were developed with prosecutors and agents prior to the Naimovich investigation remained intact. A "work together" atmosphere was still a priority for all involved.

In 1990, I was promoted to the position Corporal. In the fall of 1990, newly appointed Colonel Charles F. Henderson placed me in charge of the Special Services Section which was responsible for investigation of organized crime among other things. Colonel Henderson stressed the importance of conducting these type of investigations and encouraged a strong working relationship with the federal agencies. He told me at the time that part of the reason he appointed me to command the Special Services Section was due to my good relationship with the federal authorities. I met immediately with Special Agent Ed Quinn and established open lines of communication between us. I re-established ties with the Strike Force and shared information. We began to exchange some information.

The State Police decided to pursue organized crime members through their primary revenue generator—the "rent collection system." Targeting high level bookmakers, we attempted to infiltrate the upper levels of organized crime in Boston through intensive investigation and extensive state court authorized electronic surveillance. We were persistent, lucky and determined. When we began to meet some success in our efforts, we knew the federal statutes were more appropriate to the crimes that we were investigating. We asked Strike Force prosecutors if they would be interested in working together on the federal level in this investigation. An agreement was reached to investigate the case out of the US Attorney's Office however the FBI never assigned an agent to the state side of the investigation.

It became clear over a period of time that the Bureau was not sharing information on a reciprocal basis. To the contrary, information was received that the Bureau did not want to participate in the investigation of Bulger/Flemmi and they were convinced that our efforts would be unsuccessful.

During this time period, three major incidents occurred that damaged relationships between all agencies involved and again illuminated the fact that the FBI and US Attorney's Office were not operating in a genuine cooperative effort. In one instance, information was provided to Ed Quinn that a search warrant was to be served by the State Police in an establishment in a suburb of Boston. Quinn was not told that the State Police had an undercover officer in that location. Shortly after informing Quinn of our intentions, we were contacted by the undercover officer advising us to disregard our plans of searching the establishment. The undercover officer was told by the target that he couldn't "book" there anymore as he was told by the FBI that the State Police would be executing a search warrant there in the near future. When I received this information, I called Ed Quinn. I picked him up at his office and we rode in my cruiser. I relayed the information I had received. Quinn apologized stating that the agent handling the source shouldn't have said anything and that he has since been transferred. I told Quinn that it was a very dangerous practice to pass this information along as he did and that the life of the undercover officer could have been placed in jeopardy. I later found out that the alleged transfer of the agent was only a story and not the truth about the incident.

During this time period we were receiving significant information from state court authorized electronic surveillance detailing the activities of Boston and Providence based organized crime figures. In an effort to identify the individuals being spoken about, the Providence office of the FBI offered to review the information we had and to help provide us with the identities of the Providence faction. We were told that SA Bill Shea was very knowledgeable about the Providence OC family. We were also told that Shea was seriously ill but that he could still review the information to help us. On January 1, 1992 I met SA Mike Sutters on Route 146 in Uxbridge and provided him with the documented detailed information. On the very next day, the wiretap that had been very productive for five weeks and had great further potential was dead. I will go no further in this matter because I believe it is not necessary.

As our investigation continued, we began to indict numerous people working together with the US Attorney's Office. On one occasion we were told by AUSA Jim Farmer that there was not enough to indict an individual whom we considered a major player in the investigation. Having worked for a significant period of time in the federal system, we knew that this could not be the case. After many difficult phone calls and meetings, Farmer and Quinn admitted that the individual was an FBI source and for that reason he was not being indicted. We expressed our concern over this matter and asked for a clarification from the US Attorney's Office. We asked if this would continue to be the practice with State Police cases in the future. We have never received an answer from Farmer on this matter only his reply that the problem needs to be resolved between State Police and the FBI. We strongly disagreed then and we do now. Our relationship with your office should not hinge on conditions issued by the FBI. In a meeting with you shortly after you became US Attorney in Boston, Colonel Henderson and myself informed you of these issues in hopes of improving our working relationships. We went to you with our concerns in hopes of improving communication between agencies.

There have been other obvious and obscure issues that have only made this investigation more difficult. Some of which are minor. One such instance was the lack of cooperation in serving subpoenas. A process and time frame was agreed upon in a manner acceptable to all agencies but was never carried out properly by the FBI. Another incident involves the holding back of information that would have been crucial in our investigation of Bulger/Flemmi; specifically speaking the unavailability of witness Tim Connolly. It was only upon our finding out that Connolly was in the FBI's protection and our inquiry as to why his information was not being provided to us, did we eventually bring his information forward. Conversations with Jim Farmer regarding Connolly impressed upon us that we did not have an ally in Jim Farmer. Farmer attempted to discourage the indictment of Bulger. And even after the issues mentioned here in this letter and others not mentioned had occurred we were still working with the FBI to locate and arrest Bulger/Flemmi et al. Only to find out that information was provided to them about pending indictments. In addition, never during any of the time we were investigating Bulger/Flemmi did the FBI provide us with the information that they were working for them.

All of which brings me to my reason for writing this letter. The atmosphere that the US Attorney's Office has created for the investigators working on this case has been one of dishonesty and distrust. Your office has been divided in its support of this case. Prosecutors have been pitted against prosecutors and investigators have been pitted against investigators. Decisions have been made in your office admittedly for "political" reasons. It is for this reason that I am concerned. I have been down this road before. There is too much at stake to be making decisions on a "political" basis. It is wrong. It has gotten to the point that we cannot believe or trust information being provided to us. This feeling is not something that is grounded in speculation or assumption. The pattern has continued. Some like to diminish the significance of this investigation by saying it occurred a long time ago or call it ancient history. They cannot be any further from the truth. Nothing has changed. As result history will continue to repeat itself and these problems will continue to surface.

Within the defendants in this case, we were not responsible for developing a mistrust of the FBI. It was the activities of the FBI with Bulger/Flemmi that created this mistrust. It was upon the request of certain defendants that they wanted to speak to representatives of the DEA and State Police. It is our duty and responsibility to investigate these crimes in the best manner possible. It is also our duty to honor commitments and agreements made to these individuals. In fact, the underlying reason for our success is the fact that we do live up to our commitments and agreements with individuals. I cannot understand why the US Attorney's Office is so insistent in putting demands upon us that can clearly effect the outcome of this investigation in a negative way. Once again it has been stated to us "it's political."

Throughout this investigation, there have been times where witnesses have been "handled" strictly by the FBI. Never has there been such a movement to insure the fair and equitable involvement of the DEA and State Police. We never saw the need to insist that we be involved in every interview. The case of Sonny Mercurio is an example of this fact. It is my opinion that the best case scenario for the FBI would have been to have an independent review of Mercurio's information. It is a fact that the FBI handling of Mercurio is an issue in these hearings. Why would the FBI want to place themselves in a similar position as in the past with this individual? Once again it opens the Bureau up for questioning and criticism by defense attorneys and for future litigation. It appears again that decisions in these matters are "political"; what is best for the FBI, not what is best for the investigation.

Since the beginning of the negotiations with John Martorano and his attorney, a major concern within your office was the role that the FBI was to have in his cooperation. To your credit, you stood firm that the FBI would be told of these negotiations at a later time. You allowed us the opportunity to develop an atmosphere of trust with Martorano. This is where my earlier stated confusion lies. I do not know if you are aware or not of the pressure that is being applied by your office for us and Martorano to accept FBI involvement in his debriefings. In good conscience, I cannot accept this.

Martorano and his attorney have specifically stated that he does not want to talk to the FBI at this time. This has been stated many times, under many conditions, to many people. He is satisfied with his current situation and we are making progress. Yet the pressure and deceit continues in your office. We have relayed to your prosecutors his information and his wishes; yet Mr. Herbert does not care to take our word in this matter. Mr. Mawn will not accept anyone's word, including Martorano's own words, in this matter. These individuals are openly questioning our integrity and in doing so threatening our ability to effectively conduct this investigation.

In July, the DEA and State Police made a significant commitment of manpower and resources in order to maintain the safety and security of Martorano and to provide a positive atmosphere for his debriefing. In attempting to obtain approval for Martorano to be housed in a secure State Police facility, DOJ Washington authorities questioned the State Police's role in this matter due to the recent indictment of a Sergeant on the State Police. (Washington did not care that the investigation into the Sergeant was conducted in a joint DEA/State Police investigation.) DOJ was so concerned that it almost sidelined the whole arrangement. Once again, the integrity of our agency has been questioned even though we have willingly and aggressively pursued those that were suspected of wrongdoing. The recent revelation regarding improper relationships with the FBI and directly related organized crime figures however never has been a concern for DOJ.

It has been alleged that Martorano has specific knowledge of involvement by past and/or present members of the FBI. The question of the ability of the FBI to effectively conduct this investigation, regardless of Martorano's intentions, has never been an issue in your office. To the contrary, your office has been relentless in your insistence for their involvement. This attitude concerns me. With the information that has recently been revealed in court it is not speculation that improprieties by the FBI have occurred. It is fact.

After we lost custody of Martorano and he was returned to the Bureau of Prisons, the process of interviewing him became more difficult to manage. For several weeks we were questioned and prodded to finish his debriefing. We were told that you were asking on a daily basis as to when we would complete the interview and that you were pushing for us to meet with Martorano. We advised Mr. Wyshak on August 21, 1998 that we would be going to interview Martorano leaving on August 30, 1998. We expressed our wishes to listen to more of the Flemmi testimony in court. We openly and in advance notified your office of our plans. Prior to leaving for the interview, I gained first-hand information regarding Martorano's intentions. On August 21, 1998 SA Doherty and myself had conversation with Martorano attorney Frank DiMento. He informed us of a call he had received from SAC Mawn requesting that the FBI be allowed to participate in his client's debriefing. He again told us Martorano did not want FBI involvement at this time.

On August 30, 1998 we went to Martorano's location and resumed the interview process. After spending two days speaking with Martorano, we received a phone call from Wyshak stating that Herbert and John Durham wanted us to stay an extra day so that they could speak with Martorano. We asked what was the urgency and purpose of their trip. We were again told that Herbert wanted to speak to Martorano about getting the FBI involved in the investigation and that Durham wanted to speak to him about the corruption aspect of the case. We were told that it was "politics" and that the United States Attorney's Office was under a lot of pressure to have the FBI involved. It was a difficult concept to accept. The most difficult part to accept is that Herbert and whoever sent him would jeopardize an investigation of this magnitude based upon the interests of the FBI image and "politics." This is where it gets real scary. The government had been told numerous times by the defendant's attorney that he did not want the FBI involved; yet Herbert insisted on meeting with Martorano. Durham was sent to speak to him regarding corruption; however the agreement with Martorano had not gone beyond the proffer stage. Herbert nor Durham had asked us at this point what kind of information had Martorano provided us. In addition, the defendant's attorney was never contacted requesting permission to speak to Martorano prior to the arrival of Durham and Herbert. A two thousand mile trip without first obtaining authorization from the defendant's attorney. I can imagine what your office would do if investigators totally disregarded a defendant's attorney and insisted on speaking to him anyway. I can only say this is mind boggling. No other words describe it.

On the third and final day of our interview with Martorano we advised him of the impending arrival of Herbert and Durham. We could not answer his questions as to why Herbert and Durham would be traveling such a distance to speak with him. He spoke openly about the fact that he was providing us with the agreed upon information and that he would speak no further until a deal was finalized. He wondered as to why Herbert and Durham would not wait to see the report before any additional interviews were conducted. He had many of the same thoughts and questions that we had spoken about amongst ourselves. Clearly, this undermined our status with him. He had the understanding that we were representing the government yet we could not answer his questions. It was not difficult to see that the government was clearly divided in this process. It was a very improper and unprofessional message to send a defendant who is trying to make a deal with the government. Upon their arrival and after another of Herbert's vigorous and relentless attempts to secure FBI participation, Martorano again refused to speak to the FBI.

Our dissatisfaction with this situation was made clear. It was totally unprofessional and highly questioned our integrity. With everything that has happened throughout this investigation it was very difficult not to question the motives of your office. But it still didn't end.

On Monday, September 21, 1998 we met at the United States Attorney's Office with Wyshak, Kelly, Herbert, and SA Doherty. We spoke about the meeting the next day with representatives of the various jurisdictions involved in the Martorano investigation. At no time did anyone indicate that the FBI would participate in the meeting. It was our understanding that our agreement with Martorano and his attorney would be honored and that FBI involvement would not occur at this stage of the investigation.

On the next day, just minutes before the meeting, I was unofficially informed that the FBI would be present at this meeting. No discussion, explanation or notification was given by the US Attorney's Office. In the presence of various officials from various agencies, Wyshak entered the room and asked in a general statement if anyone minded if the FBI attended the meeting. The United States Attorney's Office has been aware of the numerous attempts by the FBI to insert themselves into this process. Calls have been made by the SAC and others to Tulsa and Miami officials insisting on FBI involvement in the case. These agencies were informed that only the FBI has the statutory authority/jurisdiction to investigate this case. Each time these agencies have declined to work with them. In another blatant attempt to force this issue, these agencies were subjected to a very unreasonable and uncomfortable request. Once again the interests of the case were secondary to the interests and image of the FBI. It was an unprofessional tactic and unrealistic to expect cooperation from these agencies when they are subject to these methods. Wyshak was informed that FBI involvement was contrary to the agreement made with Martorano and his attorney. Wyshak then began the meeting. Several minutes later, despite the concerns indicated, Herbert entered the room with SA Stan Moody who spent the rest of the time in the meeting. Your office ignored and disregarded the request of the agencies in the room. Investigators that have been working this case for years were not even informed of the fact that no matter what anyone else felt, the FBI would attend.

After the meeting many who attended commented on the insistence of FBI involvement. They expressed concern that even though they had previously made clear what their feelings were that they were being forced to meet your standards. We were placed into a position where we had to make clear that we were not in agreement with this forced issue. The credibility of your office now becomes a question. Investigators directly working the case are being forced to conform to standards set by your office in direct conflict with our agreement with Martorano. We will not accept your office's violation of the commitments and agreements that we make with defendants. We have worked closely with your prosecutors and have not misled or misinformed them regarding the agreements made with the defendant. Once again, due to your office's relentless and questionable insistence for FBI involvement, a disunified front was exposed to those we were trying to get assistance from. Once again to the detriment of this case, the priority of your office was to insist on FBI involvement, no matter what the ramifications to the case. The time has come. We as investigators can no longer be a part of a process that clearly is unethical and extremely unprofessional. We cannot participate on decisions that are made for "political" reasons. Your office has used this excuse many, many times. This case demands more. We are not condemning the FBI, however we are trying to be realistic. There are many fine professional agents who are being unfairly injured by this investigation. It is my belief and the belief of others including some prosecutors in your office; that the worst move to be made would be to include the FBI in this stage of the investigation. Questions will be asked of all of us as to how an effective investigation could be conducted under these circumstances. It is unfair to the Bureau and it is unfair to the agent that would be put in that situation. The Department of Justice has sent an experienced and well respected professional prosecutor to deal with this aspect of the case. Why is this not acceptable? For the record, I will say again. We do not and will not investigate FBI agents. We have no interest or desire to do so. That job is the responsibility of DOJ.

It is time to review our role and involvement in this investigation. We must meet the responsibilities required of us as members of the Massachusetts State Police and we must protect the reputation of our agency. Just as the FBI is concerned about their image, you must understand that we are concerned about ours. We know that if the job is done in a honest and dedicated manner then the image takes care of itself. In this case it is becoming increasingly more clear that we have little or no control over how this investigation is being conducted. The tactics being employed in your office are causing a strain on respected relationships. Demands being placed on highly respected and overworked prosecutors such as Fred Wyshak and Brian Kelly are unreasonable. Your office is asking them to meet the political requirements in the first order and then use their relationship with the investigators to get us in line. Our friendship and respect for these professionals has carried us a long way, however now it has become insulting. We cannot subject our agency to the political concerns of other agencies. We all know that politics is a fact of life, however in this case it should not and cannot be the governing and deciding fact. When we make a commitment and we are unable to ensure that the commitment will be met, then it is time to review our involvement.

I wanted to come directly to you with my concerns. I will be forwarding this letter to Colonel Hillman and Lieutenant Colonel Reagan along with my suggestions for further involvement in this investigation. I do not set State Police policy however I feel that due to my extensive experience in this investigation that I must bring this matter to the attention of my superiors. There is nothing left to do.

Sincerely,
Thomas J. Foley, Lieutenant,
Massachusetts State Police

— ACKNOWLEDGMENTS —

Tom Foley

In this book, John Sedgwick and I have made every effort to tell the exact truth about what happened in the Bulger investigation. While this book has largely been drawn from my memory of the case, my recollection has been well buttressed by a six-hundred-page, heavily detailed account that I set down at the time, as the events were unfolding. I have also gone through thousands of pages of court documents, other contemporaneous records, and published accounts to fill out my recollections of what happened. Wherever possible, the dialogue in *Most Wanted* has been drawn from written sources, and where it has not been, I have done my best to recall exactly what was said. Because the Bulger investigation began over twenty years ago, is extremely complex, and still continues, I can't guarantee that all the quotes are verbatim. But they are always true to my understanding of the speakers and to my knowledge of the facts.

It is difficult to name the many people who have helped me in my life and career, but there are some who deserve special recognition. It was my honor to work with professionals like Fred Wyshak, Dan Doherty, and Steve Johnson. No account anywhere, anytime, can give them the true recognition they deserve. These committed professionals put their lives and careers on the line, following an unpopular path and working under enormous pressure. It was the skills and personal commitment of Danny and Steve, who met with all of the victims' families to keep them informed as best as possible of the developments in the case. It was Fred's skills as an outstanding attorney that guided us through the legal minefields that seemed to change each day. My gratitude, appreciation, and respect for them cannot be put into words. I want to add a special thanks to Steve Johnson.

There were many others who played key support roles that I would like to mention. Special Agent Jim Marra, Inspector General's Office, joined us late in the investigation, but his involvement proved invaluable in getting the investigation to its final level. Jim Marra will always have my respect and admiration for his courage, hard work, and commitment. Dave Lazarus and Sandy Lemanski, IRS; Brian Kelly, USAO; Sam Buell, USAO; and Tom Duffy, Mark Caponette, Darlene Decaire, MSP, all played important roles. Mike Von Zampt, Florida assistant state attorney, for his courage, determination, and commitment in taking on a prosecution that was not encouraged or popular with federal authorities. We received outstanding support from Dan Doherty's agency, the Drug Enforcement Administration, by committing Danny full-time to the case and applying DEA resources. Thank you to DEA SACs John Gartland, Mark Trouville, and Vince Mazzilli, along with ASAC Jack Mahoney.

The investigators' hard work and dedication brought about this successful investigation but not without a price. Not only did this burden fall on these investigators and prosecutors, but also on their wives and families, who had to live with the consequences of our work resulting in long hours, nights, and weekends; missed holidays, birthdays, Little League games, school functions, and numerous other events where they had to act like two. The calls in the middle of the night, the worry about our well-being, the years of our frustration and the appearance that our likelihood to succeed was minimal all took their toll. Thank you to Marguerite, Marie, Mary, Joan, Carrie Marie, Bette Jeanne, and the families of others who worked on this investigation, for without their understanding and support we would not have been successful. I want to thank my three children—Kellianne, Patrick, and Mike—for their understanding that I could not always be there and for their support and encouragement.

I want to thank my friend Detective Lieutenant Kevin Horton for all of his support and friendship over the years. Kevin and I recently lost a close friend and mentor. Detective Lieutenant Pat Greaney passed away but his presence will always be felt. Pat was not only a true professional but also a very close friend. I also want to thank Deputy Superintendent Lt. Col. Brad Hibbard for his loyalty, dedication, and support during my term as the Superintendent.

Thank you to Cols. Charles Henderson and John DiFava for your confidence and support over many difficult years. I have utmost respect and admiration for former Massachusetts attorney general Tom Reilly for his commitment and courage. His early support and encouragement were critical in getting this investigation off the ground.

This book addresses some of the court hearings that the families of the victims of Bulger, Flemmi, and the FBI had to endure. They have been tortured and ridiculed in a manner that might be even worse than their loved ones have suffered. The Department of Justice continues its legal maneuvering to avoid responsibility. They have tried to discredit witnesses who have already been brought before the court and established as reliable by other prosecutors from the same Department of Justice. Their legal machinations have been shameful, relying on technicalities and personal attacks. More than three federal court justices have ruled against the government in favor of the families. Yet the DOJ continued to appeal some of these findings. The same DOJ that ignored the law for years that brought about this embarrassment now wants to hide behind the law to avoid responsibility. Congressman Stephen Lynch has filed a bill to compensate the victim's families where the courts don't. As frustrating as this is, that a bill has to be filed to deal with this inequity, and as frustrating as it is we do not have a Department of Justice that can see what we are all seeing, I am still confident that some aspects of the system still work because of the people like those who brought this case forward against all odds.

As a novice writer I relied upon some talented people. In 1999, the book *Black Mass* was written by Dick Lehr and Gerard O'Neill. It was the most accurate account at that time about the ongoing Bulger investigation. When they wrote their book we were still actively engaged in the investigation. Steve Flemmi's son, Billy Hussey, was furious that his father had killed his stepsister, Debbie Hussey. As a result in 2000 we traveled down to Florida where Hussey turned over two large suitcases loaded with numerous weapons from the Bulger arsenal. Dan Doherty had scheduled the DEA jet to bring us back to Boston but it was rerouted to an emergency. So we had to travel via commercial airlines. On board, Danny and I struggled to lift one of the suitcases into the overhead luggage bin. As we did so we looked down and saw a passenger reading *Black Mass.* He never was aware how close he really was to the story he was reading. I met with Lehr and he provided me direction, encouragement, and an introduction to his agent Dan Conaway from Writers House. I am grateful for his support and his advice.

Dan Conaway has been an outstanding guide and advocate for this book. His vision and knowledge of the business has made this book possible. In finding an author to work with, Dan recommended an accomplished author, John Sedgwick. Often Dan served as a sounding board and voice of reason, steering us through the process into the hands of our editor, Matthew Benjamin, and the group at Touchstone. It has been a pleasure to work with a real professional like Matt and everyone at S&S.

I want to thank John Sedgwick for his hard work and dedication to this book. John is a professional in his field and is committed to his work. This is a very complex and lengthy story that offered so many challenges in being able to put it on paper in a way that is understandable to the reader. John has met those challenges and has produced an outstanding piece of work. Thanks, John, for your effort and understanding.

Thanks to Dave Boeri for his technical help and advice in putting this book together. Dave was one of the few courageous Boston reporters who aggressively pursued this investigation over many years.

Last but not least I want to thank my parents, John and Roberta, for all the love, support, and encouragement over the years. My father passed away in 2009 but his concern and advice was greatly appreciated throughout my career. I have been fortunate to have parents that have supported me the way mine have.

John Sedgwick

I'd first like to thank Colonel Foley—Tom to me now—for opening up his life, thoughts, and feelings to me, so that I could gain an understanding of his experience on a case that, for its depth and complexity, would otherwise have seemed utterly impenetrable. I depended heavily on his own six-hundred-page account, and on extensive—he might say endless—interviews about just about every aspect of his work. I cannot thank him enough for entrusting his story to me; few things can be more frightening then letting someone else tell your tale. I'd also like to thank my own inimitable agent, Dan Conaway, of Writers House, for assembling this project and then working so hard to see it through. Thanks, too, to all the good people at Touchstone, but especially Matthew Benjamin, who has been an astute editor, reliable partner, and peerless champion of this book from the first. For all this, he has my boundless gratitude.

Beyond Tom's own writing, and his spectacularly detailed recollections, I have turned to a few books in what is now a sizeable library of Whitey-ology to round out his account. One is *The Underboss*, about the rise and fall of the Boston mafioso Jerry Angiulo, by the *Boston Globe* investigative reporters Gerard O'Neill and Dick Lehr; it helped establish the context for Whitey's own operation. Another is O'Neill and Lehr's indispensable *Black Mass*, which stands as both encyclopedia and Bible for all things Whitey. And Kevin Weeks' memoir, *Brutal*, written with Phyllis Karas, offered important insights into Whitey's mind and capacity. And finally John Martorano's powerful memoir, *Hitman*, written with Howie Carr; it provided a useful angle on the case, in detailing the life of another deadly mobster whose criminality interwove with Whitey's.

— INDEX —